Success as a Financial Advisor

by Ivan Illan

Financial adviser

A Wiley Brand

Success as a Financial Advisor For Dummies®

Published by: **John Wiley & Sons, Inc.**, 111 River Street, Hoboken, NJ 07030-5774, www.wiley.com

Copyright © 2019 by John Wiley & Sons, Inc., Hoboken, New Jersey

Published simultaneously in Canada

For general information on our other products and services, please contact our Customer Care Department within the U.S. at 877-762-2974, outside the U.S. at 317-572-3993, or fax 317-572-4002. For technical support, please visit https://hub.wiley.com/community/support/dummies

Wiley publishes in a variety of print and electronic formats and by print-on-demand. Some material included with standard print versions of this book may not be included in e-books or in print-on-demand. If this book refers to media such as a CD or DVD that is not included in the version you purchased, you may download this material at http://booksupport.wiley.com. For more information about Wiley products, visit www.wiley.com.

Library of Congress Control Number: 2018960656

ISBN 978-1-119-50410-8 (pbk); ISBN 978-1-119-50409-2 (ebk); 978-1-119-50413-9 (ebk)

Manufactured in the United States of America

C10005833_110218

Contents at a Glance

Introduction 1

Part 1: Getting Started as a Financial Advisor 5
CHAPTER 1: Looking at the Big Picture 7
CHAPTER 2: Deciding Whether You're Geared to Be a Financial Advisor 27
CHAPTER 3: Performing a Self Background Check 37
CHAPTER 4: Deciding to Work for a Firm or Build Your Own Practice. 47
CHAPTER 5: Surveying the Regulatory Landscape: The Fiduciary Standard. 63

Part 2: Mastering Core Competencies 77
CHAPTER 6: Pursuing Professional Development. 79
CHAPTER 7: Getting Budgeting under Your Belt 91
CHAPTER 8: Brushing Up on Asset Management 99
CHAPTER 9: Delving into Liability Management 117
CHAPTER 10: Excelling in Estate Planning. 133
CHAPTER 11: Tackling Taxation 147
CHAPTER 12: Getting Up to Speed on Behavioral Finance 161

Part 3: Providing Superior, Personalized Service. 169
CHAPTER 13: Formalizing Your Client Due Diligence Process. 171
CHAPTER 14: Developing a Personalized Financial Plan 183
CHAPTER 15: Offering Collaborative Value-Added Advice. 197
CHAPTER 16: Adjusting Your Service Level to Different Clients 209
CHAPTER 17: Benchmarking Performance. 221

Part 4: Building Your Clientele 233
CHAPTER 18: Earning Clients and Making a Career for a Lifetime 235
CHAPTER 19: Raising Your Profile with Networking and Marketing. 245
CHAPTER 20: Teaming Up to Build Synergies. 261

Part 5: Running Your Practice as a Business. 273
CHAPTER 21: Transitioning from Solo Practitioner to Business Owner 275
CHAPTER 22: Structuring Your Firm as a Well-Oiled Machine. 287
CHAPTER 23: Divvying Up Your Business: Equity Participation. 299
CHAPTER 24: Ensuring Business Continuity and Planning for Succession 309

Part 6: The Part of Tens 319

CHAPTER 25: Ten Tips for Being a Successful Financial Advisor 321

CHAPTER 26: Ten Business-Building Activities 327

Appendix: Financial Advisor Resources 333

Index 343

Table of Contents

INTRODUCTION 1
About This Book. 1
Foolish Assumptions. 3
Icons Used in This Book 3
Where to Go from Here 4

PART 1: GETTING STARTED AS A FINANCIAL ADVISOR 5

CHAPTER 1: **Looking at the Big Picture** 7
Understanding What a Financial Advisor Does (or Should Do) 8
Evaluating Yourself: Do You Have What It Takes?. 9
Do you have the right personality? 10
What's driving you to consider this career? 10
What are your qualifications? 11
Deciding Whether to Fly Solo or Work in a Firm. 12
Weighing the pros and cons of working in a firm. 13
Considering the option of operating as a lone wolf. 14
Thinking about starting your own firm. 15
Taking Inventory: What You Need to Know. 16
Complying with financial regulations 16
Brushing up on budgeting basics 17
Wrapping your brain around asset management 17
Knowing what liability management entails 18
Looking at what estate planning involves 18
Identifying key tax issues 19
Comprehending behavioral finance 19
Providing Superior Service to Your Clients 20
Performing your due diligence 20
Creating personalized financial plans. 20
Teaming up for superior service 21
Creating a tiered service model. 21
Assessing your performance as a financial advisor 22
Growing Your Client Base. 23
Winning lifelong clients. 23
Marketing your services 23
Teaming up with colleagues 23
Moving Up: Starting Your Own Firm. 24
Getting started. 24
Sharing revenue (or not). 25
Planning your exit strategy 26

CHAPTER 2: Deciding Whether You're Geared to Be a Financial Advisor 27

    Evaluating Your Personality Traits 28
        Do you like to teach? 28
        Are you patient and supportive? 29
        Are you willing to advocate for your clients? 29
        Are you humble? 31
        Are you well-connected? 31
        Are you hungry for knowledge? 32
    Questioning Your Motivations. 32
        Making a commitment to deliver value 33
        Avoiding the siren call of commissioned sales 33
    Balancing Leadership and Service 34
        Embracing your leadership role 34
        Maintaining a service-oriented mindset 35

CHAPTER 3: Performing a Self Background Check 37

    Choosing a Career Path 38
        Getting started fresh out of college 38
        Changing careers from within the industry. 39
        Changing careers from outside the industry. 40
    Capitalizing on Your Personal Experience 41
        Taking advantage of your childhood memories 42
        Dealing with your own financial challenges 42
        Helping others manage their finances 43
    Evaluating Your Financial Position 43
        Gauging your financial stability 44
        Recognizing the risks of financial instability 45

CHAPTER 4: Deciding to Work for a Firm or Build Your Own Practice 47

    Knowing Your Options 48
        Hiring in as an employee of an existing firm. 50
        Setting out on your own as an independent financial advisor 52
        Scoping out hybrid models 53
    Investigating Different Revenue Models .53
        Understanding the fee-only model. 54
        Collecting asset-based fees and commissions 56
        Checking out the commission-only compensation model 56
        Understanding how firm managers get paid 57
    Getting On-the-Job Training as an Employee 58
        Deciding where to go for your field training 58
        Using internships to find the right fit .59

Finding Employment as an Independent Contractor...............59
Affiliating with an independent broker/dealer 59
Finding work with an insurance-company-owned
broker/dealer...60
Becoming a Registered Investment Advisor 61

**CHAPTER 5: Surveying the Regulatory Landscape:
The Fiduciary Standard**.................................. 63
Familiarizing Yourself with Your Role as Financial Advisor 64
Recognizing the Confusion over Obligations and Care Standards 64
Sifting through the Clouds of Bureaucracy 67
Considering federal rules and regulations (DOL, SEC, FINRA) 67
Looking at state rules and regulations.......................70
Can you call yourself a financial advisor?....................71
Governing Itself: Industry Organizations Weigh In.................72
Recognizing that change comes from within 73
Taking the fiduciary pledge 73
Looking to the Future 74

PART 2: MASTERING CORE COMPETENCIES................ 77

CHAPTER 6: Pursuing Professional Development................. 79
Identifying the Core Competencies 80
Asset management.....................................80
Liability management...................................81
Budgeting 82
Estate planning 82
Taxation 82
Behavioral finance....................................83
Getting a Formal Education 83
The American College of Financial Services...................84
CFA Institute...84
CFP Board...86
The Institute of Business and Finance (IBF)...................86
Obtaining Your Licenses to Practice..........................87
Financial Industry Regulatory Authority (FINRA)...............87
National Association of Insurance Commissioners (NAIC) 88
Applying Certifications across the Financial Advisory Spectrum 89
Embracing Continuing Education 90

CHAPTER 7: Getting Budgeting under Your Belt................. 91
Guiding Clients on Household Budgeting 91
Estimating income.....................................92
Identifying and estimating expenses 92
Shaking the piggy bank: Savings 96
Establishing spending and savings guidelines 97

Exploring Helpful Technology Tools 97
Leveraging the Power of Auto Pay and Payroll Deductions 98

CHAPTER 8: **Brushing Up on Asset Management**. 99
Developing a Client's Investment Policy Statement 100
Exploring the client's goals and objectives 101
Defining your duties and responsibilities .103
Establishing portfolio selection guidelines 103
Concurring on a rebalancing frequency. 108
Setting parameters for performance monitoring
and reporting 108
Agreeing on an Investment Philosophy 109
Active, passive, or somewhere in between 109
Individual securities versus packaged products 111
Cautioning Clients on "Hot Money" Investments 115
Comparing Revenue/Compensation Models .115
Asset-based fees 116
Commissions and sales charges 116

CHAPTER 9: **Delving into Liability Management**. 117
Assessing a Client's Risk Profile 118
Following a formal process 118
Using the income replacement approach .124
Taking the needs-based approach 125
Reviewing Insurance Lines and Products 125
Life insurance. 126
Disability insurance. 127
Health insurance 127
Homeowner's insurance. 128
Auto insurance. 128
Liability insurance 128
Annuities. 129
Comparing Revenue/Compensation Models .130
Collecting a one-time, up-front commission 130
Getting paid in installments. 131
Embracing transparency 131

CHAPTER 10: **Excelling in Estate Planning**. 133
Addressing Estate Planning Essentials. 134
Naming heirs 135
Naming beneficiaries 136
Planning for business succession or continuity 136
Accounting for estate taxes 138
Managing estate liquidity (or lack thereof) 139
Considering capital market conditions at time of death 140

Preparing for Estate Settlement Complications 140
    Handling differences over a closely held business. 141
    Anticipating a struggle for control. 142
Helping Clients Pass along Values, Not Just Wealth 143
    Checking out donor-advised funds. 143
    Considering private family foundations. .144
    Brushing up on CRTs and CLTs 144
Teaming Up with Estate Planning Attorneys and Family
Accountants 145

CHAPTER 11: Tackling Taxation 147
Reminding Yourself That You're Not an Accountant 148
Adding a Tax Advisor to the Team 149
Managing Capital Gains: Don't Let the Tail Wag the Dog 151
Using Tax-Deferred Accounts to Maximize
Compounding Returns 152
Exploring Tax-Free and Tax-Lighter Investments 153
    Buying municipal bonds. 154
    Investing in tax-exempt securities 155
Slashing Taxes with Retirement, College, and Health
Savings Accounts. 156
    Contributing to a retirement plan. 156
    Socking away money in college funds 157
    Trimming taxes with an HSA 158
Taking a Nibble Out of Taxes with Charitable Contributions 158

CHAPTER 12: Getting Up to Speed on Behavioral Finance 161
Recognizing Irrational Factors That Drive Thinking
and Behaviors 162
    Myopic loss aversion. 162
    Confirmation bias 162
    Mental accounting. 163
    Illusion of control. 163
    Recent extrapolation bias. 164
    Hindsight bias 164
    Herd mentality. 164
Muting Irrational Thoughts and Behaviors 165
Appealing to the Rational Side of Your Client's Brain. 166
    Step 1: Acknowledge your client's fear. 166
    Step 2: Tell your client to take a deep, cleansing
    breath and smile 166
    Step 3: Introduce a rational argument. 166
    Step 4: Have your client explain the strategy back to you. 167
Riding Out Market Cycles: Balancing Fear and Greed 167
    Calming common fears. 168
    Reining in greed. 168

PART 3: PROVIDING SUPERIOR, PERSONALIZED SERVICE 169

CHAPTER 13: **Formalizing Your Client Due Diligence Process** 171

Deciding Whether You Want Clients or Consumers 172
Serving consumers as a broker/agent 172
Serving clients as a fiduciary financial advisor 173
Considering the Factors That Really Matter 174
Mastering the Four As of Due Diligence 176
Assessment 176
Audit 178
Action 179
Alignment 180

CHAPTER 14: **Developing a Personalized Financial Plan** 183

Obtaining Your Client's Input 184
Going Deep and Broad with Every Client 185
Copy 186
Capital 187
Consequences 188
Outlining a Client's Financial Plan 189
Focusing on cash flow 190
Considering savings and investment goals 190
Accounting for taxes 191
Addressing insurance needs 192
Connecting the financial plan to the estate plan 193
Connecting the financial plan to the client's
business succession plan 193
Making Your Job Easier with Tools and Guides 194
Reviewing the Plan Regularly 196

CHAPTER 15: **Offering Collaborative Value-Added Advice** 197

Recognizing the Benefits of a Collaborative Approach 198
Aligning your compensation model with that of
other professional advisors 199
Delivering optimal results 199
Creating a system of checks and balances 201
Leveraging the power of specialization 201
Collaborating to Serve Your Clients Better 203
Teaming up with your client 203
Partnering with your client's lawyer 204
Working with your client's accountant 205
Working on your follow-through 206

Taking on the Role of Your Team's Quarterback 206
    Acting as the central point of contact. .206
    Maintaining separation among advisors base on their roles 207
    Shopping solutions 208

**CHAPTER 16: Adjusting Your Service Level to
Different Clients** 209
Building a Tiered Client Service Model. 210
    Scaling services to different clients. 210
    Giving your best clients concierge care 211
Scoring Your Clients 212
    Considering demographics 213
    Weighing psychographics. 215
    Assigning clients to service level brackets 216
Rewarding Quality Clients 217
    Hosting special events 217
    Inviting clients to breakfast or lunch 218
    Recognizing the need to budget your time 219

CHAPTER 17: Benchmarking Performance 221
Measuring Portfolio Success Against a Chosen Index 222
    Tuning in to the clients' mindset. 222
    Recognizing the limitations of stock market indexes. 223
    Using a blended benchmark 223
    Keeping it simple with your clients 224
Riding the Personal Benchmark Trend. 225
    Establishing the client's personal benchmark. 226
    Using the personal benchmark to keep calm a client's nerves. . . .227
    Using both relative and absolute benchmarks 229
Tailoring Performance to Each Client's Needs 230
Own It! Don't Make Excuses for Poor Performance 231

PART 4: BUILDING YOUR CLIENTELE 233

**CHAPTER 18: Earning Clients and Making a Career
for a Lifetime** 235
Adding Value before Asking for Referrals 236
    Making a choice: Sales or consulting 237
    Differentiating yourself as a trusted advisor. 237
Speaking to Clients in Plain English 238
Showcasing Your Value Proposition. 240
    Ask clients about their past experiences 241
    Write your elevator pitch 241
    Quantify your value and qualify your expectations 242
Being Humble and Honored to Serve Your Clients 243

CHAPTER 19: **Raising Your Profile with Networking and Marketing** 245

Establishing an Online Presence...246
Creating a website as your home base 246
Hosting your own blog 248
Becoming active on LinkedIn.......................................249
Creating a Facebook page for your practice 250
Claiming your business in online directories 251
Making the most of your certifications........................252
Getting Connected in the Real World...................................252
Discovering what you're passionate about 253
Getting involved in a charitable cause 254
Serving on boards 254
Developing cross-industry professional alliances.......255
Building Your Own Sales Force 256
Marketing to fellow financial advisors 256
Leveraging home office leadership personnel 257
Encouraging and rewarding client referrals 258
Promoting Yourself over the Long Haul................................259

CHAPTER 20: **Teaming Up to Build Synergies**.............................261

Choosing Your Preferred Role: Lone Wolf or Leader of the Pack 262
Considering the pros of flying solo.............................262
Considering the cons of flying solo.............................263
Collaborating with Other Financial Advisors........................266
Teaming up for joint-work opportunities....................266
Sharing unique techniques and skills.........................269
Finding your niche: Minder, finder, or grinder? 270
Exploring broader practice partnerships....................271

PART 5: RUNNING YOUR PRACTICE AS A BUSINESS......273

CHAPTER 21: **Transitioning from Solo Practitioner to Business Owner** 275

Gut Check: Deciding Whether Starting Your Own Firm Is the Right Move for You...276
Determining how tethered you are to your current firm 276
Considering a change in roles and costs 277
Putting All the Pieces in Place 278
Structuring your business 278
Choosing a broker/dealer platform 279
Sketching your organizational chart............................279
Staffing your firm...281
Dotting your i's and crossing your t's 281

Getting someone focused on rainmaking 282
Battling client attrition 283
Measuring Success in Terms of Profit Margin. 283
Achieving Growth through Mergers and Acquisitions 284
Planning Your Exit Strategy 284
Bailing out with a buyout 285
Choosing a successor to take over 285
Handling your own estate planning 285
Avoiding the "die at your desk" scenario 286

CHAPTER 22: **Structuring Your Firm as a Well-Oiled Machine** 287
Organizing Your Business by Department. 288
Minding the business: Administration 288
Finding clients: Business development 289
Grinding out the work: Client service 291
Identifying Business Development's Focus Areas. 292
Getting your firm's foot in the door with 401K plans. 292
Expanding opportunities through corporate
benefit programs. 293
Networking through trusts and estates. .293
Easing the burden of household's financial manager 294
Delegating Responsibilities to Client Service Associates 294
Assigning Administrative/Operational Responsibilities 295
Managing the office. 295
Harnessing the power of client relationship
management (CRM) software 296
Coordinating the workflow for new clients 297
Outsourcing accounting and legal 298

CHAPTER 23: **Divvying Up Your Business: Equity
Participation** 299
Keeping Some Profits in the Firm 300
Adopting a Founder Mentality. 301
Playing the role of visionary. 301
Serving as the primary rainmaker. 302
Avoiding the temptation to deal with day-to-day operations. . . .303
Offering Equity Buy-in to Team Members. 304
Being selective 304
Putting your agreements in writing 305
Proceeding When Equity Ownership Doesn't Matter. 305
Maximizing annual compensation to advisors 306
Having no desire to ever sell the business 306

CHAPTER 24: **Ensuring Business Continuity and Planning for Succession** 309

Creating a Hit-by-the-Bus Business Continuity Plan 310
Protecting Your Heirs' Interests with a Buy-Sell Agreement.......312
Planning for Succession 314
    Picking a successor with the right credentials.................314
    Addressing personality and values compatibility..............315
    Considering transferable skills 316
    Sizing up a candidate's leadership potential 316
    Accounting for loyalty 317

PART 6: THE PART OF TENS 319

CHAPTER 25: **Ten Tips for Being a Successful Financial Advisor** 321

Let Your Conscience Be Your Guide 321
Beware of False Profits..................................322
Protect Your Clients from Predators 323
Don't Use Big Words 323
Remember That Good Service Makes Up for Other Shortcomings....................................324
Be Active in a Community Cause...........................324
Be Eager to Acquire New Information and to Share What You Know 325
Focus More on Skills, Less on Tools 325
Appreciate the Trust Your Clients Place in You..................326
Always Ask: What If I'm Wrong?............................326

CHAPTER 26: **Ten Business-Building Activities** 327

Schedule Client Review Meetings 328
Keep a Log of Friends and Family That Your Clients Mention 328
Sponsor One Charitable Event Each Year 329
Break Bread with Your Best Clients 329
Be Responsive: Practice the Same-Day Rule 329
Attend Every Party You're Invited to........................330
Have an Elevator Pitch 330
Welcome All Prospects, Large or Small 330
Stop Selling and Start Telling Stories 331
Be Active on Social Media................................331

APPENDIX: FINANCIAL ADVISOR RESOURCES 333

INDEX 343

Introduction

Success as a financial advisor requires that you practice as a financial advisor. Most people unfortunately who practice as financial advisors aren't really financial advisors. At best, they're portfolio managers. At worst, they're salespeople looking to score big commissions. That's not what I mean when I use the title *financial advisor*, and it's certainly not *the* measure of success in this field.

The problem is that no single standard authorizes someone to practice as a "financial advisor." Unlike other professions including medicine, law, and accounting, financial advisory has no single governing or regulatory authority charged with their members' oversight. Doctors have medical boards, lawyers have bar associations, and accountants have the Financial Accounting Standards Board (FASB), but financial advisors have no equivalent. As a result, you can find plenty of people in this profession who, for example, sell only insurance products or who are raising money in an unregistered private placement investment offering. No wonder that consumers are so confused and leery of financial advisors; too many who operate under this designation are just commissioned salespeople, not actual *advisors*.

When I say success as a financial advisor requires that you practice as a financial advisor, I mean you can achieve success in the profession by always placing your clients' needs above yours and by providing superior comprehensive and cohesive financial advice. This advice covers all aspects of a client's family finances, including buying a home, paying for children's education, saving and investing for retirement, protecting assets against unforeseen tragic events, reducing the client's tax burden, and more. Simply put, you achieve success as a financial advisor by delivering consistently superior holistic service to your clients. With this point of differentiation, you can just about corner the market wherever you practice.

About This Book

Welcome to *Success as a Financial Advisor For Dummies*, where you discover how to achieve your success by helping clients achieve theirs. The two key terms in the title of this book capture what this book is all about:

- » *Success* means not only financial success, but also personal satisfaction, job satisfaction, self-respect, and personal and professional fulfillment. The more you work with clients, the more you realize that money and what it buys is only one key component in achieving happiness and fulfillment. My guidance in this book, just as the advice you give (or should give) your clients, is holistic. By following my advice, you can achieve success in your career however you choose to measure it.

- » *Financial advisor* means a professional who delivers holistic financial advice to clients and upholds the *fiduciary* standard — always advising and recommending products and solutions that are in the client's best interest and with total compensation transparency.

This book covers all aspects of being a successful financial advisor, from deciding whether you're a good fit for the profession to starting your own firm and everything in between. To make the content more accessible, I divided it into six parts:

- » Part 1 brings you up to speed on the basics. Here, you conduct a self-assessment to figure out whether this is the right career for you, decide whether to join or firm or start your own practice, and scope out the regulatory landscape.

- » Part 2 guides you in developing the foundational knowledge you need to practice as a financial advisor. Here, I identify the core competencies, point you in the direction of where to go to obtain your formal education and get licensed, and explain asset and liability management, budgeting, estate planning, taxation, and behavioral finance.

- » Part 3 leads you through the process of onboarding new clients, so you can target your services to their unique needs; developing a personalized financial plan for each client; and offering collaborative advice by teaming up with your client's lawyer, tax advisor, and other professionals. Here you also discover how to tier you service to different clients to optimize efficiency and how to measure performance.

- » Part 4 presents three ways to acquire and retain clients, the most effective of which is to *earn* clients by delivering superior service. I also provide guidance on how to market and network to raise your profile and how to team up with other professionals to improve service while expanding your referral network.

- » Part 5 discusses how to transition from solo practitioner to business owner, structure and run your business, attract and retain talent through equity participation and other means, and develop a business succession plan to preserve your legacy in the event you choose to retire or you experience a situation in which you're no longer able to run the firm.

- » Part 6 features ten tips for achieving success as a financial advisor and ten tips for growing your practice. This part also includes an appendix that provides several lists of valuable resources, including professional development resources, professional licensing bodies, trade publications and resources, and business valuation and formation resources.

In short, this book explains first how to become a holistic, fiduciary financial advisor and then how to raise your game to build on your success.

Foolish Assumptions

As a financial advisor, or someone who wants to be a financial advisor, you should realize that all assumptions in this field are foolish and potentially dangerous, so I hate to admit to making foolish assumptions as I wrote this book. However, to keep the book focused on the right audience and ensure that it fulfilled my purpose in writing it, I had to make the following foolish assumptions about you:

>> You want to be a financial advisor aligned with my definition of what that means. You don't want to merely sell investment and insurance products and solutions to earn a buck.

>> You're committed first and foremost to each and every clients' financial success in all areas of their financial life and what that wealth represents for each client and your clients' family.

>> Your knowledge of and experience in the field ranges from nothing to substantial. At any point in your career as a financial advisor, and even before you take the first step, you can benefit from the guidance I provide in this book.

>> You're eager to acquire knowledge and skills and willing to change, especially if you're entrenched in bad habits and practices or stuck at a firm that doesn't support the highest standards of practice. My hope is that this book will be transformative to most readers, setting them on the right path to becoming holistic, fiduciary financial advisors.

Icons Used in This Book

Throughout this book, icons in the margins highlight different types of information that call out for your attention. Here are the icons you'll encounter and a brief description of each.

REMEMBER

I want you to remember everything you read in this book, but if you can't quite do that, then remember the important points flagged with this icon.

TIP

Tips provide insider insight. When you're looking for a better, faster way to do something, check out these tips.

WARNING

"Whoa!" Before you take another step, read this warning. I provide this cautionary content to help you avoid the common pitfalls that are otherwise likely to trip you up.

Where to Go from Here

You're certainly welcome to read this book from cover to cover, but I wrote it in a way that facilitates skipping around. For a quick tutorial on how to achieve success as a financial advisor, check out Chapter 1, where I touch on the key topics. Review the table of contents or the index for a topic that piques your interest. Flip to any number of chapters and start reading. For an extra Cheat Sheet chockfull of interesting tidbits that you can refer to again and again, check out www.dummies.com/successasafinancialadvisor.

1

Getting Started as a Financial Advisor

Wrap your brain around what's required to be a successful financial advisor.

Figure out whether you have the right characteristics to be a financial advisor, such as problem-solving, intention, and service-oriented.

Discover how to leverage your education, experience, and former career(s) to transition successfully into the role of financial advisor.

Weigh the options and make the call of how to practice — working for an established firm or starting your own business.

Get up to speed on the rules and regulations that govern financial advisors, so you can avoid doing anything that gets you into trouble and be positioned for where the regulatory and legislative trends are headed.

» Deciding the kind of financial advisor you want to be

» Conducting a quick self-assessment

» Getting up to speed on the basics

» Building and growing your client base

» Making the leap to starting and running your own firm

Chapter **1**

Looking at the Big Picture

B ecoming a successful financial advisor is a process that involves deciding the kind of financial advisor you want to be, developing the personal and professional attributes that make you a natural for the job, obtaining the formal education and training required, gaining on-the-job experience, and then honing your skills as you build your practice.

The acid test is whether you consistently enable clients to achieve their financial goals. This test sounds easy enough, but like any marathon or triathlon, the path to victory is strewn with potential pitfalls. Success depends on your ability to carefully balance your clients' risks and returns (their liabilities and assets) while keeping them from veering off course. To achieve success, you must serve clients in a way that they understand *how* your guidance keeps them heading in their desired direction and *why* your role is so important to them.

This chapter provides a bird's-eye view of how to become a successful financial advisor by touching on the key topics covered in this book. The remaining chapters take a deeper dive into these topics and other areas you must attend to in order to achieve success as a financial advisor.

Understanding What a Financial Advisor Does (or Should Do)

A *financial advisor* is a person who helps her clients plan and manage their finances to achieve their short- and long-term financial goals. Ideally, every financial advisor should meet the following two criteria:

REMEMBER

>> **Fiduciary:** A financial advisor has a *fiduciary* responsibility to her clients, meaning that the advice provided is in the best interest of the client instead of what's best for the advisor, such as commissions received for the sale of a financial product or solution.

Serving as a fiduciary is easier said than done, considering that so many financial advisors work for firms that have institutional agendas (to sell specific products or solutions) that compete with this standard.

>> **Holistic:** A financial advisor must attend to all aspects of a client's family finances to not only grow wealth but also protect it in ways that are carefully planned to meet the client's goals and objectives. Financial goals include buying a home, paying for children's education, affording a comfortable retirement, starting and running a business, supporting a charity, passing down assets to heirs and beneficiaries, and more. Holistic financial advice also includes ensuring that the client is properly insured against events or incidents that could undermine the client's ability to achieve those goals.

REMEMBER

A financial advisor doesn't merely sell insurance policies or manage investment portfolios, but that doesn't mean that the advisor must do everything. Financial advisors often outsource many of the tasks required, such as referring a client to a lawyer for estate planning or using a turnkey asset management program (TAMP) instead of personally managing a client's portfolio.

Unfortunately, there's quite a bit of confusion in the marketplace as to *how* someone serves clients as a financial advisor. Many financial advisors focus on certain investment or insurance-related financial products. Others are licensed to advise on a product purchase or are registered to provide holistic financial advice that's not product related. The variety of roles and the complexity involved in addressing all of a client's financial needs present big challenges, but they also offer a world of rewarding opportunities.

A GOOD TIME TO BE A FINANCIAL ADVISOR

Financial advisory is one of the most personally and financially rewarding professions you can pursue, and your timing couldn't be more perfect. Baby Boomers are retiring in record numbers, creating an epic intergenerational wealth transfer in the trillions of dollars. These Boomers and their heirs and beneficiaries are in need of reliable and trustworthy financial advice now more than ever.

Adding to this vast and growing opportunity is the fact that relatively few people who call themselves "financial advisor" meet the criteria to serve in that capacity. Most are either salespeople who have transactional relationships with their customers, or they serve as portfolio managers who ignore all other aspects of their clients' financial health and well-being. Chances are good that by acting as a true fiduciary financial advisor, you can essentially corner the market wherever you choose to practice. All you need to do is deliver optimal financial outcomes to your clients, which is what being a successful financial advisor is all about.

Evaluating Yourself: Do You Have What It Takes?

Not everyone is cut out to be a financial advisor. Certainly financial knowledge and skills are necessary but aren't sufficient. Interpersonal and communication skills are also essential. You have to love being with, talking with, and, most importantly, listening to people — all day, every day. As with any profession, your ability to acquire clients is directly related to your ability to add value to their lives. In addition, your interactions with clients and others is the fuel that keeps you going when the inevitable roadblocks, rejections, and market crashes dampen your spirits.

In this section, I encourage you to conduct a self-assessment to determine whether you have the qualities and qualifications to become a successful financial advisor, and I lead you through the process. Chapters 2 and 3 provide more detailed self-assessments, with Chapter 2 focusing on your personality and motivation and Chapter 3 examining your personal and professional qualifications.

Do you have the right personality?

This profession has a place for all personality types, as long as you choose a role that fits. All firms need financial advisors to fill the following three roles:

>> **Minders** run the business/practice, organizing, managing, hiring/firing, and setting goals and agendas. Typically, these are partners who've been in the business for many years, made the business-building mistakes, and learned from them. To be a minder, you must be a leader with excellent organizational, interpersonal, and communication skills. You may not be working closely with clients, but you'll be leading and mentoring associates and staff.

>> **Finders** source new clients. These advisors are great at filling a pipeline and marketing services and solutions. Finders can be any age and at any level of experience, but they must have excellent interpersonal and communication skills and genuinely enjoy interacting with prospective clients.

>> **Grinders** do research, analysis, illustration, and paperwork. Whether it's the research that drives discussion at investment committee meetings, or running several insurance carrier illustrations, these advisors are the worker bees of the business. This is a great position for new college grads, because it gives them the opportunity to figure out how the business runs from the inside-out. It's also great for those who aren't exactly people-persons.

See Chapter 20 for more about these three roles and how to team up with other financial advisors to build productive synergies. If you choose to practice as a lone wolf, you'll have to fill all three roles.

REMEMBER

You can be an introvert in this business and be successful, but only if you're teaming up with complementary advisors. Forcing yourself to become a finder when you love manipulating spreadsheets all day isn't the best use of your time or career development. This profession has room for all personality types, but you need to be honest about who you are and what you enjoy doing before taking the leap.

What's driving you to consider this career?

If you're looking for money, you'll find it in this business. However, just because you've uncovered methods to routinely ring your cash register doesn't mean you've achieved success as a financial advisor. If you're motivated solely by the promise of a six-figure income, you probably won't become successful for two reasons:

>> You'll be focused on your own success instead of that of your clients, and your clients and prospective clients will sense it.

>> You'll be more prone to conflicts of interest, which could get you into legal trouble or at least tarnish your reputation in the community in which you practice.

REMEMBER

Nothing's wrong with wanting to earn a good income, but your motivations should also include the following:

>> A desire to have a positive impact on your clients' lives (and a genuine concern for their well-being).

>> A desire to serve on a team and to coordinate the team's efforts and expertise to improve your clients' financial outcomes.

>> A hunger for relevant knowledge and skills to continually improve your ability to serve your clients. To be successful, you must keep up on rules, regulations, tools, and techniques.

>> A desire to teach others the importance of careful financial planning, disciplined management, and the reasoning behind the plan you develop for each client. The desire to gently but firmly guide, educate, and direct action is paramount to your long-term professional success.

>> A desire to work in a challenging career.

REMEMBER

You achieve true success when your clients arrive at their desired destination. This goal can take many years, usually decades, to achieve. When you're doing it right, you serve more as a financial steward than anything else, preventing clients from making decisions when they struggle to see the long-term consequences or negative impact of certain choices.

Being a successful financial advisor requires nerves of steel and the ability to talk people off ledges and navigate them through troubled waters. When a family crisis or market instability causes panic, you need to be the calm captain with the steady hand who keeps the ship on course.

What are your qualifications?

Just finished college studying basketweaving? That may not be the best initial training for becoming a financial advisor, but I've heard worse, such as a high school dropout who entered the business at 18 with an insurance license who was selling policies door-to-door. You don't need a great deal of formal education and training to be a successful financial advisor, because the best preparation is on-the-job training. However, you do need to have the following qualifications:

>> **Interpersonal skills:** You must be able to engage with a wide variety of clients if you hope to have any clients.

- » **Organizational skills:** Organization is essential in record-keeping, financial planning, and presentations to clients.

- » **Communication skills:** Explaining the financial plan you developed and the need to stick with the plan is essential for keeping clients on track to meet the agreed-upon goals and objectives.

- » **Analytical skills:** A big part of the job involves shopping for financial products and solutions that fit with the client's financial plan. To do so, you need to be able to analyze and compare options.

- » **Computer skills:** Increasingly, financial advisors rely on technology to do their work, so you need to be comfortable using a computer. However, you don't need high level skills such as programming.

- » **Basic education and training:** You need to know the basics about asset and liability management, budgeting, estate planning, taxation, and behavioral finance. (See the later section "Taking Inventory: What You Need to Know.") You can (and often should) outsource the more complex tasks or anything you're not really good at, such as estate planning or even portfolio management.

If you've studied economics or finance in college or graduate school, you'll certainly have a knowledge base that gives you confidence and enables you to sound super-smart. However, knowing a bunch of fancy terms and how things work is of value only if you're able to convey your knowledge in a way that's relevant and comprehensible to clients.

REMEMBER

Financial advisory is a people-business first and financial-business second. For example, if you have the best investment portfolio in the world, but your clients don't understand the path you've mapped out for them, then you won't achieve the desired level of success, and you may not last very long in the business.

Deciding Whether to Fly Solo or Work in a Firm

Critical to longevity and success in this profession is having the right work environment and conditions. For some, living the dream is hanging out in shorts on their patio with their laptop and smartphone, whereas others need to dress in a business suit and meet with clients in a professional office setting to make them feel as though they're really in this business.

The first choice is whether you want to work for a firm, operate as a solo practitioner, or start your own firm. In this section, I briefly describe the potential benefits and drawbacks of each option. (See Chapter 4 for additional guidance on deciding whether to work for a firm or set out on your own.)

Weighing the pros and cons of working in a firm

If you're just getting started or you prefer working in a more structured office environment or you want to avoid the hassles and costs of running your own operation, working for a financial advisory firm may be the best choice. Consider the pros and cons.

The pros are as follows:

>> An existing firm is likely to provide at least some training and may cover part of the cost of getting certified and continuing your education.

>> The firm covers the hassles and costs of providing office space, utilities, technology, business management, and support personnel.

>> You can focus solely on client acquisition and service. Typically, you can delegate financial planning, portfolio management, and other planning and management work to others in the firm.

>> You're an employee, so you don't pay self-employment tax, and you may qualify for benefits, such as retirement, paid vacations and leave, health insurance, disability insurance, and other fringe benefits.

>> You're in closer contact with other financial advisors and personnel, so you work in a more supportive environment.

>> You have an office and regular office hours, so you have a clearer separation between work and home.

And, the cons are

>> You have regular office hours, so your schedule is less flexible.

>> You're managed to some extent, meaning your daily activities are monitored, reported, reviewed, and assessed weekly. (Performance metrics are usually related to sales and not financial advisory work.)

>> You build a client base for the firm, not for yourself. If you leave the firm, you're likely to be prohibited from taking your clients with you.

>> You may be pressured or required to recommend certain financial products or solutions favored by the firm that are not necessarily in the best interest of your clients.

>> You earn less of the revenue you generate, but it is often offset by the amount saved (in time and money) by not having to run your own business.

Considering the option of operating as a lone wolf

Many financial advisors choose to set up shop as sole proprietors, which provides the ultimate in freedom and flexibility but burdens the advisor with the most responsibility. This option is typically practical only if you've been in the business for a few years. Before you make the break from working for a firm to working for yourself, consider the pros and cons.

Here are the pros:

>> You make your own hours.

>> You answer only to yourself and your clients.

>> You have no restrictions on your financial planning and management activities; you can recommend any financial products or solutions that are in your clients' best interests.

>> You keep all the revenue you generate, less operating costs.

>> You build your own client base for yourself, not for someone else.

And, the cons are

>> Running your own business costs time and money and distracts from your focus on client acquisition and service. All the day-to-day management, administration, and other operational concerns are yours to deal with — on top of the normal client interaction and financial advisory work.

>> Without management oversight, you must be self-motivated, and you receive no professional feedback on your performance. However, by being accountable to clients, you do receive some oversight and feedback from them.

>> You have limited contact with colleagues unless you reach out to other financial advisors and relevant professionals.

Thinking about starting your own firm

If you have some experience in the field, you've probably already thought about starting your own firm with one or more other financial advisors, associates, and support personnel. You can start your own firm in any number of ways. For example, you may hire an executive assistant to manage the business while you focus on acquiring and serving clients, team up with another financial advisor and divvy up the workload, or create a major operation with multiple advisors and support staff.

Depending on the size and complexity of the firm, the pros and cons vary.

Consider these pros:

>> You have many of the benefits of working at a firm, including close contact with colleagues.

>> You own the firm, so you call the shots. You can serve clients however you determine is best and require everyone in the firm to uphold the same standard of care.

>> You have the opportunity to earn more revenue and leverage the cost savings of scaling the business.

>> You delegate the work, so you can focus on the activities you're best at and enjoy most.

And, check out these cons:

>> Starting and running a firm is a major commitment that carries big risks.

>> Someone must run the business, either one of the financial advisors (maybe you) or an office manager you hire.

>> You must attract and retain the right mix of talent — a minder, one or more finders and grinders, and support staff.

>> Your initial investment of time and money may be significant, depending on the size of the firm. However, after it's up and running, assuming the business is a success, you can scale back your hands-on involvement.

See the later section "Moving Up: Starting Your Own Firm" for additional details on starting your own firm and the chapters in Part 5 for even more guidance.

Taking Inventory: What You Need to Know

In addition to basic skills, such as organizational and communications skills, you must master certain core competencies. In this section, I touch on each of these areas, which I cover in detail in Chapters 5 through 12.

Complying with financial regulations

Legislative and regulatory proposals and actions are giving financial advisors something extra to concern themselves with lately. The purpose behind these proposals and actions is noble; the goal is to ensure that anyone providing financial advice to consumers is acting as a fiduciary — that is, in the best interest of the consumer. Unfortunately, the legislation enacted and proposed often adds to the confusion and bureaucracy without actually benefiting consumers, as I explain in Chapter 5.

To comply with federal, state, and local rules and regulations and uphold a highest standard of service, I advise you to do the following:

>> Be a true financial advisor, which means providing holistic financial advice that covers financial planning, assets and liabilities management, estate planning, tax planning, and any other area related to a client's financial health and well-being. You don't need to be an expert in every area; you can add other specialists to your team. However, every area should be addressed in a client's financial plan.

>> Honor your fiduciary responsibility to your clients. Don't succumb to temptation or to pressure from your firm to sell products or solutions that aren't the best for your clients.

TIP

If you work for a firm that pressures you to recommend certain products or solutions, a good rule is to recommend one of those products or solutions only if something better isn't available.

>> Whenever recommending a product or solution that pays a commission, fully disclose the commission to your client.

REMEMBER

By adhering to these three guidelines, you not only comply with any current or future regulations, but you also differentiate yourself from the majority of practitioners in the market who call themselves financial advisors but are actually functioning more like salespeople.

Brushing up on budgeting basics

If a client loves to spend, spend, spend, and has credit card debt to show how good she is at her favorite pastime, you can deliver value to the client by engaging her in a financial fitness program. In Chapter 7, I present two common approaches to budgeting:

>> Set up spending categories and estimates for each category so that a sufficient amount of monthly income remains at the end of the month to allocate to the client's various financial goals.

>> Siphon funds automatically from the client's earnings to allocate to various accounts tied to the client's financial goals. This technique is commonly referred to as *paying yourself first.*

REMEMBER

One of the first steps in financial planning involves evaluating what you have to work with, and that depends on how much money your client earns and spends. Unless your client can free up some income for building and protecting her wealth, she won't have any money to put to work for her, and you won't have any assets to manage.

Wrapping your brain around asset management

Asset management involves the planning, monitoring, administering, and disposing of everything a client owns of value, especially her investment portfolio, but also including real estate properties and any business(es). You can approach asset management as a step-by-step process:

1. **Establish the client's goals and objectives and the amount of money needed to achieve each in the given timeline.**

2. **Develop an investment strategy that accommodates the client's risk tolerance while meeting the agreed-upon goals.**

3. **Establish various accounts, as necessary, such as retirement accounts and college savings accounts.**

4. **Design a portfolio of stocks, bonds, cash, and other assets to execute the investment strategy.**

    Investment choices must be based on several factors including expenses, taxes, risks, and returns.

5. **Review the portfolio regularly with the client and make any adjustments necessary to keep the portfolio and the client on track.**

    Much of your work here involves managing client expectations and reminding the client of the strategy, goals, and objectives.

As a financial advisor, you have choice as to whether to dive into the deep end in this fundamental area or outsource it to others (for example, TAMPs or specialist colleagues). Regardless, your clients will demand a portfolio return that meets or exceeds their expectations. You need to deftly set and manage your clients' portfolio and expectations, getting them from today to their future goal.

REMEMBER

Even though a great debate rages as to whether active investment management is all but dead (as reflected in the trade publications), passive management hasn't proven to be the silver bullet that it's been touted to be. No investment strategy is a panacea. Refer to Chapter 8 for more discussion about asset management.

Knowing what liability management entails

If an unforeseen event blindsides your client's household, then no matter how great the portfolio performance, your client will be spending her assets to meet the unexpected need. Whether it's a disability, illness, death, job loss, living longer than expected, or any number of other unanticipated burdens of withdrawal on a portfolio, you must make sure these risks are actively identified and hedged against. You don't need to hedge against 100 percent loss, but including some protection in the financial plan is critical to your client's positive financial outcome. Chapter 9 discusses liability management in greater detail.

Looking at what estate planning involves

Estate planning sounds like it's just for rich people, but that's far from true. Anyone with assets they plan to pass on to heirs needs a plan to ensure that more of those assets pass to loved ones than to the government and that the transfer of wealth goes as smoothly and quickly as possible. An estate plan makes that happen.

Although your client's lawyer will write the estate plan, you play a key role by doing the following:

» Making sure your client has an estate plan, and, if she doesn't, referring her to a great lawyer in your network to prepare the plan.

>> Collaborating actively with the client's estate planning lawyer and tax advisor, well in advance of any event, to ensure that the client's intentions for her assets are properly organized and administered.

>> Ensuring that all of the client's accounts have the correct beneficiaries listed.

See Chapter 10 for more about estate planning.

Identifying key tax issues

Whether your clients are employees earning a regular paycheck or business owners whose income is tied to the profits from the business, you must identify key tax issues and be sure that your clients financial plans take advantage of any qualified tax breaks, such as tax-advantaged or -deferred accounts and financial products. Charitable interests can make a big tax difference too.

TIP

Find and collaborate with one or more tax experts in your professional network. One of the best ways to deliver value to a client is with a referral to a tax advisor, if the client doesn't already have one. Don't give specific tax advice unless you have the expertise to do so.

See Chapter 11 for more about helping clients reduce their tax burdens.

Comprehending behavioral finance

Because your clients are human, you have one major impediment to your daily work — that your clients *are* human. Behavioral finance takes this fact into consideration by acknowledging the psychological and emotional factors that influence how people feel about money and how they make their financial decisions. For example, in one study, 401K plans that required participants to opt in had a 68 percent participation rate after 36 months of employment, whereas plans that enrolled participants automatically and required them to opt out had a 98 percent participation rate, indicating that people were often reticent or just too lazy to sign up for the plans.

Familiarizing yourself with a variety of investor biases and sentiments and training yourself to keep your own emotions at bay when your clients get the jitters serve you and your clients well. See Chapter 12 for more about behavioral finance.

Providing Superior Service to Your Clients

Although your daily activities as a financial advisor are likely to be diverse, they all boil down to acquiring and serving your clientele. I could even argue that being a successful financial advisor all boils down to serving your clientele, because if you do that well, you won't have to spend much time finding new clients — they will find you. In this section, I cover the basics of providing superior service to clients.

Performing your due diligence

Each client has different financial needs, so the first order of business with any new client is to perform your due diligence. I recommend a framework I developed to use in my own practice called The Four As of Due Diligence:

>> **A**ssessment: Ask big questions.

>> **A**udit: Dig into the details on current products/solutions.

>> **A**ction: Close the gap from what's in place versus what the client needs.

>> **A**lignment: Monitor changes to maintain alignment with financial products and/or services used and the household's situation.

REMEMBER

This formal process enables you to identify the areas where you can deliver the most value to your client, and it keeps you mentally organized. More importantly, it forces you to stay within a consultative boundary, thus avoiding an off-putting sales routine. See Chapter 13 for details about how to use The Four As of Due Diligence to your and your clients' advantage.

Creating personalized financial plans

As you perform your due diligence, you uncover each client's unique needs. The next step is to formulate a personalized financial plan that meets those needs. Even though certain planning items, such as retirement, life insurance, and estate planning, are mainstays, others may differ from client to client. In addition, the allocation toward each depends on household-specific factors, including whether the client is married, has children, is an employee or business owner, has a high or low risk tolerance, and more.

In Chapter 14, I present a framework for building a holistic and cohesive personalized financial plan for every client. I call it the "Three Cs of a Holistic Financial Plan":

>> **Copy:** The written documentation or family governance paperwork, typically prepared by the family lawyer, that spells out the family's intentions for its assets. Copy includes a family trust or will, medical directives, and powers of attorney, which collectively delineate how assets will be distributed and how the family is to act in the event that the matriarch or patriarch is no longer able to make decisions and issue directives.

>> **Capital:** Capital includes all assets and claims on those assets, including a home and the mortgage on that home, a family business, investments, savings, and belongings.

>> **Consequences:** Consequences are the various scenarios that a family wants to avoid, such as the loss of income when a major breadwinner dies unexpectedly. Consequences are usually covered by various insurance policies.

WARNING

Don't embrace a one-size fits all mentality. You must remain flexible to develop a plan that meets each client's unique needs and concerns.

Teaming up for superior service

One of the biggest mistakes a financial advisor can make is to try to be everything to everyone. You have two primary responsibilities as a financial advisor:

>> Assess each client's unique financial needs.

>> Ensure that all those needs are met.

No rule exists that you must be the person to meet all those needs. At the very least, you should consult with the client's attorney and tax advisor and follow up to be sure that they're doing what they need to do and you're doing what you need to do to provide holistic financial planning, management, and administration. (See Chapter 15 for details.)

Creating a tiered service model

As you grow your client base, your time becomes more precious as you have less time to devote to each client. To continue to grow beyond 100 clients or so, you need to work more efficiently. You can improve your efficiency in several ways, including making better use of technology and hiring an assistant to handle routine tasks.

Another way to improve efficiency is to create a tiered service model. In Chapter 16, I suggest a precious metals approach, dividing clients into the following four groups, which are generally based on their revenue-generating potential (either directly through services they need or indirectly through referrals):

>> Platinum

>> Gold

>> Silver

>> Bronze

Using various demographic and psychographic criteria, you can assign each client to one of these groups, so you know how much relative time and effort to devote to each client.

Assessing your performance as a financial advisor

Unlike other professions, where success may be easier to measure (for example, percentage of patients cured or lawsuits won), for financial advisors it's more complicated, and the timespan is longer. As a financial advisor, you may not witness success until your client sails into retirement on his brand new yacht. Then again, you may experience success much sooner when you hand your client's widower a check from the life insurance policy you convinced your client to purchase only a few months ago.

In Chapter 17, I provide a few benchmarks for measuring success, primarily in terms of your clients' portfolios. The two key benchmarks in the area of investments are the market indexes and the personal benchmark, which I prefer. With the personal benchmark, you measure your success based on how well your client's portfolio meets the agreed-upon goal. With this approach, you have a fixed benchmark tied to the client's needs and dreams instead of to a fluctuation benchmark index.

REMEMBER

To hold yourself accountable and provide your clients a clear assessment of how well you're doing managing their assets and liabilities, you need a benchmark that quantifies success. This benchmark enables you and your clients to know when all is well and when adjustments need to be made. It may also give your clients peace of mind by letting them know they're making progress even when they're convinced they're losing ground.

Growing Your Client Base

Obviously, your success hinges on your ability to acquire and retain clients. Client acquisition is particularly important when you're just getting started and haven't established yourself as one of the top financial advisors in your area. In Part 4, I share several strategies and techniques for attracting prospects and scoring clients. In this section, I share the highlights.

Winning lifelong clients

Building a client base finds is rooted in a value exchange. In short, you're in the value-exchange business. If you deliver value, you receive value in return. The value you give is in the form of sound financial advice, savvy financial planning, product and solution recommendations, listening carefully to and evaluating clients' needs, and holistic, cohesive service that addresses all aspects of a client's financial life. The value you receive in return is in the form of advisor fees, commissions, and referrals. In other words, you receive fair pay for helping your clients achieve their financial goals.

REMEMBER

The best way to acquire and retain clients is to earn them. Marketing is secondary.

Marketing your services

I'm not big on marketing in the traditional sense of the word, and I don't believe in nonsensical networking. If I don't have a clear idea of *how* I can deliver value to someone I'm meeting, then it's a waste of both our times.

However, nobody knows the value you offer if they don't know you exist. You need to meet people, especially when you're getting started in the business. In Chapter 19, I present various ways to raise your profile online, in your community, and among other professionals in fields related to yours.

TIP

The best marketing is an intellectual capital campaign. Sharing your specialized knowledge or perspective should be your crusade. Don't engage in mundane, dialing for dollars activities.

Teaming up with colleagues

You're likely to have a tough time achieving success as a financial advisor if you try to fly solo. At the very least, team up with your client's lawyer and tax advisor to develop a holistic, cohesive financial plan for each client. Beyond that, you can achieve even greater success by teaming up with other financial advisors through joint-work opportunities, especially if you specialize in one area and they specialize in others.

In addition to providing your client with knowledge and skills you may not have, teamwork enhances your skill set, provides you with different perspectives you may not have considered, and adds to your professional network, which can be a valuable source of referrals.

REMEMBER

One of the best aspects of this profession is that you get to meet and interact with some of the most fascinating and wonderful people on the planet. I've been lucky to meet, and keep, financial advisors who share similar core values and life purpose. I encourage you to do the same, to enhance your skill set and your revenues.

Moving Up: Starting Your Own Firm

You can achieve success as a financial advisor by working at a firm for the entire course of your career or by running your own practice. However, if your goal is to help more people with your unique approach to providing financial advice, you may want to consider starting your own firm. To make your decision, you need to answer two questions:

» Do you have any previous commitments that prohibit you from starting your own financial advisor firm? In other words, are you willing to lose the clients you already serve, which is a real possibility if you make the leap from employee to business owner.

» Do you really want to start and run your own firm? Take into account that starting and running a business is a major time and money commitment and that it's risky. Also, your role is likely to change; you may need to spend more time in management and administration and less time serving clients.

One more consideration to make is what's involved in starting your own firm. The chapters in Part 5 provide detailed guidance. Here, I touch on the key points.

Getting started

The first steps are the most challenging when you're starting any business. In Chapter 21, I provide a checklist and additional details for putting all the pieces in place:

>> **Choose a business structure:** Limited liability company (LLC), S-corporation (S-Corp), C-corporation (C-Corp), or partnership.

>> **Choose an independent broker/dealer platform:** Find a list of independent broker/dealers online, do your research, and choose one.

>> **Create an organizational chart:** You need to know the roles to fill and start thinking about the people who would be the best fit for each role. Get acquainted with a typical financial advisory firm structure and adapt it as necessary to fit your firm. (*Hint:* If it's your firm, you should probably be the rainmaker and chief cheerleader.)

WARNING

Trying to establish your own firm without going through the time-consuming task of understanding whom you need and what each person should be focused on sets you up for failure from day one.

>> **Evaluate your staffing needs:** Hire an assistant to handle the paperwork and other routine tasks, so you can focus on acquiring and serving clients and getting the business up and running.

TIP

Plan on having a 3-to-1 ratio of advisors to assistants.

>> **Formalize the business and file the necessary paperwork:** Better yet, hire a lawyer to do it for you.

>> **Finance your startup:** Use your own money, get a loan, find investors, partner with your firm's other financial advisors, or figure out some other way to get your mitts on enough cash to keep the firm running for at least 12 months, when your cash flow should be sufficient to keep the business going.

>> **Get someone focused on rainmaking:** You need to start acquiring clients pronto. One or more (or all) of the financial advisors in your firm should be focused, initially, on client acquisition. As you acquire clients, each advisor can specialize more as minder, finder, or grinder.

Sharing revenue (or not)

How you compensate your team members can vary greatly, depending on the level of turnover you expect. If you pay your team a fair wage for fair work, you'll get to keep and develop personnel for years. However, if you're hiring people who have to eat what they kill, and not much else, expect to see that revolving door in perpetual motion.

TIP

One way to attract and keep your financial advisors and other key personnel is to set up a revenue sharing plan. Such a plan may be in the form of bonuses based on the financial success of the firm or offering shares of ownership in the business.

Planning your exit strategy

When you're starting a business, the last thing you want to think about is your exit strategy, but you should recognize from working with clients the importance of planning ahead for the unexpected. If you build a thriving business and experience a tragedy in your life, who's going to run the business? Who's going to benefit from all your hard work? How will your family manage? You probably have plenty of time to plan a business transition before you retire, but you really should be thinking about the future of the business even in its early stages. How will you ensure that the next generation of leadership continues your firm's philosophy, service model, and financial stewardship?

REMEMBER

Follow the same advice you give your clients. Identify the best people to carry on your legacy. This challenge may even affect your decision on whom to partner with and whom to hire. You need not only the most skilled advisors, but also the most trustworthy and authentic ones to carry on your firm's mission.

Chapter **2**

Deciding Whether You're Geared to Be a Financial Advisor

Prior to making any career decision, conduct a self-assessment to ensure that the financial-advisory career is right for you and that you're likely to be a good fit for it. Many people spend a great deal of time and money pursuing a career that they're not well suited for only to discover later that they don't like the work or aren't qualified to do it.

Being a successful financial advisor requires the right mix of nature and nurture. Nature and formative life experience provide the personality traits, values, and motivation required to be successful in the field. Nurture (education, training, and job experience) provides the knowledge and skills. Although you can acquire knowledge and skills later in life, personality, values, and motivation can be difficult to change. For example, if humility and supportiveness aren't built into your DNA, they can be tough to develop.

In this chapter, I provide guidance for performing a self-assessment to determine whether you have the right stuff to become a successful financial advisor and enjoy doing it. Though this chapter doesn't include every conceivable trait or skill that's necessary or useful for building a successful and satisfying career, it does contain the key qualities I've observed across the broad spectrum of financial advisors I've known, all of whom I like, trust, and respect.

Evaluating Your Personality Traits

Savvy employers look for candidates who not only have the requisite qualifications for an opening in their company but also have the right personality to be successful and to fit in with the organization. Personality traits are part of the soft skills that separate equally qualified candidates from one another. Even though hard skills are certainly essential, soft skills also contribute to determining whether a candidate is likely to succeed or fail.

In this section, I lead you through the process of evaluating your personality traits by asking you a series of questions. Think of it as part of your interview for the financial advisor position.

Do you like to teach?

The best financial advisors are those who like to share their acquired knowledge. I've always believed that the happiest clients are those who are routinely educated by their advisors. Education prepares clients for the unexpected, such as a stock market crash or an unplanned life-changing event. When clients are prepared, they worry less because they know the plan that's in place to proactively and successfully deal with the situation and perhaps even capitalize on it.

In many ways, the desire to enlighten others comes from an excitement to inspire people to either shift their own perspective or to take action in some new direction. Some of the best motivational speakers are the most powerful teachers. They communicate ideas in ways that create emotional connections to their subject matter, enabling the audience to see themselves in the story. Likewise, as a successful financial advisor, you must find a way to identify your clients' core values and the emotional factors that drive their financial decisions and behaviors, so that you can educate them about finances in a way that resonates with them. People who love to teach have an inherent knack for connecting with their students.

TIP

One of the greatest teachers in history, Socrates, developed a teaching method that has remained extremely effective to this day — dialog. Instead of merely presenting information and insight and hoping that your clients will absorb it, ask pertinent questions to make your teaching moments more interactive, thus improving your clients' retention. Asking questions opens the client-advisor dynamic to healthy interaction. You discover what your clients are thinking, and they become more receptive to the facts and figures you share with them.

Are you patient and supportive?

Being a financial advisor can be frustrating and emotionally draining. You must deal not only with the daily fluctuations of the market and the constant stream of world news, good and bad, that panics markets and clients, but also with stressful life events that weigh on your clients' emotions and drive their behaviors. After all, as an advisor, part of your job is to counsel clients and be the calm captain on the raging seas.

If you're easily frustrated when people don't understand what you're trying to tell them, work on simplifying your communications. Ask questions to figure out why your clients aren't getting it or why they're resisting the proposed plan or recommendation. Although clients may appear to be dense or difficult, the problem is usually with the presentation or with an unexpressed objection to what you're recommending.

REMEMBER

Be patient with yourself and your clients. Taking time for reflection is often helpful for allowing you and your clients to step back and let the information settle in and for allowing you to think of a different way to present the information. The more patient and supportive you are in the transmission of knowledge, the better chance your clients will adopt whatever recommendation you're making.

Patience and support also extend to emotional situations. Many times, I've had clients cry when describing a painful life event or memory that has shaped their perception and sensitivity. When your clients share their emotions, being connected with them and having earned their trust are good signs. Continue to earn it by showing genuine empathy.

Are you willing to advocate for your clients?

Being an advocate means you fight for someone else's benefit — not your own. It's an entirely selfless act. You need to be willing to step into difficult situations to protect your clients from any financial harm and, sometimes, from themselves. Here are a few examples:

>> If a client has a strong impulse to make a foolhardy financial decision, do your best to talk him off the cliff.

>> If a friend or relative is slowly (or quickly) bleeding your client dry, stand up to your client's urge to give the friend or relative more money. (Rarely does giving a friend or relative large sums of money for nothing help the friend or relative, and it usually ends up destroying relationships.)

>> Encourage clients to tell you about any investment opportunities they're thinking about before investing, so you can be their sounding board. (You can't advocate for a client if you don't know about potential scams he's being exposed to.)

REMEMBER

If you're heart's in the right place, you're the type of person who gives advice in the best interest of your clients, even when it generates less revenue for you. As an advocate, however, you must be willing to do even more by defending your clients and their money against external threats.

Of course, your motivation isn't *entirely* selfless; you need to earn an income from the services you provide. However, charging a client for the services you provide and being his advocate isn't mutually exclusive. Ethical professionals in nearly every field do it all the time.

STRIKING THE RIGHT BALANCE

Standing between a client and a friend or family member who's slowly bleeding your client dry is a difficult position to place yourself in. Your client has a desire to help a loved one, and it's the client's money, after all. As a great financial advisor, your job is to deftly navigate the divide between protecting your client from the world around him while honoring his desires and intentions for the use of his money.

As a client advocate, I've found myself in this position. Although I have no problem with clients giving away their money to loved ones who need a reasonable, fixed amount of money to handle a temporary cash flow problem, I have a big problem with anyone who tries to bleed a client dry while being reckless with their own finances or too lazy to earn their own money.

A client's child who never left the nest, or a sibling who continues to wonder at age 50 what they'll be when the grow up, are two examples of undue burden that should be addressed. Obviously, the continued support of these folks will drain resources designed to provide for your client. Framing the consequences in possible lifestyle pivots could be helpful. Suggesting a change of geography or housing status may make enough of an impact to help your client realize that he's being dragged down, and not doing something about it will have a financial impact on him eventually.

Are you humble?

Humility is a job requirement for a financial advisor for two reasons:

>> A client's trust in you is an honor and a challenge. You can congratulate your client on making a good decision, but you should also let your client know that you value his trust and are committed to earning that trust by providing superior service and advice. Accept the responsibility with humility.

>> You're not infallible. Overconfidence is a sure sign that you're on the path to a disappointing career. To maintain your humility, constantly ask yourself, "What if I'm wrong?" Also, remind yourself that your job is to deliver added value to your client and that job never ends. As long as you've invested yourself in a process to reveal the best solution, you can be proud of the work you've accomplished; just don't think that your work is done.

REMEMBER

Practice what you preach. As a financial advisor, you encourage your clients to live within their means and put their money to work for them. Follow this advice yourself, as well. Take a look at your credit card debt and your lifestyle. Living beyond your means may be a sign of a lack of humility and of misplaced priorities.

Are you well-connected?

If you're planning to operate as a lone wolf, being well-connected is a sign that you have an outgoing personality required to be your own rainmaker. If you're planning to work for a firm or team up with another financial advisor who's talented at client acquisition, being well-connected is less important.

REMEMBER

Charismatic financial advisors have the advantage of not only attracting new clients but also adding team members and joint-work partners to their practice to handle a greater influx of new clients. (See Chapter 20 for more about joint work.)

Being well-connected is just the first part. You also need to be passionate about your work — excited to contact, meet, discuss, and educate your network. Having a drive to engage with your network is an incredibly valuable trait to develop, especially if you're new to the field. You may not be fully aware of your talents or where you're lacking until you challenge yourself through interactions with colleagues.

WARNING

Don't be discouraged if you're not well-connected or outgoing, even if the sales manager at the firm where you work tries to make you feel otherwise. Industry-wide, sales managers encourage newbie financial advisors to become social animals to ferret out new business prospects. If you love that part of the job, great, more power to you. However, if you discover that you hate it, don't worry too much. Shift your role toward another part of the financial advisory business by partnering with a rainmaker and contributing your unique skills to achieve great synergies. (See Chapter 21 for more about the three key roles of financial advisors — minders, finders, and grinders — and how to create productive synergies.)

Are you hungry for knowledge?

Like most professions, the financial services industry is constantly evolving. The constant introduction of new technologies, regulations, and capital markets requires that financial advisors be lifelong learners. Maintaining your core competencies in an ever-changing field while growing (or just maintaining) your practice is a never ending pursuit. The good news is that you'll never be bored in this business.

TIP

Be curious. Whenever you notice something unfamiliar in the field, ask questions such as "How does this work?," "Why are people using this technique?," and "How can I use this to help my clients?" A natural (or well-developed) curiosity leads you to discover more ways to add value to your clients' lives and improve the way you operate your practice. Becoming a lifelong learner is not only empowering (especially after being in the business for 20 years or more), but it's also a surefire way to stay humble — even if you've had some degree of success in your career thus far.

Questioning Your Motivations

The most successful professionals in any field are usually those who enter the profession for the right reasons — typically because they're passionate about the profession, and they want to make a positive impact in some way. Most professionals also consider the compensation to some degree.

Prior to choosing financial advisory as your lifelong work, I encourage you to question your motivations for two reasons:

>> I want you to be happy and successful in the field, or to choose a different field that you'd be more passionate about and enjoy more.

>> I like to see people enter the field who are passionate about it and passionate about their clients.

In this section, I present two ways to ensure that your motivation aligns with your clients' interests.

Making a commitment to deliver value

Consider the valuable advice moments in your own life. Maybe it was a parent giving you counsel on getting over a broken relationship or your first boss giving you pointers on how to succeed in life. Everyone has all been the beneficiaries of good advice — sometimes they're receptive to it and sometimes not so much.

As a financial advisor, you're prime directive is to provide your clients with sound financial advice and planning, both of which add value to their lives. Your job is to guide them to achieving the best financial outcomes possible. By accomplishing this goal, you not only secure a nice living and successful career, but most importantly gain a deep sense of self-fulfillment, purpose, and achievement.

If you're interested in how you can create a positive impact on your clients' lives and on how you can add value to their lives, then you're well on your way to becoming a successful financial advisor. Make the commitment to add value, and then strive to honor that commitment daily for each and every client.

WARNING

If you're getting into the financial services business just to make a bunch of money, you're selling yourself short. No doubt plenty of money can be made in this career, but that's just the tip of the iceberg. Later, when you're reflecting on your life's purpose and how you've contributed to the world around you, you want to feel that you've had a profound positive impact on those around you and in your community.

Avoiding the siren call of commissioned sales

One of the first decisions you need to make when you're entering this field is whether to be a financial advisor or a salesperson. Here's the difference:

>> Financial advisors improve their clients' short- and long-term financial outcomes by providing solid financial advice and planning. Their compensation is tied to the financial success of their clients.

>> Salespeople sell financial products to customers and collect a commission on each sale. Salespeople may develop long-term relationships with their customers and sell them products that are in their best interests, but that arrangement isn't built into the transactions.

Many so-called financial advisors make their living selling products and collecting up-front commissions. In doing so, the advisor's and customer's interests aren't aligned, and the time frames differ significantly. A customer buys a financial product with the hope and promise of a positive future financial outcome, but the commission rewards the salesperson immediately, so the salesperson has no vested interest in the future outcome. This misalignment is a conflict of interest that's common in the financial services industry. The best way to align your motivation with that of your clients is to build a practice based primarily or solely on asset-based and service fees, not commissioned products.

REMEMBER

In reality, most financial advisor practices are a combination of both fees and commissions. However, I've found that firms that base their compensation solely on the financial outcomes of their clients are most consistent in providing clients with advice that's in their best interests. The most common compensation models that align advisor and client interests are asset-based fees or financial advisory fees. (See Chapter 7 for more about compensation models.)

TIP

Differentiate yourself by being open and honest with clients about how you're compensated. Full disclosure can be a powerful way to build trust and earn new client referrals.

Balancing Leadership and Service

The best leaders are servants; they provide the opportunities, knowledge, and resources that those they lead need to be successful in their roles. *Servant leadership* is actually a style of business leadership that seeks to be the beacon of hope and guidance while serving the personal goals and objectives of those who follow. As a servant leader, you deliver value to your clients through exceptional service, advice, and personal accountability, and in return they follow you with their money and time and by rewarding you with the self-satisfaction of helping them achieve their dreams.

The following sections take a closer look at servant leadership and how you can accept your role and sustain it in your interactions with your clients.

Embracing your leadership role

As your client's financial advisor, you're the quarterback of the financial team, which includes the client and may include other advisors (such as an attorney or accountant), trusted family members or friends, and, in more sophisticated households, named trustees and beneficiaries. As quarterback, you communicate with and coordinate the efforts of the other players on the financial team to optimize the client's financial outcomes. Strong leadership is necessary to oversee and direct the many aspects and many people involved in a client's finances.

You're in the best position to take on the duties and responsibilities of managing the overall financial plan for a household. Attorneys are great for drafting and amending solid family governance documents and preventing your clients against monetary losses related to legal cases. An accountant is fantastic at keeping the tax liabilities optimized and managed through different techniques or structures. However, setting the family's financial agenda is your responsibility. In this capacity, you're considered the wealth manager, a moniker that's been newly minted and marketed by many financial advisory firms.

Maintaining a service-oriented mindset

This profession delivers an intangible product. You can't wrap it up with a nice bow and present it to your client. Instead, the results of your efforts are measured by your clients' ability to live the life they've dreamed of — putting their kids through college, traveling and having a work-life balance, and retiring to a fulfilling and enjoyable lifestyle.

TIP

Because you're offering an intangible product, you should develop yourself into a product of sorts. Your clients should come to expect a certain type of interaction on a given frequency, and they certainly don't want to be sold the hot financial product du jour. (Over the years, I've had more than one new client hire me and fire another financial advisor, just because I had a defined client service model and because they understood that they'd be served, not *sold to*, on a regular basis.)

Chapter 3

Performing a Self Background Check

Successful financial advisors don't merely have the right stuff in terms of personality and drive (as Chapter 2 explains); they also have the right background in work and life experience and are on a solid financial footing. Having a lot of rich friends (a ready-made market) is certainly helpful, but relevant work and life experience is much more valuable for long-term sustainability and growth. The right experience (background) enables you to develop an intellectual and emotional connection with the field and with clients and prospects that makes you more of a *natural* — a person who's suited to and likely to be successful at something without a great deal of training or effort.

Defining the ideal background for the perfect candidate for this field is difficult, and it's more qualitative than quantitative, but there are certain hallmarks of successful advisors. For example, the most successful financial advisors have backgrounds in which they had a great deal of experience interacting with people, especially in the role of coach or teacher. Great financial advisors are also successful at managing their own finances — a skill developed mostly through life experience, because very few people receive formal training in this area when they're growing up.

In this chapter, I introduce factors related to a person's background that are likely to make them more qualified to become a financial advisor, and I break them down into three key areas:

>> Professional background

>> Personal background

>> Personal finance background

REMEMBER

Life experience and financial stability play a much larger role in a person's success as a financial advisor than most people realize. You develop the abilities to communicate with clients and manage money over the course of your life. These abilities aren't something you develop solely or even primarily through classwork.

Choosing a Career Path

Many paths lead to a career as a financial advisor. These paths can be broken down into three categories based on your starting point: right out of college, within the industry, and outside the industry.

Getting started fresh out of college

If you just graduated from college with a degree in finance or economics, you may have determined already that becoming a financial advisor is the path for you. After all, studying related subjects at a college or university prepares you perfectly for this profession, right? Wrong. Having some education in the financial arena can be helpful to understand financial terminology and concepts and to pursue further professional designations. However, it doesn't adequately prepare you for the day-to-day work involved in being a financial advisor.

One of the most common ways graduates get their feet wet is to work for one of the big investment banking firms (see Chapter 4). Years ago, these firms offered months-long training programs that focused on developing the sales skills and product knowledge required to be a functional financial advisor. Today, training is much less robust, and newbies must fend for themselves to acquire clients.

TIP

To give yourself a leg up, join an existing team or apprentice with a solo practitioner. Broker/dealers have wide variety of practices within their networks. If you're working with a recruiter for one of these firms or, better yet, proactively approaching one, tell her you're looking to *apprentice* to an existing solo practitioner or advisor group within the branch. Don't hesitate to make this request. After all, you're fulfilling a need that most firms are struggling with — namely, replacing an aging workforce with younger tenured advisors. In addition, your targeted self-promotion and assertiveness gives you an edge over shyer candidates who don't have what it takes to grow the business.

As an apprentice, expect to earn a salary and perhaps a bonus based on revenue growth. The biggest benefit, however, is that you get hands-on experience in the field, just as residents at medical centers and associates at law firms gain practical experience on their way to becoming fully fledged members of the profession. You'll also avoid the rat race of having to find new clients right out of the gate, something that's difficult for new college grads whose network consists mostly of fellow twenty-somethings who are also looking for jobs.

WARNING

Avoid firms that hire new college grads merely to increase their product distribution instead of to develop highly qualified financial advisors. Unfortunately, this exploitation of new college grads is common in the industry. These work opportunities are fine if you're looking to make a quick buck in commissioned product sales, but if you're pursuing a lifetime career as a professional, don't settle for less than a position that offers mentorship and continuing education.

Changing careers from within the industry

If you're working in the financial services industry and are beginning to crave a greater purpose — by adding valuable financial advice and guidance to the lives of people in your community — then becoming a financial advisor may be just the right move for you. You probably have all the skills and experience required to succeed. You simply need to redirect them.

REMEMBER

Applying your accumulated knowledge and insight on how and why the financial world works the way it does is a great way to deliver value to clients. Not only do you have a specialized background that can be of great benefit, but you're also in the perfect position to be a true client advocate, looking out for your clients' interests in a way that only someone with financial services experience (for example, banking, securities trading, or product wholesaling, to name a few) can. It's a great differentiator too, which can help you attract more clients in your early years.

The evolution of financial technology has driven many traditional Wall Street jobs to extinction. As one major example, a stock exchange floor specialist used to be the best job you could have on Wall Street. The role required a complicated combination of brute force and intellect, which had at its core the responsibility of managing the market around a particular set of stocks. This role is almost a relic of the past, as technology has reinvented how markets facilitate the meeting of buyers and sellers.

Today, institutional bond market traders are slowly getting the message that their roles are disappearing, too, as many more transactions are being organized and executed through peer-to-peer networks and exchanges. Gone are the days where a client would need an well-connected bond broker with a great network of bond traders at various dealers across the country to find a good deal. With the advent of technology, profit margins have been squeezed even more, benefitting investors while slowly eroding the status quo.

These backgrounds and others in the financial field can significantly ease the transition to becoming a financial advisor, providing the knowledge and insights to serve clients more effectively.

Changing careers from outside the industry

Few things in life are worse than feeling stuck in a job or on a career path you don't like. After college, most people who major in general studies set out on a career path by happy (or unhappy) accident as they look for ways to apply their education to a worthy endeavor. Years may pass, and then one day, they wake up to realize that they're unfulfilled and losing hope for ever being so. They know they need to change careers but aren't sure which career path would lead to their dream job.

WHERE I GOT MY START

I started in the mid-1990s at a large institutional investment management firm. For ten years, I played various roles in the financial product development and distribution machine. My clients weren't retail households but financial advisors who worked for other large institutions. In truth, very few of these clients behaved like real financial advisors. They were more like traditional brokers, selling products to customers and serving as intermediaries between the product manufacturer and the end customer.

Having added value and made lots of money for big financial institutions, shifting my accumulated knowledge and skills to benefit regular folk became a personal crusade. I figured that because I knew where all the proverbial bodies were buried in the financial product distribution machine, I could use that knowledge to significantly improve the investment plans in which many clients found themselves and help them avoid ugly surprises. My background and personal crusade provided the perfect combination to differentiate myself by offering lower fees, fewer conflicts of interest, and greater transparency, along with a passion for helping my clients use their assets most effectively to achieve their dreams.

Dissatisfied professionals with a wide variety of educational backgrounds can find the answer as a financial advisor, especially those who understand people and appreciate the role of money, and its limitations, in enabling people to pursue their own happiness and fulfillment. Several backgrounds in particular ease the transition into becoming a financial advisor:

>> **Psychology:** Anyone who has an intimate knowledge of human psychology and factors that drive thoughts, emotions, and behaviors has a good start. If you like to spend time with people — talking with them, listening, connecting — then you're already at an advantage.

>> **Fundraising/charity:** People who work for charities, especially in donor development, already value the importance that strong financials can have on a cause or outcome. If this category includes you, you merely need to shift your focus from nonprofit fundraising to family wealth stewardship. If you've received formal education and training related to charitable gift planning strategies, you're even better positioned to make the transition.

>> **Professional networker:** If you're in any industry that requires you to have a broad network of colleagues, communication skills (writing and speaking), and relationship management skills, you're probably suited for a position as a financial advisor. Communication and relationship management skills are highly transferrable.

Capitalizing on Your Personal Experience

The best financial advisors draw on their personal experience to provide exceptional service to their clients. Three types of personal experiences in particular are useful in helping you serve clients:

>> Childhood memories of your family's money-management expertise or shortcomings

>> Your personal history of managing and perhaps mismanaging your own personal finances

>> Your history of helping others manage their personal finances, either professionally or by providing assistance to family members, friends, colleagues, and acquaintances in a less formal role

In this section, I explain how these three types of personal experience can benefit you and your clients.

REMEMBER

Your personal experiences are what give you the passion for what you do. By sharing your experiences with clients and prospects, you help them to understand the source of your passion — your reason for choosing this profession. As a result, your clients and prospects will be more engaged and action-oriented.

Taking advantage of your childhood memories

How your family managed its finances when you were growing up has a tremendous impact on your own approach to managing finances. Perhaps your parents demonstrated the value of careful financial planning and discipline, or maybe they taught you, by example, how *not* to manage finances. After all, childhood memories aren't all sunshine and moonbeams. Divorce, illness, job loss, the untimely death of a breadwinner, and even poverty can provide valuable lessons that help you serve your clients better.

TIP

Use your childhood memories to connect emotionally with clients and prospects. Regardless of whether your parents taught you how to manage or how not to manage money, sharing your story can be a powerful way to instill the importance of financial planning and discipline in your clients.

WARNING

Be careful not to get preachy or to present your personal experience in a way that draws sympathy, even if that's not your intent. Either scenario turns off clients. For example, a story about how mom or dad lost a job and struggled to keep food on the table for you and your siblings can come across as a sob story, even though the intent was to use it to teach a valuable lesson.

Dealing with your own financial challenges

As a financial advisor, you're more than a numbers-cruncher; you're also a heart-and-soul counselor. As such, you must be empathetic; that is, you must be able to understand and share the feelings of others, especially in terms of their financial goals and the poor choices and life challenges that can disrupt progress toward those goals.

If you've experienced financial hardship, made terrible choices, or suffered from the terrible choices of others, you're more likely to be able to empathize with clients and prospects and be less prone to judging them. If you've had experience being taken advantage of by financial salespeople in the past, you'll be even more sympathetic to the needs of clients.

WARNING

Sharing your financial setbacks is like walking a tight wire. You want to empathize by demonstrating that you're human, but you also need to show that you've gained valuable insight and developed knowledge and skills that enable you to help clients avoid and recover from these setbacks. A little self-deprecation can be very effective, but to build trust you have to follow up by demonstrating your expertise in financial planning and management.

Helping others manage their finances

Whether you've managed finances for clients professionally or for friends, family members, or colleagues, you have plenty of vicarious life experience from which to draw. You have stories of people you helped, those you tried to help but chose to go their own way, those who've made terrible financial decisions and suffered as a result, and those who were disciplined and followed a plan to build wealth.

Feel free to share the relevant success and horror stories you've gathered with your clients and prospects when you think these stories will help them make the right decisions. Just be sure to fictionalize the stories enough to protect the identities of those involved.

REMEMBER

Using emotion to connect clients with the importance of financial planning, management, and discipline is manipulative, but it's manipulative in a good way. As long as you use the emotional connection to inspire relevancy for the client, so she can then move forward in developing a financial plan, playing her emotions may be the only way to get her attention and drive home a valuable lesson. However, use this technique carefully and conscientiously.

WARNING

If you don't have experiences, direct or vicarious, don't make them up. (You may need to fictionalize stories just enough to make them more engaging and to protect the identities of those involved.) Made-up stories aren't only fraudulent, but often ineffective because they just don't ring true. If you don't have good stories to tell, you can develop new clients in many other ways (see Chapters 18 and 19). The point of this section is that if you have personal experience, don't overlook the opportunities to leverage it to the benefit of clients and prospects.

Evaluating Your Financial Position

If you're planning to launch your career as a financial advisor as a lone wolf or by starting your own firm, first crunch the numbers to figure out whether you can afford to do so. Starting without a substantial nest egg makes you more susceptible to conflicts of interest. You'll have a difficult time serving your clients' needs when you have to worry about your own needs.

In this section, I tell you how much money you should have to get started and explain the importance of having this money set aside. I also share some words of caution by explaining what typically happens when people start their financial advisor careers without a substantial nest egg.

REMEMBER

You can enter the field by accepting a salaried position, in which case this discussion about the importance of having a nest egg is irrelevant. Many companies are actively seeking to hire financial advisors to focus the majority of the their efforts on business development. This is often called an *eat-what-you-kill compensation model*. As long as you're effective and consistent at client or customer acquisition, and you enjoy it, you needn't worry about having savings in place to cover your venture.

Gauging your financial stability

Regardless of your background or experience, you won't have a positive cash flow as soon as you decide to start your own financial advisory practice. Client acquisition takes time, and even after you acquire a few clients, sufficient cash may not start flowing into your bank account for weeks or months to cover what's flowing out. Prior to quitting your day job, make sure you have at least 12 months cash in a savings or money market account to cover your monthly expenses.

If you don't have at least *12 months* of cash set aside, you'll be putting yourself at a disadvantage, especially if you have a family to support. Worrying about how you're going to make the monthly housing or car payment or keep the utilities on and food on the table makes it all the more difficult to be present and focused on the needs of clients and prospects.

After six months or so, the revenue stream from your financial advisory business should start to slow the cash burn and begin to replenish your nest egg, giving you more time to build your business. If you're still burning through cash and have no reason to believe that the situation will improve, you may need to work as a broker/agent on the side temporarily to earn extra money, as discussed in the next section.

REMEMBER

As a financial advisor, I know full well that risks always accompany rewards. No guts, no glory, as Frederick C. Blesse, a Major General in the U.S. Air Force once wrote. Pursuing a career as a financial advisor, where you must build your own client base from scratch, is a risky venture that has the promise of great rewards. But, unlike other ventures, the start-up capital required is nominal; it's not like opening a restaurant or building houses. Also, small wins in the early years give you staying power.

Recognizing the risks of financial instability

Without the proper preparation, embarking on building your own client base from the ground up takes you to the brink-and-back mentally, emotionally, and financially. Assuming you can manage the first two using meditation and exercise, the financial factor becomes all-important. After all, financial success alleviates a great deal of mental and emotional stress.

When you're financially compromised or feel as though you're losing ground, making decisions in other people's best interests isn't natural. When you're desperate for income, you have a natural survival instinct to serve your own interests *first*. Nothing's wrong with that; if you go belly up, others, including your clients, suffer too. If you reach this point, the best and most common option is to shift from being a financial advisor to acting as an investment/insurance broker/agent until you regain your financial footing.

REMEMBER

Nothing's wrong with being a broker/agent and earning up-front commissions. It's just not the role of a financial advisor. In your role as broker/agent, be up front with your customers and let them know how you're being compensated. In addition, be careful to separate your clientele into clients and customers. You can serve as a financial advisor to clients while selling products to your customers, but don't "sell" products to your clients.

WARNING

Don't market yourself as a financial advisor if what you're really doing is selling products to earn up-front commissions. As a financial advisor, you'll more than likely be required to adhere to a certain set of SEC rules (see Chapter 5) that define the advisor-client relationship. If you're an investment broker or insurance agent, make this clear to your customers.

In practice, many financial advisors have functioned as investment brokers or insurance agents at different points in their careers. Using broker-customer sales transactions to buy yourself more time and afford to serve in an advisor-client relationship has been common industry practice. Just beware that federal and state regulators are heavily debating this trend.

ADVISOR CASE STUDY

As I explain in Chapter 5, the industry's regulatory environment is currently undergoing a paradigm shift. For decades, financial services firms have employed legion representatives to sell products manufactured by asset management and insurance carriers. Compensation primarily has been through up-front commissions, upon the product sale's completion. The retail client has assumed that this brokerage relationship has been *fiduciary*, meaning the broker was acting in the client's best interest. However, the regulators have required only that these sales recommendations be suitable *at the time of the sale.*

Consumers are beginning to wise up thanks in large part to information campaigns sponsored by various professional industry groups and from articles and blog posts by individual financial advisors. Their goal is to educate the retail client marketplace that true fiduciary financial advisors provide a higher standard of care. You can benefit from the efforts of your colleagues and these industry groups by showcasing this service and care differentiation to win new clients. When prospects want to know why they should choose you over other financial advisors operating under the guise of fiduciary duty, educate them about the difference.

Regardless of how you receive compensation or how you choose to serve your clients or customers, revealing the amount of money you earn places you in rarefied air. Few financial advisors, and even fewer brokers/agents, communicate the specific dollars earned from a product sale. If the recommendation is sound, the compensation you earn shouldn't be a limiting factor but rather a helpful disclosure that reveals the underlying economics of how a product is expected to perform.

IN THIS CHAPTER

» Considering the choices for working independently or for a firm

» Exploring different ways to receive compensation from clients

» Joining a firm that provides education and training

» Gaining freedom as an independent contractor or registered investment advisor

» Scoping out different firms: what to look for

Chapter 4

Deciding to Work for a Firm or Build Your Own Practice

As a financial advisor, you can choose to work for a mega, traditional, full-service broker/dealer, set out on your own as an independent registered investment advisor, or build a successful career at any firm along that spectrum. As you evaluate your options, consider the following key factors:

» Your knowledge, skills, experience, and background (see Chapters 2 and 3)

» Whether you prefer to work as an employee or as an independent contractor

» The roles and responsibilities you'll engage in your day-to-day operations

In this chapter, I lead you on a tour of various work options where you can provide clients with holistic financial planning and management with varying degrees of independence from an institutional agenda. Also, you get tips on what to look out for before committing to a firm to avoid any nasty surprises.

Knowing Your Options

If you've been working in the industry for a few years or a few decades, you probably have a pretty good idea of its diversity in terms of financial advisor roles and responsibilities. If you're just starting out, the level of diversity may surprise you. However, you can group the variety of opportunities into the following three categories:

>> Traditional employee who works for a firm

>> Independent financial advisor broker/dealer (B/D)

>> Independent financial advisor registered investment advisor (RIA)

These three modes of operating as a financial advisor differ in numerous ways, but here are five key differences, which I summarize in Table 4-1:

>> **Autonomy:** If you like to be the master of your day's schedule and come and go as you please, then a working arrangement that provides more autonomy may be appealing to you. However, with such freedom (not only in scheduling, but also in business operations) comes the challenge of keeping motivated to meet your goals (if you've even bothered to set goals, along with other self-starter issues).

>> **Payout:** Also called *grid payout*, this refers to the amount of net revenue paid out to the financial advisor, after the firm keeps its share of the gross dealer concession (GDC) or advisory fee revenue. This percentage is typically in the 30+ percentage range at full-service (employee) firms and goes all the way up into the 90s percentage range at independent B/Ds and for RIAs.

>> **Support:** Full-service firms provide support for their financial advisors. Support includes all aspects of administrative, marketing, technology, trading, and custody platforms, along with support personnel. You get less day-to-day support as you move from employee to independent financial advisor.

>> **Expenses:** As a traditional employee, you get the benefit of having a firm pay for business development, personnel, office space, stationery, licensing, and other costs related to operating your practice. However, the firm owns the

client, which complicates the process of moving to another firm or creating your own firm if such an option appeals to you later in your career.

>> **Book:** Short for *book of business,* this refers to the client list that you develop during your tenure at the firm. As an employee, the firm owns the client list. When operating an independent practice, financial advisors typically build their book of business under their own doing business as (DBA) name, which causes less confusion over who owns the book of business when an advisor switches firms. (Most independent B/Ds and RIAs operate under their own DBA or entity name.)

TABLE 4-1:   **Financial Advisor Roles and Their Associated Features**

	Traditional employee	Independent financial advisor B/D	Independent RIA
Autonomy	Low	High	Full
Payout	Lowest, plus sometimes paid base salary	High, salary determined by business owner	Highest, salary determined by business owner
Support	Highest	Some to none	None
Best for	Focus on financial advisor work only, no management or administration	Financial advisors who want to build/manage their own business	Financial advisors who want to build/manage their own business
Expenses	Paid	No support	No support
Book	Owned by employer	Owned by financial advisor	Owned by financial advisor

The three modes of operating as a financial advisor offer a broad spectrum of ways in which you can have a fulfilling career as a financial advisor. Here are a few examples:

>> Join an existing firm as an associate to one of its top financial advisors, so you can figure out everything when you're getting started in the industry.

>> Join or contract with an existing firm after you've developed knowledge and skills, so you can focus all your time on client interaction without the burden of running a business.

>> Start your own firm as an RIA and run it as a solo operation, preferably with a talented, hard-working assistant to do the grunt work.

>> Start your own firm, manage the business as its minder, and hire finders, grinders, and other personnel to carry out the daily operations. (See Chapter 21 for more about minders, finders, and grinders.)

>> Partner with other financial advisors with each of you serving as minder, finder, or grinder.

REMEMBER

As with any investment or career pursuit, the more risk you take, the greater the potential reward. If you're highly ambitious and looking for an opportunity to earn considerable income and have a significant positive impact on more people's financial lives, starting your own business may be the best choice. However, if you get nauseous at the idea of being in debt, trying to build your own business, working 15 hours a day marketing yourself and staying on top of market conditions, you'd probably be wise to join an existing firm or at least team up with other advisors so you can focus on acquiring and/or servicing clients instead of on business management and growth.

The following sections take a deeper dive into the various ways of operating as a financial advisor.

Hiring in as an employee of an existing firm

If you're thinking about hiring in as an employee of an existing firm, consider the following:

>> **You become a statutory employee.** When a firm hires you, you become a statutory employee — an independent contractor under IRS common law who is treated as an employee for tax purposes. You may or may not receive a regular salary, but you're compensated for the production you generate from your business activity (fees and commissions) through a W-2 pay structure. This arrangement is generally good, because you can qualify for corporate benefits, such as a 401K plan, medical insurance, paid vacations and holidays, and other fringe benefits, and you don't have to pay self-employment tax.

>> **You're building business for the firm, not for yourself.** As an employee of a company, you're not an independent business owner. You're building business for the company that employs you, typically a large, full-service firm.

>> **The firm owns the business you develop.** Financial advisors who join any of the large, full-service firms are often required to sign noncompete agreements. If you switch firms or start your own business later, you may be prohibited from soliciting business from clients you had developed while under the firm's employment.

The types of firms in this "traditional employee" category include:

>> **Full-service brokerages:** Examples include Morgan Stanley, Bank of America, Merrill Lynch, Wells Fargo Advisors, and UBS Wealth Management. These firms provide their own investment research, securities order execution, and financial advice to their clients. They also operate investment banking divisions (for taking companies public), as well as providing traditional lending/banking services.

Full-service brokerages are also referred to as *wirehouses,* because in their early days they were connected directly to their branches and to the stock exchanges by way of wires (proprietary telephone and telegraph cables) for timely market price reporting and for placing trade orders.

>> **Banks:** Examples include JPMorgan Chase, Bank of America, Wells Fargo, Citigroup, Goldman Sachs, US Bancorp, TD Group, PNC Financial Services, Bank of New York Mellon, Capital One, BB&T, and SunTrust. These firms are where most people keep their checking and savings accounts and get home mortgage loans. Financial advisors who work for banks are often tasked with quotas requiring cross-selling of other bank products or affiliated companies' products.

>> **Regional broker/dealers:** Examples include Hilliard Lyons, RBC, Baird, Oppenheimer, D.A. Davidson, Janney Montgomery Scott, and Stifel. Like wirehouses, regional B/Ds offer a full-service employee advisor model. They often have their own investment banking and securities underwriting departments, proprietary research, and even lending and banking — pretty much all the same bells and whistles that a large firm would offer. They're just smaller and more geographically regionalized. They've also become more adaptive by encouraging free thinking among their financial advisors. As a result, they've been successfully retaining and growing their numbers, whereas larger firms continue to have advisors jump ship for independent RIAs.

>> **Insurance company broker/dealers:** Examples include MassMutual, Northwestern Mutual, Guardian, New York Life, Ohio National, and many others. Though the broker/dealer aspect of these companies tends to have more of an open-architecture compared to full-service brokerages and banks, they usually require you to produce a certain amount of insurance related revenue each year.

Setting out on your own as an independent financial advisor

As an independent financial advisor, you have your FINRA licenses held with an independent B/D. The independent B/D category is a broad and diverse group. Examples include LPL Financial, Raymond James Financial, Ameriprise, Commonwealth Financial Network, MML Investors Services, Northwestern Mutual, Cambridge Investment Research, and AXA Advisors. (Search online for "financial planning top 50 independent broker/dealers" to find a link to a longer list.)

The independent contracts offered by these companies vary considerably. Some require a certain threshold of demonstrated revenues to earn consideration to join their ranks. Others are owned by insurance product manufacturers with requirements to generate a certain amount of production using their proprietary products each year. Regardless of the details, the common thread tying them together is a philosophy of independent thinking and freedom, but usually with imposed guardrails (for example, risk profile assessments, limits on individual securities versus mutual funds, no access to junk bonds, and so on). This way, the B/D doesn't have to worry that an financial advisor's self-designed investment strategy blows up a client portfolio.

TIP

If you crave more freedom, you can establish your own independent RIA firm. The reasons to pursue this option were more plentiful in the past, because independent B/Ds had far more restrictive program guidelines, making it difficult for an original thinker to construct a client portfolio precisely as they'd prefer. Today, most independent B/Ds have corporate RIAs with the flexibility and range of investments that satisfy the majority of independents. Nonetheless, independent

RIAs continue to proliferate, because starting your own business doesn't require a B/D affiliation.

Typically, an independent financial advisor earns self-employment income (reported on a 1099), which gives the advisor the option to run his own business, but that also means paying all of the business's operating expenses. Studies have shown that on average, the *net income* of full-service versus independent financial advisor differs only slightly, if at all. An independent advisor earn a higher grid payout, but it doesn't necessarily make up for the added expense, especially in areas where office space costs more to rent and employees earn more.

In other words, don't become an independent advisor just for the promise of higher income, but rather to be free to choose when, what, and how you run your business. Also, independents have the opportunity to build equity value in their business, as Chapter 19 explains, which employees of full-service firms can't.

Scoping out hybrid models

The decision of whether to work as an employee or an independent financial advisor isn't a clear either/or choice. Some independent B/Ds pay both employee (W-2) and independent contractor (1099) compensation depending on the business revenue produced. Also, some independent RIAs affiliate with an independent B/D, so they can serve clients who may need securities transactions or other FINRA regulated product sales, such as variable annuities and other products. Every firm has its own nuance.

REMEMBER

When conducting your due diligence, be sure to take your time and ask lots of questions. In the following sections, you pick up more detail on which firms favor certain aspects of financial planning and how to make sure you pick the best firm for your career goals.

Investigating Different Revenue Models

At most firms, you have a variety of ways to make money. This section covers the three big revenue models:

>> Financial planning fees

>> Investment advisory fees

>> Commissions

GETTING TO KNOW NAPFA

The National Association of Personal Financial Advisors (NAPFA) is the leading association of fee-only advisors with roughly 3,000 members across the United States. NAPFA requires its members to hold the Certified Financial Planner (CFP) designation, and it doesn't allow its members to sell any product, so deferring to another financial advisor to execute the plan is the member's only option.

Some companies offer additional ways to earn, such as referral fees to loans and other banking functions. Additional bonus income may be tied to hitting certain production targets or referrals into other company business lines as well.

TIP

Know which FINRA licenses and other professional designation(s) or certification(s) permit you to operate various business lines. Each firm has the ability to interpret rules and regulations according to its own comfort level, so no two firms are exactly alike when it comes to platform offerings.

Understanding the fee-only model

Fee-only financial advisors don't accept any compensation based on product sales, so they have fewer inherent conflicts of interest. If you choose this model, you can structure your fees in various ways, including the following:

>> Percent of assets under management (see the next section for details) or household net worth

>> Flat retainer

>> Hourly rate

>> Per task or project

When the time comes to implement the fee-only financial advisor's plan, this type of financial advisor (often called a *financial planner*) either defers to a broker/agent who shops the market for solutions and products that would meet the plan's requirements or implements the plan himself. The latter is the more commonplace approach in the industry, but clients generally don't get it. It begs the question about the veracity of the plan being developed and whether the plan has a built-in bias toward specific products that the financial advisor has a quota to sell. Nothing's innately wrong with having a bias or belief that certain products should be foundational components to *any* plan, but you need to account for the client's perception.

Although most financial advisors don't rely solely on fees (fee-only is most common among independent RIAs), this compensation model is becoming a more sought-after solution as retail investors seek personalized advice without being sold to. The specific terms of the fees and what services are being provided appear in the firm's Form ADV, which is used to register both with the Securities and Exchange Commission (SEC) and state securities authorities.

REMEMBER

The fee-only model isn't the perfect solution for a couple reasons, such as the following:

>> **You have no control over the product selection.** Imagine developing the perfect financial plan that's botched by another broker/agent who uses an investment or insurance product that doesn't perform as expected.

>> **Financial advisors have no specific incentive to form a comprehensive plan.** For example, a financial plan should include disability insurance for any client who's currently employed or self-employed to provide sufficient income (in addition to any employer-provided disability insurance) to replace income in the event the client is unable to work. However, a financial advisor who doesn't believe in robust liability management strategy may be more prone to overlook this need.

REMEMBER

Bottom line: The combination of sound financial advice *and* product selection is key to long-term value creation for clients.

SWITCHING HATS WITH A TWIST

I'm not a big fan of the fee-only approach. After all, if you're creating the plan, nobody is better suited to implement that plan by choosing the best products. Unfortunately, the reality is that demand for fee-only fiduciary advisors is likely to rise dramatically as clients seek unbiased advice from financial advisors who have a fiduciary responsibility to their clients.

The best approach is to switch hats with a twist. Charge a fee to prepare the client's financial plan or to give advice and then, as a precursor to providing the solutions named in the plan, explain the distinction between the two services you provide: advice and product shopping and selection. For planning, advice, and management, you charge only a fee. For product shopping and selection, you receive a commission. Explain that you select only those products you think are the best for implementing the plan, and be transparent about the income you receive from these products. Point out that if you were to outsource this task to another advisor, that advisor would receive commissions, and you would have no control over what products he chose.

Collecting asset-based fees and commissions

The vast majority of financial advisors earn their incomes in the following two ways:

>> For asset management, through fees based on the market value of their client portfolios

>> For insurance products, in the form of built-in commissions

Here I explain these two ways in greater detail.

Tying your compensation to the portfolio's success

When managing a client's investment portfolio, consider charging a fee in the 1 to 1.5 percent range annually, earned monthly in arrears or quarterly in advance.

Regardless of the frequency, the industry generally considers this compensation model to be in the client's best interest because when the client's portfolio performs better, the financial advisor earns more money, and when the portfolio's value drops, the advisor earns less. This approach also aligns the client's and advisor's time horizon; both desire a long and prosperous result.

Earing commissions on insurance policies

Insurance products are typically structured with built-in commissions. These commissions aren't deducted from the money put into a product but rather paid directly by the carrier. In the past few years, more carriers have begun offering products for fee-only and asset-based fee advisors by doing away with large up-front commissions and replacing them with smaller, annual recurring payments. Again, the pressure from regulators and legislators is showing up in compensation formats that seek to place both client and advisor on the same time frame of caring what happens. Big up-front commissions mean that a broker could sell a product and collect some nice money, but the broker has no incentive to monitor how well that allocation does for the client over the next 10 or 20 years.

Checking out the commission-only compensation model

Under today's rules (at the time of this writing), finance professionals can still call themselves "financial advisors" even though they're just brokers or agents selling products on commission. (As Chapter 5 explains, change is coming in this regard.) However, brokers and agents will always serve a role fulfilling the product needs of customers for two reasons:

>> Many people are reluctant to pay ongoing fees because they don't see the value in *advice*. Instead, some customers just want a broker to shop the market for them and give them a spreadsheet on where they can get the highest quality benefit for the lowest cost. For this service, they're happy to have the broker earn a commission. This is how most insurance agencies operate.

>> Some customers just want to buy an investment that'll make them rich. They're not interested in having a proper and prudent portfolio or learning about making good decisions. They're just on the hunt for big returns in low risk investments. Of course any financial advisor knows that this client will never be happy, because high-return, low-risk investments live in the same town with unicorns and leprechauns.

Nonetheless, the marketplace is diverse, and until legislators and regulators determine that all investors must be protected, even from themselves, the commission-only broker or agent will still be able to operate as a "financial advisor."

Understanding how firm managers get paid

If you're working at a firm, find out how your managers are paid. You don't need specifics, but your firm owes you an explanation of how its managers are paid, so you can decide for yourself if any bias is built into how the firm operates that may negatively impact the way you serve your clients. If management insists that you perform your duties in a way that clashes with what you believe is best for your clients, the disconnect will only add to your job-related stress.

Ask these two big question:

>> Does your manager make more money when you use a certain product versus another?

>> How much more, a little or a lot?

Just as your advice should align with your clients' interests, your firm's policies and practices should align with the way you serve clients.

REMEMBER

Don't be shy about asking these questions. The more understanding you have, the better your ability to detect a pressured product sales environment or potentially even worse schemes.

Getting On-the-Job Training as an Employee

One of the biggest perks with being an employee of a firm is that you get on-the-job education and training, especially if you're just starting. In this section, I introduce you to your training options and provide insight into how to maximize the value of this benefit.

Deciding where to go for your field training

When you're setting out on your path to become a financial advisor, you have several options of where to work to get your field training: a wirehouse, a bank, or a regional broker/dealer. In this section, I discuss those options.

Considering wirehouses

Wirehouses used to be the places to go for novice financial advisors to receive their field training. That was 30 or more years ago. Today, as with most companies, the training programs available at these companies are mostly seen as distractions from what you should be doing to build your own book of business — finding clients.

REMEMBER

A wirehouse may be a good choice if you want to focus all of your time on serving clients, and you're not interested in managing a business. Otherwise, you're better off working as an independent B/D or RIA. You can still get on-the-job training by working as an associate or intern first.

Checking out banks

Considered the easiest way to enter the financial services industry, banks offer an opportunity to become part of the industry at entry-level positions. In-branch financial advisors are typically trained on bank savings and lending products, as well as affiliated investments and sometimes insurance products. Depending on the type of bank — local, regional, community, credit union, or large national — you may have the opportunity to climb the corporate ladder through bank branches and divisions.

Looking into regional broker/dealer firms

Regional B/Ds are generally smaller than wirehouses and banks and have a more uniform culture throughout their office networks, so they're usually better places to work if you're looking for on-the-job training.

Using internships to find the right fit

TIP

If you're still in college or junior college, start searching for an internship program. The internship should be paid (minimum wage is typical), and you shouldn't be asked to make cold calls from a phone book. The ideal internship exposes you to the firm's culture and workflow. Getting hands-on experience with portfolio analysis and portfolio review techniques, including investment or insurance product analysis, is ideal.

Interning also gives you a sense of the various roles that exist within a firm and which roles are more valued. As you check out various establishments that offer internships, try to find out whether the firm is more interested in new client sales or serving an existing client base. Determining the firm's culture, values, and focus helps to shape your own thinking on where you'll want to work and the specific career path you many want to take to become a financial advisor.

Finding Employment as an Independent Contractor

When you've acquired the education, training, and experience to be a financial advisor, consider setting out on your own as an independent contractor. In this section, I introduce two options:

>> Getting affiliated with an independent B/D

>> Working for an insurance company owned B/D

Affiliating with an independent broker/dealer

To find independent B/Ds, search online for "financial planning top 50 independent broker/dealers" and start doing your homework. Visit their websites and take notes. Because independent B/Ds recruit actively, most of the B/D websites have a page that explains what the company offers in the way of independence and support. They also typically list a phone number to call to speak with a recruiter.

REMEMBER

Some independent B/Ds are loosely structured and governed, providing more freedom to run your practice in a way that you think is best for your clients. Other independents have more compliance and structure, which can help protect your burgeoning career. Additional perks include the ability to network with other affiliated financial advisors and use the independent B/D's platform for research and servicing clients.

Finding work with an insurance-company-owned broker/dealer

To have the best of both worlds, consider working with an insurance-company-owned B/D. This approach gives you exposure and access to insurance products, while you focus on providing clients with holistic solutions, including financial planning and asset management.

To find a list of the top insurance B/Ds, you can use the same list for top independent broker/dealers (see the previous section), but then ask the recruiter (or visit the B/D's website) to determine if an insurance company owns the B/D. Often the name of the B/D doesn't indicate an insurance-affiliated relationship.

When I was establishing a financial advisory practice many years ago, I knew that my own professional interest and inclination were toward asset management. To meet my goals, I sought out an insurance-company-owned independent B/D to force me to be diversified. Otherwise, I was afraid I wouldn't focus sufficiently on the risk management aspects in financial plans.

REMEMBER

To be a holistic, comprehensive financial advisor, make sure you have a well-rounded practice involving both asset and liability management. Diversity of core competencies and solution expertise will benefit your client's overall financial outcome and make you a more successful financial advisor.

Becoming a Registered Investment Advisor

If you've been in the profession for several years and have an established client base, you may want to consider becoming a registered investment advisor (RIA). See the earlier section "Setting out on your own as an independent financial advisor" to find out about the benefits of becoming an RIA.

TIP

The easiest way to register as an independent investor is to use a turnkey solution, such as RIA in a Box at www.riainabox.com/start-an-ria-firm. A turnkey solution gives you all the support and guidance needed to process the registration and get started as efficiently as possible. This option may be a bit expensive depending on your budget (from $2,500 to $4,500), but it's worth it. Turnkey solutions ensure that you properly attend to all the details, including filing requirements, ongoing compliance and regulatory demands, and structuring your business. A misstep in any of these areas may limit your services and business revenue opportunities.

» Getting up to speed on your duties and responsibilities

» Knowing why clients are often confused about what financial advisors do

» Examining federal and state rules and regulations

» Becoming familiar with how the industry governs itself

» Checking out what's in store for the future of the industry

Chapter **5**

Surveying the Regulatory Landscape: The Fiduciary Standard

The financial advisory industry today is at an evolutionary inflection point. Change is in the air, and it's being driven by three primary forces:

» **Legislation and regulation:** In an attempt to protect consumers from charlatans, legislators and regulators at the state and federal levels are passing and enforcing new regulations and standards that often just add to the confusion and uncertainty for both consumers and the industry.

» **Technology:** New software and systems are providing better support for true fiduciary financial advisors while displacing those who sell products or act as intermediaries (as agents of distribution between product manufacturers and consumers).

>> **Financial advisors:** Fiduciary financial advisors committed to the industry and consumers are driving much of the change to the industry. As they educate consumers and spread the word among colleagues about how they deliver value by serving their clients' best interests, they're challenging the so-called financial advisors to do the same.

This chapter gives you an up-to-date briefing (current with the writing of this book at least) on the regulatory environment for financial advisors, including a recently court-vacated Department of Labor fiduciary rule and the Security Exchange Commission's (SEC) financial advisor definition proposal. I explain how real change happens from within an industry of proactive professionals and share a peek into the future, so you'll know what to expect.

Familiarizing Yourself with Your Role as Financial Advisor

The most successful financial advisors are *fiduciary*, meaning they're obligated to provide advice that's in their clients' best interests. To join this elite group, you must take a comprehensive, holistic approach to planning, managing, and protecting your client's financial assets and well-being. Your standard of care should involve giving advice, guidance, and recommendations regarding the following:

>> Asset management

>> Risk protection

>> Lending and other financing needs

>> Estate planning

If the firm you're affiliated with doesn't offer these services in the form of products, you should still provide advice regarding these matters, even if your advice is in the form of a referral to another professional in your network who provides the service.

Recognizing the Confusion over Obligations and Care Standards

Unlike in other professions, financial advisors aren't currently subject to a single standard of care. Doctors have *MD* after their name, accountants have *CPA*, and attorneys show *JD* (maybe *Esquire* too if they're fancy), while the FINRA website alone lists more than 150 designations (to scroll through the list, visit `www.finra.org/investors/professional-designations`) in the financial services industry. Industry professionals often tack on additional acronyms as they complete certain study programs. This plethora of designations and accreditations has given way to a client and customer marketplace rooted in *caveat emptor* (buyer beware).

The main source for this confusion in the industry is the fact that the financial advisory profession was never considered a profession. One good definition of *profession* is a calling requiring specialized knowledge with long and intensive academic preparation and prolonged on-the-job training. This definition is true for CPAs, MDs, and JDs, but no such single course of study or on-the-job training standard exists for the financial advisor profession.

Moreover, society at large doesn't see any *real* difference between a *financial advisor* and someone who holds a *Chartered Financial Analyst (CFA)* or a *Certified Financial Planner (CFP)* designation. After all, most consumers believe that all are just a bunch of salespeople. And, why would they think any differently when the vast majority of licensed representatives who call themselves financial advisors show up in the marketplace daily *selling* financial products or services?

Society would think much differently about medicine and law if most practitioners in those fields were knocking on doors selling medications or lawsuits. Certainly, those fields have their own salespeople, evidenced by the flood of pharmaceutical companies and lawyers advertising their products and services on TV, the Internet, and in newspapers and magazines with the same result — a growing confusion and distrust among consumers. However, doctors and lawyers have, so far, remained immune to the rampant confusion and distrust among consumers that's characteristic of the financial services industry. When they meet with an MD or JD, consumers know that these professionals have met a minimum education, knowledge, and training rigor. Financial advisors have no such reputation.

Contributing to this confusion and distrust are the charlatans who use their clients' money to engage in Ponzi schemes, pyramid schemes, fraudulent private placement offerings, and other capital allocation disasters. Due to the frequency and well-publicized incidents of financial services failures and corruption, the industry is often seen as not only a haven for crime and incompetency, but a purveyor of them. As a result, the investing public has a difficult time distinguishing between crime, incompetency, bad investments, and good investments that are in a temporary slump.

WARNING

Being a fiduciary financial advisor whose interests and timeframe are aligned with your client's doesn't automatically qualify you as a successful financial advisor. You also must make portfolio allocation decisions that increase the client's portfolio value over the given timeline. Market value fluctuations are normal; permanent capital loss should be avoided completely.

SELLING HOT FUNDS THAT GO COLD

In the late 1990s, almost every large, reputable mutual fund company launched its own version of a technology fund. These funds were marketed through the financial advisors of various distribution channels, from wirehouses to independent broker/dealers (B/Ds) to banks. No registered rep was left out in the cold nor wanted to be, as customers lined up to buy funds and stock shares that were in the *dotcom* sector.

After the market crashed in 2000 and a recession set in, many investors lost money. Investors who had put all their eggs in one dotcom basket lost everything. Many of these investors had dived headfirst into the stock market and bought shares directly through a discount brokerage firm, while many others had been sold a fund by their financial advisor. The customer's assumption is that when a financial advisor is recommending a fund to purchase, while earning an up-front commission on the sale, that the recommendation is in the best interest of the customer. (**Note:** I'm using *customer* instead of *client* deliberately, because a *customer* has a transactional relationship with the person or company she's buying from or selling to, whereas a *client* is engaged in an ongoing relationship with a fiduciary financial advisor.)

The dotcom era was fraught with peril. Experienced advisors were caught up in the mania and the greed as customers and clients demanded access to this seemingly new investment paradigm (for example, no corporate revenues, no problem!). But, if *actual* financial advisors were functioning in their professional role, they wouldn't have been so eager to satisfy client/customer demand.

Unfortunately, many "financial advisors" succumbed to the mass hysteria, because technically an investment broker who's paid a commission upon the sale of a security 1) isn't obligated to the financial outcome of the investment, 2) nor is her compensation tied to the eventual investment outcome. Instead, as long as the broker determined that the sale was suitable for the client, she's satisfied her duty.

A financial advisor paid an asset-based fee wouldn't have had an added incentive (via commission) to add dotcom stocks or funds to a client's portfolio. Also, by being tied to the performance outcome, the financial advisor's revenue would have been reduced had she made a bad decision to incorporate those ultimately worthless holdings. The point here is that removing incentive compensation and replacing it with a smaller, ongoing trail revenue based on portfolio market value would have given advisors a better decision-making perspective.

Sifting through the Clouds of Bureaucracy

A major change is in the making. Legislators and regulators are challenging the notion that the investing public has the ability to differentiate between a broker/agent and a financial advisor. Here is a quick rundown:

>> *Broker/agent* sells a product to a customer that is deemed a "suitable" (meaning that's an appropriate recommendation based on client objective and risk profile) transaction, earns a commissions, and isn't tied to the product's or customer's financial success.

>> *Financial advisor* has the client's best interests at heart and is paid over the course of and in alignment with the client's time horizon, acting as a steward of the client's desired financial outcome.

As a successful financial advisor, I can attest to the fact that the investing public has little understanding of these two different roles. Brokers, agents, and financial advisors are all lumped into the same category. Where I differ with the legislators and regulators is that I think the investing public does have the *ability* to differentiate between these two roles. Through client education and transparency, successful financial advisors can differentiate themselves favorably, earning even more client relationships and referrals and having more fun and in that role.

This section reviews the legislation intended to protect consumers of financial products and services. The bottom line, though, is whether you can call yourself a financial advisor. You can find the answer to that question near the end of this section.

Considering federal rules and regulations (DOL, SEC, FINRA)

Various self-regulatory authorities and government agencies have been attempting to force an industry-wide evolution toward a single, fiduciary standard of care in relation to working with financial services clients. So far, over the past two years, as this topic has heated up, the efforts have been an exercise that can best be described as three steps forward and three steps back.

DOL: The fiduciary rule

As I write this (the summer of 2018), the U.S. Fifth Circuit Court of Appeals has confirmed its decision to vacate the U.S. Department of Labor's (DOL's) fiduciary rule. Just two years ago, the DOL issued this rule in its final form, with requirements scheduled to be phased in between June 2017 and July 2019.

From its beginning, the DOL rule had jurisdiction only relevant to the Employee Retirement Income Security Act (ERISA) or qualified plan accounts (such as 401K, IRA, and other qualified retirement accounts). For example, if you had a client with an IRA and a regular, taxable individual account, you'd be subject to two different care standards, one for each account:

>> In the regular, taxable account, you could sell products based on client suitability and earn commissions.

>> In the IRA account, you'd have to function in a fiduciary capacity and prove that your recommendations were in your client's best interest forever, regardless of whether you're her financial advisor in the future.

Having a two-tiered investment account care standard would have been confusing for clients, not to mention for financial advisors, who'd have to overhaul their entire practice to accommodate the expected loss in commission revenues.

Meanwhile, many companies took steps to become compliant with the rule well in advance of its 2019 effective date, spending tens of millions per firm on technology and compliance-enabled systems. According to recent news, some of these big firms are set to roll back their announced changes (such as going from a no-commissions-allowed policy for an IRA to permitting commissions once again).

SEC: Regulation best interest

In April of 2018, the Securities and Exchange Commission (SEC) proposed a package of new rules and interpretations on relationships between investment advisors and broker-dealers, which is regarded as the SEC's answer to the failed DOL fiduciary rule. As part of these proposed changes, investment professionals would provide customers/clients a document that discloses whether they're working in a suitability/customer/transaction or a fiduciary/client/ongoing relationship capacity. The proposal restricts broker/dealers and their financial professionals from using titles such as "financial advisor" (including the alternate spelling, "adviser") unless they have certain registrations.

The 90-day comment period, which ended in August of 2018, inspired a flurry of articles. Just search the web for "SEC best interest" to get a sense of the diversity of opinions. Plenty of debate and rewrites to the proposal are anticipated before a final rule is adopted. Here are a few highlights from the SEC's 400+ page proposal:

>> "Best interest" isn't defined. The proposal leaves room for interpretation, which makes any potential rule more administrative than transformative.

>> The proposal seems to be calling for a higher care than the current suitability standard, though not as strong as a fiduciary (only requiring some additional disclosure).

>> Brokers can still make more money using proprietary or affiliated products, as long as they disclose doing so and make an effort to reduce this conflict — whatever that's supposed to entail.

>> The proposal doesn't create a single, uniform standard for financial professionals. The industry would still have separate standards for advisors and brokers/dealers.

REMEMBER

Of everything being proposed, the most potent many be the simplest. Restricting the use of "advisor" or "adviser" to only those who have the proper licensing and registration could be helpful. However, for the many financial advisors in the marketplace today who are *dually* registered (meaning, both a Registered Representative (RR) through FINRA to act as a transactional broker, *and* registered as an Investment Adviser Representative (IAR) through the SEC to act as a fiduciary advisor), clients still won't understand when they're being served by one standard or another because a dually registered financial advisor can switch back and forth depending on the product or service recommended.

Furthermore, many financial advisors also hold state insurance licenses. Insurance products typically pay large up-front commissions and have their own separate customer standard of care requirements (usually subject to a variation on the theme of suitability), which varies from state to state. How would a client possibly know that the recommendation being offered is potentially subject to three different standards of care? For this reason alone, manifesting a uniform care standard across all financial services will be a slow process, particularly in relation to investment and insurance products.

FINRA: New SIE exam

Although you won't see any new proposals on fiduciary rules, the Financial Industry Regulatory Authority (FINRA) has been actively upgrading its registration and licensing requirements. The organization has also been doing a great job with a tool called BrokerCheck that enables anyone to search a would-be financial advisor to see if she's been the subject of any complaints or other unsavory disclosures (brokercheck.finra.org).

The biggest update comes in the form of a new Securities Industry Essentials (SIE or simply Essentials) exam, beginning October 1, 2018. After the effective date, the new exam structure will allow individuals to take one SIE exam, which tests general knowledge (for example, basic products, structure of securities industry, regulatory agencies, prohibited practices, and so on) that used to show up over and over on each Series exam, and then a separate representative-level exam covering responsibilities and functions of representatives.

Unlike the current exam registration process, the new process doesn't require someone taking the exam to be associated with a broker/dealer firm, which is a big win for folks who are interested in joining the industry but haven't yet been hired by a firm. Minimum age to sit for the exam is 18. Results are valid for four years, giving you time to study for a subsequent securities exam, for a more specific securities license (for example, Series 6 or Series 7) after you're affiliated with a firm.

Looking at state rules and regulations

Not be left out of the political bonanza, state legislatures are getting in on the fiduciary bandwagon too. As of April 2018, several states have introduced bills that seek to impose or amend current care standards toward giving financial professionals a fiduciary duty within their states. Their goal is to more clearly protect their constituents if they think the national regulations aren't stringent enough. Such action could create even greater confusion for consumers by adding legislation atop existing legislation.

States where a fiduciary duty is *under development*, include the following:

>> Connecticut

>> Illinois

>> Maryland

>> Massachusetts

>> Nevada

>> New Jersey

>> New York

WARNING

Don't assume that just because your state isn't on the list you're safe. New legislation often gains momentum, passing from one state to another as states don't want to be perceived as being behind the times.

Depending on the bill, each state has focused on different aspects of what a financial advisor serving as a fiduciary entails. In certain instances, as with the New York Department of Financial Services (NYDFS), the proposal requires a "best interest" standard on all life insurance and annuity product recommendations to clients, which takes direct aim at variable life and variable annuity sales practices. What's interesting here is that their proposal doesn't apply to mutual funds or other securities, as long as they're not related to a life insurance or annuity product. Regardless of whether you do business in New York, stay tuned to how this proposal evolves into rules, because New York is the pace setter for most other states.

Nevada's law, passed on July 1, 2017, imposes a fiduciary duty on broker/dealers, their registered reps, and investment advisors. It doesn't apply to insurance product sales, except when accompanied by investment advice. So, if you're a comprehensive, holistic financial advisor in Nevada, you now have to make sure you're acting as a fiduciary across all investment and insurance recommendations.

WARNING

I foresee an active plaintiff's bar developing around breaches of these various regulations as attorneys are able to ferret them out. I imagine lawyers right now scoping out potential class-action opportunities.

Can you call yourself a financial advisor?

Regardless of the legislation that's proposed, passed, or revoked, you can consider yourself a financial advisor only if you're able to offer your advice for fee-only and/or trail compensation (instead of larger up-front commissions) and then implement the various planning components in a fiduciary capacity (for example, fairly shop the market and disclose the compensation you receive). Furthermore, by being and referring to yourself as a true financial advisor, you can differentiate yourself from all the other financial advisors who don't subscribe to this standard.

REMEMBER

Don't call yourself a financial advisor unless you are one. More than a million people in the U.S. financial services industry call themselves financial advisor or some variation thereof. In addition to the *actual* title of financial advisor, other common titles include

>> Broker

>> Comprehensive wealth planner

>> Financial coach

>> Financial consultant

>> Financial planner

>> Financial services professional

>> Insurance agent

>> Investment advisor representative

>> Registered representative

>> Vice president or president

>> Wealth manager

MY HOPE

My hope is that within 5 to 10 years, the financial advisor profession will be understood as a significant contributor to society and its general welfare and benefit. The largest generational wealth transfer in the history of the world will be taking place, right here in the United States, over the next 25 to 35 years. Some estimate this figure to be around $30 trillion in assets. Considering the gravity of this eventuality, real, fiduciary-based financial advice is going to be needed more than ever.

Think about it: If the medical field foresaw an epidemic that could wipe out segments of the population, wouldn't those professionals band together and prepare? Certainly they would. In the case of the coming generational wealth transfer, I hope for and expect a more unified response by financial services industry professionals with the full support of the federal, state, and local governments. What's true for physical health should also be true for financial health. As wealth passes from one generation to the next, it should be protected through proper oversight, advice, and unbiased care.

Depending on the advisor's licenses, issued by various bodies including FINRA, the SEC, and state insurance commissioners, some of the preceding monikers may be more appropriate than others. Insurance agents could use the title financial services professional or vice president, although they don't have the ability to give *financial advice*. Similarly, a wealth manager or registered representative (without an insurance license) can't include insurance products in their client discussions or provide *financial advice*. What they're permitted to do is sell investment or insurance products that are *suitable* based on the customer's fact pattern.

Governing Itself: Industry Organizations Weigh In

The two leading organizations providing technical knowledge and ethics training for financial advisors are as follows:

>> The Certified Financial Planner (CFP) Board

>> The Certified Financial Advisor (CFA) Institute

However, when you read their commentary on the various fiduciary rules and best interest care standards being proposed by the SEC, DOL, or others, their bold clarity of purpose reveals the immense pressure they're feeling from the large financial services companies who employ the majority of their charter holders and certificate holders.

Positive, lasting change will come from within the industry — from financial advisors, including you, who are committed to upholding the fiduciary standard, as I am about to explain.

Recognizing that change comes from within

Given the conflicting interests of these industry governing organizations and the added confusion and bureaucracy of federal, state, and local governments, what's clear is that raising the professional financial advisor industry standard is best accomplished as a grassroots movement driven by practitioners, practices, consumers, and technologies. As FinTech and market demand shift in favor of the fiduciary financial advisor, the large institutions will follow the money.

While the industry overall can look forward to progressing in this direction, insurance product sales are routinely left out of the fiduciary discussion. I'm not sure why financial advisors are so hesitant to disclose what they earn on financial products that pay commissions. Clients always want to move forward on executing a solid financial plan, as long as they understand the long-term benefit to them. They want us to make a living, and a good living at that. As long as you're open and honest about how you're paid, earnings from insurance product sales aren't generally a deal breaker.

REMEMBER

Successful financial advisors should be models of financial success, just as your trainer at the gym has the physique you wish you had. The financial advisor's model of financial success should be based on compensation and conflict transparency. If you were hiring a trainer, you'd probably want to know whether she looked like she does solely from a disciplined diet and routine exercise or with the help of diet and steroid supplements. That difference would probably be a major consideration in your choice of trainer. The same goes for the advisor-client relationship.

Taking the fiduciary pledge

To serve clients in the most beneficial manner, an industry-wide standard of care must be delivered. My own firm has enacted The Fiduciary Pledge, joining many other firms around the country, who aren't afraid to shine a light on any form of compensation or potential conflicts of interest. Unlike many firms, my firm applies this standard of care to both asset management *and* risk management (insurance) products and solutions.

To give you a head-start, use my firm's Fiduciary Pledge as a model (see Figure 5-1). You can customize it to your own needs, editing as you feel ready and comfortable to do so. The more financial advisors who engage in documenting their fiduciary responsibility and communicating it to prospects and clients, the greater the client flow toward financial advisors who deliver this standard of service. The outcome: A win for you, a win for your clients, and a win for the industry.

I, the undersigned, pledge that *Your Name and Your Firm's Name* will exercise its best efforts to always act in good faith and in the best interests of our client, *Client Name*, and will act as a fiduciary advisor.

We will provide written disclosure, in advance, of any conflicts of interest, which could reasonably compromise the impartiality of our advice.

Moreover, in advance, we will disclose any and all fees, commissions or other compensation that we will receive as a result of any recommended transaction or solution, and we will disclose any and all fees we pay to others for referring a client relationship to us, if applicable.

This pledge covers all *investment* and *insurance* products and/or services provided. Should other products or services be offered by us in the future, those too will be included under this pledge.

X_____

Date_____

FIGURE 5-1: My firm's fiduciary pledge.

Looking to the Future

Assuming you follow the news, you've probably come across reports about *robo-advisors* — artificially intelligent software that manages investment portfolios with minimum human involvement. These reports send shivers down the spines of those financial advisors who function more like brokers/dealers and insurance salespeople. If you're a holistic, fiduciary financial advisor, however, robo-advisors pose no threat. In fact, they may benefit your business.

Established companies including Charles Schwab and Vanguard have joined start-up firms such as Betterment and Wealthfront in offering automated investment portfolio solutions. Though I see great value in robo-advisors for investors who want ultra-low-cost, index performance, and diversified portfolios, many clients seek out an opportunity for better than index performance, through actively managed solutions. Whether that means pursuing *alpha* (a risk-adjusted performance measure) through individual security selection or discriminating macro-asset and sub-asset allocations, financial advisors with a specific investment passion for helping clients achieve their financial goals will not be displaced.

More importantly, emerging technologies will enable the future financial advisor to deliver more value through improved assessment and monitoring of current household financials. Providing guidance on a mortgage refinance, encouraging a second opinion on tax returns with another CPA, and reviewing a client's family trust document for required updates are all ways that financial advisors can add *real* value in the form of money saved or earned through proper holistic planning. An algorithm won't be able to do this for quite some time, if ever.

FinTech will also drive financial advisors to become more sophisticated and smaller firms to consolidate, so they can offer greater scale and operational efficiency to achieve more comprehensive services under one roof. Expect firms of the future to have all the collaborative advisors located at one firm — attorneys, CPAs, portfolio managers, and financial planners, all working together within the same financial advisory firm and with a unified commitment to their fiduciary responsibility.

2
Mastering Core Competencies

Acquire the fundamental education and training you need to practice as a financial advisor and get certified in specific areas.

Discover the basics of managing a client's assets, reach consensus on an investment philosophy, and steer clients clear of doing anything crazy.

Navigate the minefield of liability management so your clients don't lose their shirts when they're trying to build their wealth.

Brush up on estate planning basics to ensure the right heirs and beneficiaries get the wealth, and the government doesn't take too much of it.

Navigate tax rules and regulations and pick up some techniques that enable your clients to keep more of their hard-earned cash.

Recognize the emotional side of financial management, so you have a better understanding of why clients often behave destructively around money.

» Finding out what you need to know

» Going back to school

» Getting licensed and certified

» Committing to continuing education

Chapter **6**

Pursuing Professional Development

S pecialized knowledge is the foundation for any professional, including doctors, lawyers, and financial advisors. However, unlike other professions that have governing boards and standards (for example, a medical board and state bar exams), the financial advisory profession has no clear professional education or certifying standards. Even so, you need specialized knowledge to deliver value to your clients, and you need to be licensed to conduct transactions related to certain financial products.

This chapter reveals the core competencies you need to develop in order to advise clients. I introduce you to the various governing and licensing entities that offer a range of programs for becoming a fully functional and competent financial advisor. Finally, I stress the importance of continuing education and recommend a few ways to stay on top of the ever-changing financial landscape.

Identifying the Core Competencies

As a financial advisor, you must have the following six core competencies and be able to coordinate advice from various other advisors, including attorneys and tax specialists:

>> Asset (investment) management

>> Liability (risk) management

>> Budgeting (household or business focus)

>> Estate planning

>> Tax management

>> Behavioral finance

Financial advisors who provide a single holistic solution are often referred to as *wealth managers*.

Asset management

Broadly speaking, *asset management* is the ongoing assessment of where and why a person invests in any variety of assets. Assets can be grouped into the following three categories:

>> **Tangible assets:** All types of real estate, commodities (for example, precious metals), and collectibles

>> **Intangible assets:** Intellectual property, human capital, and goodwill

>> **Financial assets:** All types of financial instrument and manufactured products (for example, stocks, bonds, mutual funds, and derivatives)

Your job in this area involves maximizing the use of the client's assets to help achieve his goals.

REMEMBER

Even if you focus on only one of a client's three asset categories, your asset management program needs to include a risk assessment across *all* assets. Risks specific to a portfolio (collection) of assets include

>> **Market price volatility:** How much the price moves up and down

>> **Liquidity:** How quickly, with no capital loss, assets can be converted to cash

>> **Correlation of price movement across portfolio holdings:** How each holding's price moves relative to other portfolio holdings' prices

>> **Concentration of asset type:** How many eggs does the client have in one basket (degree of diversification)

TIP

Many investment portfolio tools are available that can improve your insight into a client's portfolio risk. For example, Morningstar offers several professional services to financial advisors and asset managers to properly design, manage, and monitor investment portfolios.

See Chapter 7 for more about asset management.

Liability management

Liabilities and assets are flip sides of the same coin. As a financial advisor, you need to manage both sides. If a client with a great asset portfolio is blindsided by an unexpected and unprepared for life event, the resulting liabilities can quickly wipe out the assets or slowly erode them.

REMEMBER

Your duty is to guide your clients through a process of identifying possible and probable risks and then to find the most appropriate cost-benefit solution that aligns with the client's risk tolerance. Risks include the following:

>> **Unexpected death:** Losing a household's breadwinner or a business's key employee

>> **Expected death:** Loss of an elderly or ailing relative, which, without proper planning, would place the burden of liquidating assets on heirs

>> **Disability:** A client's short-term or long-term inability to earn employment income

>> **Economic recessions:** Economic conditions that depress assets, challenging retirees to make ends meet

>> **Inflation:** The slow and often indiscernible reduction of purchase power that retirees often fail to plan for

>> **Diagnosis of serious illness:** Illness that triggers the one-two punch of lost income and high medical bills

Although most clients would prefer to discuss how to make more money in the stock market, an unexpected liability can do far more damage to a household's net worth than a bad investment. As a financial advisor, you're doing a great service to allocate as much, if not more time in your client discussions to this area of financial planning. (See Chapter 8 for details.)

Budgeting

Psychologically, budgeting is a mental third rail for most clients. People are adaptive, and when a certain amount of money flows into their checking account each payroll cycle, those funds have a funny way of disappearing completely, just in time for the next direct deposit. Without a family budget, your clients are unlikely to be able to free up any money to put toward their financial goals.

Many people try budgeting and give up because it's too complicated and the record keeping is too involved. Your job is to simplify it for them. You can find plenty of tools for simplifying the budget process: personal finance software, such as Quicken; budgeting apps for your client's smartphone; even a basic Excel budget template you can download online may be sufficient.

REMEMBER

The key first step is to gain a clear understanding of the client's income and spending patterns. Only then can you properly advise clients on how to modify their spending today in order to achieve future goals and obligations. (See Chapter 9 for more guidance on how to help clients budget.)

Estate planning

All clients have an estate comprised of all their assets. *Estate planning* is the process of determining how assets will be distributed to heirs or beneficiaries after one dies or is incapacitated. However, estate planning isn't restricted to financial assets. With estate planning, clients can, for example:

>> Create a will naming heirs and an executor

>> Limit estate taxes by establishing trusts

>> Name a guardian for any surviving dependents

>> Name or update beneficiaries on life insurance and qualified plans

>> Request funeral arrangements

See Chapter 10 for more about estate planning.

Taxation

Part of financial planning involves minimizing the amount of taxes your clients pay, so they have more money to put toward their financial goals. Common tax-reduction strategies include the following:

- » Buying a home instead of renting living space to take advantage of homeowner's deductions

- » Maximizing contributions to tax-deferred annuities, such as an IRA

- » Paying healthcare bills with pre-tax dollars by using a health savings account (HSA)

- » Paying child-care bills with pre-tax dollars

The net tax impact of the 2017 Tax Cuts and Jobs Act on a per household basis remains to be seen. States are likely to adjust their taxes in response to lost federal revenue, so the impact is likely to depend on the state in which your clients live. Some tax-saving strategies that worked in the past may no longer be beneficial.

Your job is to help your clients navigate the ever-changing tax landscape to take advantage of any tax savings they qualify for. See Chapter 11 for details.

REMEMBER

Taxes shouldn't be the tag wagging the dog of money management. Paying taxes is a symptom of having made money, which is the ultimate desire for any investor.

Behavioral finance

Behavioral finance involves understanding the emotional and psychological factors that influence a client's attitude toward money and how it affects her financial decisions. For example, a client who had a relative who lost a lot of money in the stock market may get the jitters when you present investment options.

REMEMBER

To serve your clients well, you need to be able to not only crunch numbers and offer financial advice but also understand their financial goals and the motivations that drive their financial decisions. By understanding your client's motivations, you're in a better position to offer advice that addresses their concerns and aligns with their aspirations.

See Chapter 12 for more about behavioral finance.

Getting a Formal Education

You don't need a college degree, a special certification, or even a high-school diploma to qualify as a financial advisor. To achieve success as a financial advisor, however, you need to know what you're doing, and having the education and credentials helps differentiate you from those less qualified.

If you're already a certified public accountant (CPA) or loan officer or you've worked in finances and you have plenty of life experience, you have a good start. However, you should get some additional, formal training under your belt and earn one or more financial advisor certifications.

A number of independent education institutions offer advanced and specialized financial advisor training. The few highlighted in this section don't constitute an exhaustive list, but they offer the more recognized, marketed, and substantive education and certification programs specifically for financial advisors.

TIP

I recommend working at a role in the field that would expose you to the world of financial advisory work before enrolling in a program to ensure that you want to be a financial advisor and you intend to stick with it. In many of these programs, you have to work in the field for several years before you can receive the designation. In addition, most programs require at least 30 hours of continuing education (CE) every two years. In other words, getting certified is a huge commitment, so you want to be relatively sure you're going to stick with it.

The American College of Financial Services

The American College of Financial Services (ACFS, www.theamericancollege.edu) offers many professional designations and degree programs. The more popular programs include the Chartered Financial Consultant (ChFC) and Chartered Life Underwriter (CLU). For a full list, visit ACFS's website and click Designations & Degrees.

Established in 1927, ACFS is one of the older organizations in the field and has supported more than 200,000 people in their financial careers. The college's website proudly highlights that the college's "sales training can boost production by up to 40 percent" and that recipients of their "financial planning designations increase their sales by as much as 51 percent."

I see this focus on financial benefits as a missed opportunity to stress the importance of education in delivering value to clients. Regardless, this institution does a solid job developing an advisor's expertise in various financial products and processes.

CFA Institute

The CFA Institute (www.cfainstitute.org) is considered the gold standard in developing professionals focused on investment management, especially portfolio managers and research analysts. The CFA Institute offers three programs:

>> **Chartered Financial Advisor (CFA):** This program is for "portfolio and wealth managers, investment and research analysts, professionals involved in the investment decision-making process, and finance students who want to work in the investment management profession." To earn the CFA designation, you must pass three exams, have four years of relevant experience, and join the CFA Institute as a regular member. This is on average a four-year program.

The program's focus is deeply enriching, addressing all aspects of asset management. Special emphasis focuses on ethics and conduct and every conceivable analysis to be performed on any asset (particularly risk and valuation analysis).

>> **Certified in Investment Performance Management (CIPM):** This program is for "portfolio managers, investment consultants, financial advisors, sales and client service professionals, and other investment professionals involved in selecting portfolio managers, evaluating portfolio performance, or communicating with clients." To earn the CIPM designation, you must pass two exams, have two years' experience in investment-performance activities or four years' experience in investment decision-making, and become a CFA Institute regular member or join the CIPM Association. The program takes a minimum of one year to complete.

>> **Investment Foundations:** This program is for "anyone who works with or supports investment decision-makers in the investment management profession." To earn the Investment Foundations certificate, you must pass one exam that takes up to six months' preparation.

CFA Institute prominently displays its core message of delivering "professional excellence for the ultimate benefit of society." The institute's extensive global standards and mission to build market integrity "by improving investor protections and investor outcomes," aren't only admirable, but a consistent fixture in CFA Institute membership discussions. The academic rigor of its programs and its global network of more than 120,000 professionals make this organization highly respected among the most sophisticated financial advisors.

PURSUING MY CFA

After 20 years of working as a financial advisor, I decided to pursue the CFA designation. I passed Level I, but I've been unable to continue through the other levels due to lack of time and commitment. Running a financial advisory business, writing, and trying to live a balanced life are key hurdles. If you're interested in achieving this credential, I strongly encourage you to do so immediately after graduating college, when the mind is still in study mode, and your time is more free from the trappings of an experienced professional.

CFP Board

The Certified Financial Planner Board of Standards (CFP, www.cfp.net) is widely regarded as setting the gold standard in the financial planning profession. CFP designees must complete a comprehensive program and commit to completing ongoing continuing education. The core subjects this credential covers include all the main financial planning areas: as investment, insurance, tax, retirement, and estate planning, along with professional conduct and regulation. These are the initial certification requirements (referred to as the "four Es"):

>> **Education:** Certification requires a bachelor's degree and the completion of a college-level program of study in personal financial planning or an accepted equivalent, including completion of a financial plan development (capstone) course registered with CFP Board.

>> **Examination:** You must pass the CFP Certification Exam, which you can take after completing the required coursework. (You don't need to have your bachelor's degree to be eligible for the exam.)

>> **Experience:** You're required 6,000 hours of experience through the standard pathway or 4,000 hours of experience through the apprenticeship pathway. ("Qualifying experience may be acquired through a variety of activities and professional settings, including personal delivery, supervision, direct support, indirect support, or teaching.")

>> **Ethics:** You must agree to adhere to the CFP Board's standards of ethics and practice as outlined in its *Standards of Professional Conduct*. After you fulfill the education, examination, and experience requirements, you must complete a CFP Certification Application to disclose information about your background. CFP then performs a background check that you must pass in order to receive your certification.

The Institute of Business and Finance (IBF)

Since 1988, more than 16,000 professionals have leveraged the Institute of Business and Finance's (icfs.com) programs to deepen their knowledge to "develop successful careers — and successful clients." IBF offers six programs, including Certified Fund Specialist (CFS), Certified Annuity Specialist (CAS), Certified Estate and Trust Specialist (CES), Certified Tax Specialist (CTS), Certified Income Specialist (CIS), and Master of Science in Financial Services.

TIP

If you're a busy professional, IBF certifications are a great option, because you can integrate the learning more easily into your other responsibilities at work and home. The curricula are robust, so you still benefit from actionable substantive knowledge.

Obtaining Your Licenses to Practice

Knowledge and certifications are fundamental, but getting licensed by the proper regulatory authorities is essential if you want to transact in mutual funds, stocks, bonds, or insurance products. In this section, I cover several licenses you'll need to conduct basic transactions.

Financial Industry Regulatory Authority (FINRA)

The Financial Industry Regulatory Authority (FINRA) "protects investors and market integrity through effective and efficient regulation of broker-dealers." Although not a part of the U.S. government, FINRA is authorized by Congress to "protect America's investors."

To protect investors, FINRA ensures that

>> All investors receive the basic protections they deserve.

>> Anyone who sells securities has been tested, qualified, and licensed.

>> Every securities product advertisement used is truthful and not misleading.

>> Any securities product sold to an investor is suitable for that investor's needs.

>> Investors receive complete disclosure about the investment product before purchase.

I recommend that any would-be financial advisor study and pass the following FINRA exams: (To register for any FINRA exam, you must be sponsored by a registered broker/dealer firm.)

>> **Series 6 – Investment Company and Variable Contracts Products Representative Exam:** A 135-minute test with 100 questions related to packaged financial products such as mutual funds, ETFs, closed-end funds, and variable annuities. Great for advisors who don't plan to provide clients with sophisticated asset management services.

>> **Series 7 – General Securities Representative Exam:** A 360-minute test with 250 questions, this is the most comprehensive exam for financial advisors to pass, because it covers a wide range of financial products and instruments, including everything in the Series 6 exam, plus all other publicly traded securities, including derivatives such as option contracts. It's a must for any financial advisor who prefers offering more diverse portfolio solutions.

>> **Series 63 – Uniform Securities Agent State Law Examination:** Passing this 75-minute, 60-question exam enables you to execute general securities transactions and effect sales within a state jurisdiction. It's an exam for NASAA (North American Securities Administrators Association) that is administered by FINRA.

>> **Series 65 – Uniform Investment Adviser:** Passing this 180-minute, 130-question exam earns you the investment advisory representative (IAR) designation, permitting you to accept fees for services related to financial advisory or investment management. Series 65 is also a NASAA exam administered by FINRA.

>> **Series 66 (a combination of Series 63 and 65):** This 150-minute, 100-question exam conveniently combines the Series 63 and 65 exams into a single exam. (You must have passed the Series 7 to sit for this exam.)

A background check, finger-printing, bonding, and additional state fees are all related requirements for these exams. Additionally, every year, you have to pay renewal fees to keep all these licenses in good order.

WARNING

Don't forget to pay your license renewal fees annually. Failing to renew is a common mistake, especially when a financial advisor is between broker/dealer affiliations. A two-year window is a customary grace period, after which you have to retake these exams.

National Association of Insurance Commissioners (NAIC)

The National Association of Insurance Commissioners (NAIC) is a national system of state-based insurance industry regulators in the United States, the District of Columbia, and five U.S. territories. NAIC's mission is to

>> Protect the public interest.

>> Promote competitive markets.

>> Facilitate the fair and equitable treatment of insurance consumers.

>> Promote the reliability, solvency, and financial solidity of insurance institutions.

>> Support and improve state regulation of insurance.

To sell insurance products, you must pass your state's resident state insurance licensing exam, through the NAIC, which varies from state to state. Regardless of where you initially pass your exam, you'll be able to apply for nonresident licenses for many other states. Sometimes, certain states have additional requirements beyond the basic nonresident online application process, which can be challenging and bureaucratic.

Applying Certifications across the Financial Advisory Spectrum

Leverage the power of your competencies and credentials by using your expertise in a given area to get your foot in the door. You can then expand your service offerings to accommodate the client's needs in other areas in which you may be less confident and lacking in credentials.

WARNING

Don't try to be everything to everyone. For example, if you've earned a Chartered Life Underwriter (CLU) certification, it probably makes the most sense for you to lead into a prospective client discussion with how you could optimize the client's cost-benefit experience in their insurance planning. After the prospect becomes a client in an area of your highest confidence, core competency, and credential, then you can introduce other areas of service, where you may add more value.

WARNING

Don't let a lack of credentials, education, or expertise in some areas discourage you. You can find plenty of clients who need the services in your areas of specialization along with *your* unique style, approach, advice, and guidance. The market for financial advisors is an extremely big sea with lots of fish and every fish needs something a little different.

TIP

Many clients are equipped with rudimentary knowledge and understanding on financial matters, which equates to low confidence. If you're able to educate and support their good decision-making, their decisions are likely to produce better financial outcomes, and they'll be more willing to seek your advice (and pay for it) in the future.

For example, a client owns a few stocks she heard about on cable news, but she routinely sells during periods of market volatility typically at a loss. She has three dependents but no life insurance or disability insurance. You can deliver tremendous value to her. You can start by educating the client on the wisdom of a diversified portfolio that gives her the confidence to stay invested during tumultuous times. Then, you can advise the client on the importance of basic liability management and planning to protect from catastrophic loss. (Her family will thank you.) Although the client can't recover the money lost on erratic investment decisions, the money saved by having a balanced plan in place is likely to make up for the past losses and then some.

Embracing Continuing Education

Many great financial advisors studied finance or economics at the university level and obtained degrees in those disciplines. However, that education, though helpful, is only the beginning. With pre-med or pre-law studies, those bachelor degrees are precursors to the post-graduate and doctoral degrees required to start a practice. Even though you don't need a master's or doctorate to practice as a financial advisor, continuing education can give a big boost to the value you offer clients and your attractiveness to prospects.

Following are several suggestions for engaging in continuing education, some formal and most informal:

>> Enroll in one of the certification or licensing programs described in the previous section. Don't stop at one program. Take classes regularly. All certification programs require that you take classes regularly and record your hours to maintain your designations. This requirement ensures that advisors stay up-to-date on key industry trends and news, as well as the latest research and practices.

>> Read at least one daily business newspaper, such as *Financial Times* and *The Wall Street Journal*. As a professional and/or a certified or chartered financial advisor, your greatest asset is your mind, followed by your ability to communicate what's on it.

>> Read at least one weekly or monthly financial news magazine, such as *The Economist* and *Bloomberg BusinessWeek*.

>> Follow well-regarded experts in your areas of interest on social media.

The best financial advisors follow the daily fluctuations of the global capital markets and gain insight into the complicated machinations that drive market activity. Sharing your long-term perspective and insight with clients in a way that improves their understanding and helps them make wiser financial decisions delivers great value to clients and helps you retain clients and attract new prospects.

Chapter **7**

Getting Budgeting under Your Belt

B efore you can help your clients build wealth, you (and they) need to figure out how much monthly income is flowing in, how much money is flowing out, and where it's going. This is what budgeting is all about. By taking control of the household budget, your clients can begin to free up some of their income to invest in building wealth.

In this chapter, you discover how to help clients take control of their household budget. Here, I highlight the eight key spending categories to focus on and how to set spending limits for each category. I also introduce some handy budgeting apps and other tech tools and reveal the savings power of auto pay and payroll deductions.

TIP

For a variety of personal household budget templates, simply Google "budget template," and find one that you're comfortable using with your clients.

Guiding Clients on Household Budgeting

To construct a proper financial plan for your clients you must have a thorough understanding of their household's income and expenses. If your clients have a budget, ask for a copy, so you can review it prior to your next meeting. If they don't have a budget, one of your first tasks is to guide them through the budgeting process. In this section, I lead you through the process.

REMEMBER

Some of the most successful people I've met have little interest or inclination to create and manage a household budget, but if you can get them to start doing it, they soon recognize its value. Introducing your clients to budgeting and making it easier for them is a great way to deliver big value to them.

TIP

If clients are reluctant to budget, for whatever reason, point out that they'll have more money to spend on what they enjoy and value most if they curb spending on things they have nothing to show for. Budgeting provides the visibility needed to make great spending decisions.

Estimating income

The first step in creating a budget is to get a relatively accurate estimate of the household's net income (after taxes). If a household member is a paid employee and receives a W-2 at the end of the year, your job is easy —you can calculate the person's monthly income based on the two or four paychecks per month.

Estimating net income for a household member who owns a business or is self-employed is more complicated. This person probably receives payments from numerous clients, receives a nontraditional W-2 or a 1099 from each of them, and pays estimated quarterly income taxes. In addition, you need to subtract business expenses, such as mileage, meals, travel, phone, and other expenses, which may be tightly woven into the household expenses, making them difficult to discern.

TIP

When you're dealing with households that have business or self-employment income, you may be better off not trying to estimate the household income and instead focus on expenses, as explained next. If the household members are racking up a lot of debt, you can tell that they're living beyond their means and need to rein in their expenses or create other sources of income (or both).

Identifying and estimating expenses

Clients often earn considerable income and wonder where all that money goes. When they take the time to list their monthly, annual, and semiannual expenses, they quickly see exactly where that money goes and can begin to identify expenses they can and can't trim back.

REMEMBER

A reluctance to budget can often be traced to how complicated the process is and the number of expense categories that must be tracked. In the following sections, I whittle the expense categories down to eight, so you can simplify budget management for your clients.

Housing

To estimate your client's housing costs, make sure you include all housing related expenses:

>> Rent or mortgage payment

>> Homeowner's or rental insurance

>> Homeowner association (HOA) fees

>> Property taxes (if not included in the mortgage payment)

>> Average monthly household maintenance and repair costs

TIP

If a major life change makes your client's current housing unaffordable, don't hesitate to discuss the situation. For example, clients often retire in the home they lived in during their working years only to discover that the home is far beyond their needs. You'll be surprised at how many clients nearing retirement age are already thinking of downsizing into a smaller home, condo, or an assisted living community (if they're more advanced in age).

DOWNSIZING WITH A REVERSE MORTGAGE?

A house can be a money pit in more ways than one, especially for retirees who own more home than they need. Housing costs for retirees are often above the 20 to 30 percent threshold recommended for the household budget. In addition to the housing, a big house typically costs more to heat and cool. By downsizing, the household can slash its housing and utility costs and (by selling the existing home) unlock any dormant equity built up in it.

Another option is a reverse mortgage, but reverse mortgages or HECM lines of credit carry risks that most homeowners don't fully grasp. You and your clients need to tread carefully when considering this option. Give special consideration to the legacy goals and desires of your homeowner clients because a reverse mortgage may severely hamper, if not completely remove, the home's value from the inheritance picture.

SYMBOL OF STATUS OR OF DEBT AND EXCESS?

Owning a car in Los Angeles is like having a front-row seat to a fashion show; everyone wants to be seen by everyone else. Cars have become not only statements of financial success but, more typically, statements of debt and excess.

Unfortunately, you can't do much, in terms of financial planning, for a client who's eager to spend a third of her take-home pay on her tricked-out ride.

Transportation

To estimate transportation costs, consider the following:

- » Monthly car payment or lease payment
- » Auto insurance (average monthly over 12 months)
- » License and registration fees
- » Vehicle maintenance and repair (average monthly over 12 months)
- » Fuel cost
- » Public transportation fees, tolls, and monthly parking

Depending on where your clients live and their travel needs, a car (or a second car) may be a necessity or a luxury, and it's often a major expense. In Los Angeles, where I live, the cost of transportation is often a big expense for many households, especially if the commute is long and gas prices are high.

Utilities

Utilities include gas, electricity, water/sewer, trash/recycling, phone, TV, Internet access, and security systems. Ask your client to gather the monthly utility bills, total them for the year, and divide by 12 to determine the monthly average. *Beware:* Using bills for this exercise during peak cost seasons, like winter for natural gas, will make for a high annualized estimate.

Healthcare and childcare

Healthcare and childcare can be another big-ticket category when you start to consider all the bills:

- » Insurance premiums for medical, vision, dental, disability, and (perhaps) long-term healthcare
- » Copays
- » Costs of prescription and over-the-counter medications and supplements
- » Eyeglasses and contacts
- » Other medical/health aids
- » Gym memberships and exercise equipment
- » Childcare (babysitting, education, child support)

Consumer debt

Consumer debt includes credit card balances, student loans, and other installment payment programs other than secured loans, such as mortgages and car loans. Most clients have some consumer debt.

REMEMBER

Carrying month-to-month consumer debt means the household is consuming more than the income is able to support. Something's got to give. Work with your clients to address any deficit spending proactively. Otherwise, you and your clients may be dealing with the issue reactively later when fewer options are available.

Food and groceries

This category includes groceries and food-delivery services for dining in. It excludes dining out, which is in the entertainment category.

Personal care and clothing

Personal care and clothing is a broad category that includes the costs of the following items:

- » Salons (hair and nails) and haircare products
- » Personal hygiene products
- » Clothing, laundry supplies, dry cleaning, shoes, and shoe repair
- » Seasonal and random gifts

I'm always surprised by the costs associated with this category. I mean, who knew personal care and clothing could cost so much? Personally, I spend very little on haircare, because I'm bald, but others in my household treasure their locks and don't hesitate to spend money to maintain their hair's luster. Some of my clients are very good at slashing expenses in this category by focusing on clothing — never spending full retail; they wait for sales or shop at outlets.

Travel, entertainment, and dining out

This is another broad category that includes many of the most enjoyable expenses, such as:

>> Movies, theater, and music, including live entertainment, movie rentals, and streaming

>> Books and magazines

>> Outings to sporting events and cultural events, visits to museums, amusement parks, zoos, and so on

>> Travel and lodging for business or leisure (including vacations)

>> Dinners out (fast food or fine dining)

>> Hobbies and pastimes, such as golf

>> Pet care, including food, supplies, and veterinary care

Most people struggle with this category. After all, people want to enjoy life. To chide some clients for overspending on luxuries would be akin to asking them to become homeless. I've found that would-be clients who engage in conspicuous consumption are the most challenging to manage toward a favorable financial outcome.

Shaking the piggy bank: Savings

As your clients get their spending under control, they should be able to free up some cash to place in savings as a buffer to protect against unexpected financial setbacks and to start building wealth.

Give your clients this age-old advice: *Pay yourself first!* Right off the top, they should stick about 10 percent of their income into savings, which should quickly fund an emergency fund, and then allow further progress toward funding a retirement account, college savings account, and/or other savings vehicles.

REMEMBER

Advise clients to build and maintain an emergency fund to cover any events that disrupt income, such as job loss or temporary disability. They should set aside the equivalent of 3 to 12 months of basic household expenses (excluding discretionary spending). If your client is an established senior manager with significant benefits at a stable company, three months may be more than adequate. On the other hand, clients who participate in the gig economy should place enough money in a savings account to cover 12 months.

WARNING

Don't start your clients with an investment plan until they have 3 to 12 months of bank savings. Otherwise, your clients may find themselves having to sell investments when the market is down. Nobody knows what the market value of an asset will be if and when a client *needs to* sell it.

Establishing spending and savings guidelines

In the previous two sections, you simplified budgeting for your client by identifying nine categories (eight expense categories plus savings). Now, you can provide targets for each category:

Category	Target (%)
Savings	10
Housing	25
Transportation	10
Utilities	10
Food and groceries	10
Entertainment	10
Personal care	5
Debt	10
Healthcare and childcare	10
Total (equivalent to net income)	100

REMEMBER

These targets are starting points. Every household's expenses and spending priorities differ. Work with your clients to tweak the percentages to align them more closely with their preferences, but be sure the total doesn't exceed 100 percent of net income.

Exploring Helpful Technology Tools

This is the golden era of personal finance programs and apps. Full-featured personal finance programs, such as Quicken, have been around for some time, and they include budgeting features. What's relatively new are budgeting/savings apps, including Mint, Acorns, Pocket Guard, and Albert, for smartphones and other portable electronic devices. Some apps can automatically categorize spending into the various expense categories and create a budget based on the user's spending habits. Encourage clients to Google something like "budget apps" or "top 10 household budget tools" and check out what's available, or recommend a budgeting app you think they'll like.

REMEMBER

The best budget tool is one that your clients will use. What's important is that everyone in the household uses it. Budgeting is rarely successful when only one person in the household is vigilant and disciplined.

Encourage your household clients to round up the family members for a quarterly income and spending meeting. Make this an opportunity to achieve transparency, not a gripe session about how certain people spend too much. Kids especially are much more supportive when they see all the ways they're supported financially and how the costs really add up. The family meeting also prevents households from enabling entitlement behavior — spending more money than they've earned.

Leveraging the Power of Auto Pay and Payroll Deductions

Humans and their ancestors have managed to survive on this planet for more than six million years due to their ability to adapt to and control their environment. Today, the upgraded Neanderthal brains quietly adapt to the financial environment; that is, when people have less money, they spend less money. This phenomenon is what makes auto pay and auto deductions such powerful tools to curb spending.

TIP

Encourage your clients to harness the power of auto pay and payroll deductions to automatically siphon money from their paychecks to pay themselves first and then pay for all the essentials — mortgage, taxes, car payments, utilities, and so on. Have the money removed as closely as possible to the client's biweekly payroll deposit. Out of sight, out of mind.

Most clients will adapt their spending accordingly. The more aggressive spenders will start to accumulate debt. The most conservative clients will start to accumulate cash savings. Either extreme isn't great over the long term, but the cash saver is easier than the debt loader to redirect.

Chapter **8**

Brushing Up on Asset Management

Asset management (often referred to as *investment management, portfolio management,* or *wealth management*) is the practice of monitoring and optimizing the use of things that have monetary value to achieve one's financial goals. *Assets* typically include cash, stocks, bonds, and properties (home, business, cars, boats, and so on). In this chapter, I focus on managing investments in securities — primarily stocks, bonds, mutual funds, and exchange-traded funds (ETFs).

I explain how to build the best asset portfolio for your client. Here you find out how to align your advice with your client's objectives and investment philosophy. You get up to speed on different investment philosophies and discover how to help your client avoid the most common pitfalls. To cap it all off, I examine your broker/advisor compensation options and provide guidance on how to choose the right one for you and your client.

Developing a Client's Investment Policy Statement

An *investment policy statement (IPS)* is a document that states the client's financial goals and objectives, the overall strategy for meeting the goals and objectives, the agreed-upon investment guidelines, and more. The power of having an IPS tailored for each client is that it leaves nothing to the imagination, and it saves time when you have to remind clients why they're invested the way they are. Here's a basic IPS template you can use:

» Objectives

  • Risk tolerance (Does the client mind riding a roller coaster to meet her objective?)

  • Growth, income, or blend (What's the client's goal for using the money?)

  • Liquidity needs (When will the client need money from this account?)

  • Time horizon (How long will this money be invested?)

» Manager duties and responsibilities (Explain what you'll do for your client.)

  • Create asset allocation, monitor holdings, and serve as custodian.

  • Select/recommend investment vehicles.

  • Report on and control costs.

» Portfolio selection guidelines (guardrails)

  • Equity (stocks)

  • Fixed income (bonds)

  • Alternatives

» Rebalancing frequency (How often you plan on reviewing the client's portfolio and making or recommending changes.)

» Performance monitoring (Specify metrics and timelines for success.)

In this section, I lead you through the process of gathering the information you need to plug into this template to create an IPS for a client.

REMEMBER

Having a dependable framework like this holds you and your client accountable to a documented investment strategy. An IPS is a great way to formally confirm to your client that you've heard and you understand her. An IPS is also helpful in future meetings with clients because it provides a point of reference. Great financial advisors routinely reference and discuss IPSs, demonstrating their diligence and accountability to clients. Also, having an IPS in your client's file makes your compliance department very happy.

Exploring the client's goals and objectives

"What are you hoping to achieve with this investment?" is a silly question. Universally, regardless of age or net worth, people jokingly respond, "Make a lot of money!" The more enlightened clients will say "Not to lose this money." The most successful investors keep to a game plan with a set target in the form of an average annualized expected return, say five or six percent.

To explore your client's goals and objectives, assess the client's risk profile, time horizon, liquidity needs, and plans for spending the money.

Assessing your client's risk profile

Understanding your client's risk tolerance (or aversion) is crucial both for setting realistic goals and expectations and for choosing the right investments. The most effective way to gauge risk tolerance is to take a look at the client's current investments and how long she's had them and then ask how she feels about those investments.

TIP

Listen carefully to what your client says and doesn't say, examine your client's current financial status and goals, and then consider that information in the light of these two factors:

>> **Your client's *willingness* to take investment risk:** Is your client comfortable with short-term market fluctuations? Is she willing to be exposed to a permanent capital loss?

>> **Your client's financial *capacity* to bear investment risk:** How would a significant loss impact her life? For example, someone worth $10 million can lose half her wealth and still not end up in the streets, whereas a client with only $100,000 living off Social Security benefits would be severely impacted by a 50 percent loss.

WARNING

Don't gauge risk solely on what your client says. Most clients feel confident in a bull market. If their portfolio isn't packed with high-flying stocks, they'll readily express their fear of missing out (FOMO), and you'll get calls asking why their account isn't performing as well as their friend's account. In a bear market, these same clients will be calling to complain that their investments are losing too much value.

Risk assessment tools are built into asset management programs and are available online in the form of questionnaires.

Understanding the client's financial goals

Although a dollar figure or a percentage is a specific and measurable goal, encourage clients to share their plans for spending the money. Are they investing to retire? If so, at what age, where, and at what standard of living? Are they saving for a child's or grandchild's education? Are they planning to leave money to their heirs? How your clients plan to spend their money and when can provide valuable insight into the type of investment portfolio that would serve them best:

>> **Growth:** When clients have long-term goals, they're likely to do best with a *growth portfolio* — mostly shares of companies with above-average growth that reinvest their earnings.

>> **Income:** An *income portfolio* is usually best for clients who need a stable source of income (from both bond interest payments or dividends from stocks) — for example, in their retirement years.

>> **Blend:** A *blended portfolio* features a balance of growth and income that's generally best for investors with a low to average risk tolerance who still want to benefit from long-term growth but don't have the stomach for riding the stock market roller coaster.

Assessing your client's liquidity needs

Liquidity is the availability of cash. Your client's investment choices may be limited by her liquidity needs. For example, a client who's planning to buy a house probably shouldn't be investing a considerable portion of her savings in a mutual fund she would need to cash out in two or three months to cover the down payment.

Engage clients in a discussion of their short-term and long-term plans, so you understand how liquid their finances need to be. Also, be sure that they have sufficient funds set aside to cover emergencies *before* they start investing. See Chapter 7 for details on budgeting.

REMEMBER

Clients tend to believe that because they own something (a house, a car, a business) it's worth more than an investment. My definition of wealth is having money when you need it, without having to accept a compromised value to access the capital. When advising clients, keep liquidity in mind, especially when clients are close to needing their money.

Looking at the time horizon(s)

Think about the commonly known quote: "A goal without a deadline is just a dream." As a financial advisor, you want to make your client's dream(s) a reality, and to do that, you must know the timeline you're dealing with. Whenever your clients mention a financial goal, have them specify when they want to achieve that goal. For example, if they want to have enough money to retire comfortably, ask when they plan to retire, and then write the answer on the IPS.

Defining your duties and responsibilities

To avoid any misunderstandings, specify in the IPS what you promise to do for your client. This list should do the trick:

>> Create asset allocation, monitor holdings, and serve as custodian.

>> Select/recommend investment vehicles.

>> Report on and control costs.

Establishing portfolio selection guidelines

Ultimately, your job as investment advisor boils down to helping clients make decisions about which assets to invest in. In this section, I explain the four classes:

>> **Equity (stocks):** Equities include U.S. and international, large cap, small cap, high dividend, and value. (*Cap* is short for capitalization, which refers to the total amount of money invested in a company.)

>> **Fixed income (mostly bonds):** Investments that are geared to deliver a steady income stream, including U.S. municipal, corporate, government, and global bonds and U.S. and global real estate investment trusts (REITs).

>> **Alternatives:** Long-short mutual funds, managed futures, hedge funds, commodities, and derivatives.

>> **Cash:** This includes money market funds, bank savings and checking accounts, or physical cash buried in the back yard or under the mattress.

REMEMBER

I can't possibly cover all you need to know about the four asset classes and many other investment options. Check out the newest edition to *Investing For Dummies* by Eric Tyson (John Wiley & Sons, Inc.), do your own research, or enroll in a financial advisor education program at the CFA Institute (see Chapter 6). Another option is to outsource this task to a competent turnkey asset management program (TAMP). In the following sections, I take the middle ground, providing enough guidance about the four asset classes to get you started in the right direction.

Don't represent products you don't fully understand (a far too common practice). Focus instead on asset management products or service solutions that you understand and can easily explain to a ten-year-old. Swimming out of your depth is not only dangerous for your client, but it also shifts the professional responsibility from you to your firm or to the product manufacturer. Don't pass the buck. Always be accountable for the asset management solutions you recommend or use.

Equity

Equity is the value of the shares issued by a company to investors (shareholders). In the broadest sense, an equity is an asset class that offers an opportunity to earn more value over time with a given level of risk. Equities are widely considered assets that can hold their value (store value) even in an inflationary economy. Investments in equities tend to grow faster than inflation, so equities are a required allocation in almost every basic diversified portfolio.

Financial advisors commonly deal with the following two types of equities:

>> **Common stocks:** Publicly, exchange-traded businesses (including stocks held in mutual funds)

>> **Real estate:** Residential, industrial, commercial, and specialty

As you advise clients on equity investments, highlight the following two considerations:

>> **Return/risk tradeoff:** Risk is proportionate to the expected rate of return. As you and your clients evaluate equity investments, keep this fact in mind: The higher the rate of return, the greater the risk. As the financial advisor, you must also consider the client's willingness and capacity for risk, as discussed in the previous section "Assessing the client's risk profile."

>> **Liquidity:** *Liquidity* is the ability to sell assets for cash. Large cap U.S. stocks have little liquidity risk, because they rarely suffer huge losses from lack of matching buyers and sellers. As you move further down the market cap spectrum, liquidity increases exponentially, because share prices can swing dramatically based on small changes in supply and demand.

Trying to figure out whether a market price is a good deal, relative to the equity's true value (whatever that might be), is a challenging endeavor. Here are three applicable valuation methods:

>> **Price multiples:** A *price multiple* is a ratio of the share price to another financial metric, such as price-to-earnings (P/E), price-to-book, and price-to-sales. For example, the P/E is the price per share divided by the earnings per share. These ratios are easy to calculate and provide a measure of whether the share price is relatively high or low, as compared to other stocks in that sector or to the broader market as a whole.

>> **Capital asset pricing model (CAPM):** This model estimates the expected returns for an asset given its risks, building on an established risk free rate (in the United States, it's typically the 10 Year Treasury Bill).

>> **Dividend discount models:** This model assumes that the stock price should reflect the net present value of all of the company's future dividend payments.

Every asset management program and research analyst service has reports for determining valuations, primarily using price multiples. You can find additional tools online through Google Finance or Yahoo! Finance.

Regardless of the equities a client chooses (or you choose for your client), you need to devise methods to approximate the relative impact of one equity's value fluctuation to another. The goal is to allocate a client's investments across various ones to maximize the probability that they'll achieve their desired financial goals. Using correlation matrix reports (readily available within portfolio management programs) to verify that your selected equities are sufficiently diversified.

Fixed income

The defining attribute of a fixed income asset is that its price is based on its *yield* — the promised income stream for a duration of time. Unlike growth investments in which investors make money primarily from selling shares for more money than they paid for them, investors in fixed-income investments make money primarily from the interest or dividends the shares produce.

Bond prices move inversely to their yields, because current yield is calculated by dividing the annual coupon payments (cash flow) by the market value (current bond price). For example, if you buy a bond for $1,000 that pays an annual coupon of $100, the current yield is $100/$1,000 = 10 percent. If the bond price drops to $800, the yield increases, because the owner still earns $100 annually but has paid less for the bond; the new yield is $100/$800 = 12.5 percent. When interest rates increase, bond prices drop while yields rise, because as companies or governments issue new debt, they're offering yields at prevailing market rates, forcing prior issue (secondary market) bonds to reprice themselves to remain attractive.

The common belief that bonds are a risk-free investment is a blanket fallacy. Bond investors must consider three possible sources of risk:

>> **Rising interest rates:** If interest rates are higher now than when you bought the bond and you have to sell it, you'll most likely be selling the bond for less than you paid for it.

>> **Inflation:** If the yield on a bond is less than the inflation rate, the return on your investment won't keep up with inflation and your client will lose purchasing power over time.

>> **Credit default:** If a government collapses or a company goes bankrupt, you'll lose all or part of the money you paid for the bond (principal) and/or receive no further or modified coupon payments.

To mitigate the risks and maximize the potential return, consider the following factors when advising clients to invest in bonds:

>> **Duration and maturity:** The holding period over which the issuer promises to make payments and pay back the principal.

>> **Credit quality:** The underlying financial condition of the issuer — for example, on the verge of bankruptcy or a pillar of the economy.

>> **Coupon rate:** Payment frequency and amount — for example, $500 paid annually.

>> **Market liquidity:** The ease of selling the bond for a decent price when necessary. Bonds trade in a highly fragmented dealer marketplace, so some bonds may be easier or harder to sell than others.

Bonds can be extremely complicated. The United States alone has more than 250,000 issuers of government debt. The worldwide bond market is valued at about $85 trillion compared to the global stock market capitalization of $70 trillion. The variety of debt issuers and other fixed income investments is huge. Every entity from small municipalities to federal governments, to small private companies to the largest public companies, and on and on are involved in the debt markets. Other related fixed income investments include real estate investment trusts (REITs) and master limited partnerships (MLPs), because they're traded based on their current yield.

Alternatives

Alternative investments are any investments that aren't equities or fixed income, including the following:

- » Gold, other precious metals, and commodities

- » Hedge funds

- » Managed futures (*futures contracts* are agreements to buy or sell a commodity or financial instrument for a certain price on a certain date)

- » Derivatives contracts (*derivatives contracts* are agreements to buy or sell a certain asset for a certain price on a certain date)

- » Privately held or family businesses (private equity)

- » Collectibles (art, jewelry, cars, Hermès handbags)

I've had conversations with clients, where their greatest equity asset is a painting that their mom bought 50 years ago that now is worth $5,000,000. Never underestimate the possibility that just because a client's investment or bank statement doesn't look large means there isn't a huge opportunity to add valuable advice because of some obscure asset. In practice, the most valuable household asset is usually the family home or business.

Cash

Cash is king. You've heard it many times before, and it's true. When a client has cash readily available, precisely when she needs to spend it is when things go smoothly. If an asset has a depressed market value or an unfavorable sale price, then converting it into cash comes at a high price. The only way to avoid such a scenario is to have liquidated the asset in advance of its price decline, which is easier said than done. Most investors and financial advisors can't accurately predict the perfect time to sell appreciated assets and squirrel away the cash to meet future expenses.

Generally, cash allocations in portfolios can be in the one to three percent allocation range to be considered *fully invested*. Higher cash allocations indicate a more conservative portfolio. Anything higher than 10 percent signifies that the portfolio manager perceives an imminent threat to the portfolio's value if that money were allocated to other asset classes.

The big downside to holding too much cash is that inflation erodes its purchasing power. Cash typically earns money market rates, currently averaging 0.5 percent for large institutional money market funds. If inflation is at 2.5 percent, then your client is essentially losing 2 percent of that money's value. Compound this out over a ten-year time frame, and your client will lose 22 percent buying power.

Concurring on a rebalancing frequency

Most clients falsely assume that their financial advisor is checking their accounts regularly and making necessary adjustments. In fact, most financial advisors don't actually manage money themselves; they outsource this service to another provider or TAMP. Be clear with you clients, and be sure they understand who controls the timing of portfolio rebalancing and how the rebalancing is executed.

The two main ways to rebalance are using calendar timing and market price triggers, or a combination of the two. For most clients, an annual rebalancing may seem too relaxed, while monthly adjustments may generate too much unwanted short-term capital gains. As a general guide, using a quarterly rebalance feature is a standard feature on most TAMP platforms.

More sophisticated platforms introduce *drift rebalancing,* which monitors the value of a specific holding relevant to other portfolio components. When a holding has exceeded a certain percentage threshold, an alert is generated to review the allocation for possible trimming back.

Setting parameters for performance monitoring and reporting

Reviewing portfolio performance with clients is a basic duty for a financial advisor. If clients understand the reasons behind the returns they've earned, they're much more likely to stay the course. The challenge is figuring out how to present the portfolio's returns in a way that reflects the investment goals you've agreed to.

A common mistake clients often make is to choose the wrong benchmark. For example, a client has a balanced portfolio of 60 percent stocks and 40 percent bonds. She sees that the S&P 500 had gained 15 percent the past year, but her portfolio earned only 10 percent, and she's disappointed. She doesn't consider that her portfolio is balanced to prevent big losses if the stock market dives.

One way to avoid such disappointment is to use a blended benchmark (common in TAMP platforms), which mixes together the asset allocations and combines indexes to illustrate a weighted average. However, if asset allocations in the portfolio change frequently, this blended benchmark methodology doesn't help your client's understanding.

REMEMBER

Benchmarks, blended or not, aren't always the best way to evaluate a portfolio's performance. A better approach is to explain the pros and cons of the approach you agreed to. Your client's understanding of the strategy and goals will go a long way to improving her continued confidence.

Agreeing on an Investment Philosophy

Investors differ in their approach to investing. Some like to buy and sell often in an attempt to take advantage of market fluctuations and trends. Other investors like to buy and hold, trusting in the consistency of a long-term strategy. Some investors prefer to purchase individual stocks and bonds, while others are more comfortable in mutual funds.

Whatever your client's investment philosophy is, you should know it, and you should work with your client to ensure that the philosophy aligns with the client's goals, strategy, and risk tolerance. These sections examine various investment strategies.

Active, passive, or somewhere in between

Asset managers can choose to be active, passive, or somewhere in between. Here's how those three approaches differ:

>> **Active:** Frequently buy and sell individual stocks and/or bonds with the goal of outperforming a *benchmark* — a market index such as the Dow Jones Industrials, S&P 500, or Nasdaq.

>> **Passive:** Buy and hold investments with the goal of generating a steady income or performing as well as a chosen market index minus the cost of portfolio management.

>> **Somewhere in between:** Buy, monitor, and adjust the portfolio on a regular basis — a mix of active and passive investing.

REMEMBER

Whether you recommend an active, passive, or somewhere-in-between approach to investing, make sure it's rooted in credible research, that it's the best approach for your client's needs and aligns with her investment philosophy, and that you can explain it to clients. I believe no approach is superior; each approach has advantages and disadvantages. As a successful financial advisor, make up your own mind and consider the approach that's best for each client. What follows are some quick highlights of the pros and cons of each approach.

Active asset managers

To beat their benchmark, active managers select individual securities, believing they can see something others don't in a particular company or bond issue. They're interested in making investors more money with the same or less risk than their fund's benchmark.

One general method to tell when a portfolio is actively managed is by looking at its *turnover ratio* — the percentage of stocks or bonds in a portfolio that have been bought or sold over the past year. A higher turnover ratio indicates a more active asset management style; for example, a turnover ratio of 100 percent means that all the securities in a portfolio have been bought in the past year.

The hoped-for benefit of active asset management is that the investment portfolio will outperform the benchmark that the manager is trying to beat. Here are some potential drawbacks:

>> Rarely do actively managed portfolios outperform their benchmarks. Statistics show that over 1-, 3-, 5-, 10-, and 15-year periods, only a small percentage (5 to 15 percent) of active managers beat their benchmark.

>> Actively managed portfolios require closer monitoring and management, which introduces complications that most clients aren't prepared to handle.

>> High turnover usually translates into higher management fees due to increased transaction fees and ongoing work required to manage the portfolio.

>> High turnover may also result in higher capital gains taxes when the sale of securities results in a profit.

REMEMBER

Most active managers, regardless of their specialty or focus, have a difficult time outperforming their benchmark with any consistency. During the writing of this book, automated, indexed strategies are the preferred approach to investing, but I'm not convinced that the era of active fund managers is over. Changing market conditions can inspire investors to look for solutions that don't have them riding the bus with everyone else. Delivering superior risk-adjusted returns is the promise of active managers, and they'll have their day in the sun once more, as the pendulum swings back from passive to active management once again.

Passive asset managers buy and hold. The portfolios they manage have little or no turnover. The most popular form of passive investing is through *index funds* — mutual funds that contain a mix of stocks or bonds that track (align with) a given index, such as the Dow Jones Industrials or Nasdaq. For example, Vanguard 500 Index Fund Admiral Shares (VFIAX) invests in 500 of the largest U.S. companies, and its performance is nearly identical to the performance of the S&P 500.

Index funds offer the following advantages:

>> **Simplified diversification:** When you buy shares of an index fund, you're typically investing in a large number of companies or bond issuers.

>> **Less worry:** By tracking indexes, investors can be more confident that their investments won't underperform an index. However, index funds can

outperform or underperform an index slightly due to a phenomenon known as *tracking error*.

>> **Lower cost:** Index funds have lower turnover ratios, resulting in lower transaction fees and less work for the management team with the savings passed along to the investor.

REMEMBER

Investors in index funds still must know how much of their portfolio to invest in each fund. You can offer value to a client by providing guidance on allocations, as I explain in the next section.

Passive investing also includes a buy-and-hold approach with any asset. For example, a client may choose to purchase high-dividend stocks or high-yield bonds and hold onto them, using the dividends as income or to purchase more shares. This approach has two possible drawbacks:

>> The investments may not perform as well as other investment options.

>> Investors must purchase and manage shares in a wide variety of companies and bond issuers to match the diversity available in a single index fund.

Somewhere in between

The somewhere-in-between approach involves building a balanced portfolio, typically a collection of index funds, with an additional layer of active management and room for discretionary allocations.

Many RIAs and TAMPs have started to offer investment solutions that invest solely in passive index funds with the addition of timely rebalancing, either on a scheduled basis or in response to changes in the client's financial needs. For example, as a client ages and has less time to recover from a significant loss, higher-risk investments may be sold to purchase lower-risk investments.

The somewhere-in-between approach is a basic level of active management, but plenty of research points to its effectiveness in providing better risk-adjusted total returns over time, as compared to strictly passive portfolio management.

Individual securities versus packaged products

Buy a stock, fall in love with it, never sell it, company declares bankruptcy, lose all the client's money — this catastrophe is what you're looking to avoid. However, owning an individual stock or bond has many advantages over investing in mutual funds or ETFs that provide pre-packaged diversification.

COMPARING MUTUAL FUNDS AND ETFs

Mutual funds and exchange-traded funds (ETFs) are similar in that each contains a mixture of stocks, bonds, precious metals, or commodities. They're less risky than owning individual stocks and are both overseen by professional portfolio managers. They differ in the following ways:

- Mutual funds often have a minimum dollar investment, whereas the minimum investment in an ETF is the price of one share.

- A mutual fund's share price is calculated after the markets close, whereas an ETF's share price changes during the trading day.

- Some mutual funds have an early withdrawal penalty (redemption fee); for example, one percent if you withdraw your funds sooner than 90 days after purchase. ETFs have no minimum holding period.

- ETFs more closely track indexes, because the selection of securities is automated based on the composition of the index. On the other hand, many mutual funds are actively managed by managers who select securities in order to beat an index.

- Because ETFs are managed more passively, their management costs are typically lower.

- With mutual funds, you may have to pay capital gains taxes even if you buy and hold shares, because the mutual fund manager may need to sell holdings to pay investors who are selling shares. With ETFs, you generate a tax even only when you sell your shares.

- You can schedule automatic investments or withdrawals with a mutual fund, but you can't do so with an ETF.

In this section, I explore the advantages and disadvantages of individual stocks versus mutual funds and ETFs, so you can help your clients make well-informed decisions.

Expenses

As you guide clients through the maze of investment options, compare costs:

» **Individual stocks or bonds:** Investors pay relatively small transaction fees to buy and sell individual stocks and bonds, but these fees can add up when you're trying to diversify or actively manage a portfolio.

» **ETFs:** With ETFs, investors pay a transaction fee plus an annual fee based on the ETF's gross expense ratio, which is typically (but not always) lower than the gross expense ratio of a comparable mutual fund. (*Gross expense ratio* is the cost of management fees, administration fees, and operating expenses divided by the total invested; for example, if the gross expense ratio is one percent, an investor would pay $1,000 on a $100,000 investment.)

>> **Mutual funds:** Mutual funds have a variety of costs, including the following:

- **Sales charge (load):** A percentage of the investment when buying shares (front-end load) or selling shares (back-end load). No-load funds don't have a sales charge.

- **Gross expense ratio:** A percentage of the average value of the investment annually. The gross expense ratio is typically small for passively managed funds (0.03 to 0.20 percent), but it can be steep for large managed funds (up to 2.0 percent).

- **Transaction commissions:** The broker fee for handling the transaction.

- **Redemption fees:** Early withdrawal penalties.

Investors often overlook fees when considering investment options. They tend to focus more on performance. Don't overlook these expenses when presenting your clients with investment options or analyzing investment options they present to you. Although fees are often hidden, your clients will appreciate your calling attention to them.

TIP

You can find fees related to ETFs and mutual funds on the fund's prospectus. Better yet, subscribe to the Morningstar Advisor Workstation (or other portfolio analytic).

Diversification

Diversification is simply the wise practice of not putting all your client's eggs in one basket or, in the case of investing, not putting all your client's money in one investment option. A quick, easy, and affordable way to achieve diversification is to invest in mutual funds or ETFs where each fund holds a larger variety of securities. Clients can further diversify by investing in several different funds.

However, investing in mutual funds and ETFs isn't the only way to diversify. I've seen (and built) plenty of well-diversified portfolios that include a few individual stocks, ETFs, and bond funds.

REMEMBER

With diversification, focus more on the correlation among investments in the portfolio than on sectors or market areas. For example, a common misunderstanding is that high yield bond funds will act more like bonds, while the truth is that they act more like stocks.

Spend more time evaluating how each portfolio holding will react when stress-tested in various economic scenarios, and then apply your own educated judgment on probabilities. For example, Blackrock offers a portfolio management analytical program called Aladdin that features forward-looking stress testing. Morningstar Advisor Workstation also provides this capability, but on a backward-looking basis. Better yet, partner with a money manager who has a proven track record and who may do all this work for you.

Tax management

To maximize the amount of money your clients can invest, consider the tax implications of different investment options:

>> **Individual stocks** provide the ultimate in tax management as long as you control the timing of sales. For example, if your client holds investments for longer than a year, she pays the long-term capital gains tax that's typically less than the short-term capital gains tax on investments held for one year or less.

REMEMBER

In most separately managed accounts, investments are run through a modeling program to maximize tax savings. Clients have little input unless they express their concerns.

>> **Mutual funds** are generally the least tax-efficient investments, because an investor may be subject to taxes on capital gains distributions triggered by other investors' decisions. When more investors are withdrawing from the fund than contributing to it, the fund manager is often forced to sell securities to cover the withdrawals. Any capital gains from these sales are distributed to investors in the fund and are subject to tax.

REMEMBER

>> Actively managed mutual funds tend to be less tax efficient than passively managed funds, because the increased buy-and-sell activity tends to trigger more tax events, such as capital gains distributions.

>> **ETFs:** With ETFs, investors don't pay taxes on distributions when other investors sell their ETFs, but the sale of a single share may result in both short- and long-term capital gains.

>> **Bonds:** Bonds earn the regular capital gains associated with a profitable sale, but they offer other interesting tax features, the most important of which to understand is *amortization* — an accounting method that gradually reduces the cost value of an asset. When buying a bond at a premium to its par (face) value, a small amortized amount each year prevents the holder from claiming a loss of principal when the bond matures at par value.

Cautioning Clients on "Hot Money" Investments

Investors often get caught up in what former Federal Reserve Chair Alan Greenspan calls "irrational exuberance." They follow the "hot money" — investments that are soaring in value. This approach is usually a recipe for disaster, as evidenced by the boom-to-bust Dotcom era that wiped out many billions of dollars of market value.

At the time, even conservative investment firms couldn't ignore the siren call that captivated investors. I had worked at a company that was well known as a conservative municipal bond specialty investment management firm. It, too, launched its own tech fund. In fact, most large, well-distributed packaged investment product manufacturers (including mutual funds, unit investment trusts, and defined portfolios) jumped on the bandwagon.

REMEMBER

A big part of your job as a financial advisor is to steer your clients' ships through stormy seas with an aura of calm confidence. Many clients will demand action in good times or bad when inaction is the best course.

Comparing Revenue/Compensation Models

As an asset manager, you may be paid in one or more of the following ways:

>> **Asset-based fees:** You earn a percentage of the value of the client's investment portfolio.

>> **Commissions or sales charges:** You earn a commission or fee when you sell a particular investment product.

>> **Flat fee:** The client pays you a retainer or pays a fixed hourly rate for specific services.

In this section, I explain the pros and cons of these revenue/compensation models.

Asset-based fees

With *asset-based fees*, clients pay an annual percentage of the value of their account monthly or quarterly. The percentage you charge may be on a sliding scale based on the total value of the account; for example, you may charge 1.5 percent up to $250,000; 1.25 percent from $250,000 to $1 million, and 1.0 percent above $1 million. Keep in mind that this percentage is on top of the percentage any fund managers charge. For example, if you charge 1.5 percent, and the portfolio contains mutual funds that collectively charge 1.0 percent in management fees, your client is paying 2.5 percent annually.

The benefit of charging asset-based fees is that your compensation is linked to the success of your client's portfolio. You earn more when the client's portfolio performs well and less if its value drops, so your interests align. Charging asset-based fees is generally the best approach, because it avoids conflicts of interest and motivates you to do your best to make your clients wealthier.

Commissions and sales charges

Earning a commission when you deposit a client's money into a fund has the potential of creating a conflict of interest. You may be motivated to sell a product that costs more and earns you a higher commission than another product that costs less and isn't in the client's best interest.

The commissionable products I'm referring to here are primarily REITs, MLPs, direct participation programs (DPPs), business development companies (BDCs), annuities, hedge funds, and retail mutual fund share classes. Sometimes, paying a commission is in the client's best interest. (A *DPP* allows income, expenses, gains, losses, and tax benefits to pass from a business to investors. A *BDC* typically invests in small- and medium-sized startups. An *annuity* is a contract with an insurance company that promises the investor a steady income upon retirement. A *hedge fund* uses high-risk methods, such as investing with borrowed money, to earn a profit.)

A classic example is that of the retiree who has no growth needs. Having saved well more than she'll ever be able to spend, a fiscally fit retiree can afford to buy into a *simple laddered* bond portfolio (buying bonds that have a staggered maturity schedule). Through a series of commissioned transactions, this strategy costs very little to maintain and to execute annually, and it's particularly effective during times of very low interest rates. You'd have trouble justifying an asset-based fee of one percent on a totally fixed-income portfolio if the yield-to-maturity is only 2.5 percent, which would equate to taking 40 percent of the portfolio's projected return.

Chapter **9**

Delving into Liability Management

L iability management involves making sure your client has enough insurance to cover the cost of any big-ticket surprises, such as serious illness, property loss, or death of a major breadwinner. Think of asset and liability management as your team's offense and defense. With asset management (see Chapter 7), you're trying to gain ground. With liability management, you're trying not to lose ground.

Although clients typically get more excited about maximizing their assets, you need to remind them of the importance of protecting against losses. After all, a single unexpected tragedy has the potential to completely devastate a high-performance portfolio.

Including liability management discussions with your asset management clients is important. Without effective liability management, your client could lose everything or, at the very least, suffer a loss greater than any bear market could cause. And if your compensation is based on the value of your client's investment portfolio, you stand to lose income if liabilities ravage your client's investment portfolio.

In this chapter, I lead you through the process of analyzing your client's exposure to risk, introduce you to insurance solutions and a variety of insurance products, and invite you to explore the delicate psychology around protecting clients from the bad things that happen in life.

REMEMBER

A great variety of business models and specialties is available among financial advisors, and they all have value. Don't assume (or let your clients assume) that one area is more important than another. Protecting against the loss of assets is just as important as maximizing the growth of existing assets.

Assessing a Client's Risk Profile

A client's *risk profile* is the level of risk the client is willing to accept. Assessing a client's risk profile is a not-so-simple process of engaging the client in cost-benefit analysis. The client must decide how much he's willing to pay for protection. Everyone conducts this cost-benefit analysis when they buy any type of insurance. For example, if you drive a clunker, you drop comprehensive insurance to save money; if you were to total the car, you wouldn't get a big payout from your insurance company.

In the following sections, I present several ways to assess a client's risk profile.

REMEMBER

Many certification programs can provide you the formal knowledge of how and when to apply different solutions, but nothing can replace real-world experience. Evaluating a client's appetite for big-ticket risks and finding the right products is more art than science. You'll get better at it over time. In the meantime, the following approaches can get you started in the right direction.

Following a formal process

Regardless of the approach you use to arrive at a dollar amount for insurance purposes (for example, the needs-based or human life approach presented later in this section), follow these five steps to assess a client's risk profile, identify the client's insurance needs, and present your plan to your client:

Step 1: Assess the client's exposure to risk

Assessing a client's exposure to risk is an exercise in answering the question "What's the worst that could happen?" You and your client need to answer that question about the following areas:

» **Death:** How much income would be lost by the breadwinner's death? How much would it cost to bury a family member?

» **Health/illness:** Do certain serious illnesses run in the family? Are certain family members at greater risk of physical injury and illness than others? What would happen to the family finances if someone in the family contracted a long-term illness?

» **Job loss:** What impact would a job loss have on the family finances? Does your client have sufficient savings to weather a job loss?

» **Disability:** If a breadwinner became disabled, what impact would that have on the family's finances?

» **Marriage/divorce:** What would be the financial impact of a marriage or divorce?

» **Family issues:** If your client has one or more burdensome family members, what financial risks do they pose? For example, substance abuse interventions and treatments can be costly.

» **Personal property:** What if the family home were destroyed by fire, flood, or some other disaster? What if a vehicle were totaled? What if items of value were stolen?

» **Business ownership:** How would damage to or destruction of a business impact the family finances? What if a customer sued the business for damages?

Your client may already have plans or insurance policies in place to cover losses in some or all of these areas. Your job at this point is to gain insight into how well he is positioned to deal with possible losses and to increase his awareness of what he stands to lose if certain tragic events occur.

TIP

Don't hesitate to pry into the lives of your clients. The financial fallout from an unplanned event is far more uncomfortable that the temporary awkwardness of discussing personal or family problems openly. Many times in my own financial advisory career, I've received a call from a client asking me to wire money to cover an *anticipated* liability that I didn't know was even a possibility.

Ask clients about their family and how everyone's doing physically and mentally. Ask them how work is going and whether their family is dealing with any issues that you need to know about. Although you don't want to grill your clients, you need to play detective and find out about any major events or situations that could rock their financial boat, such as a marriage, divorce, job loss, or illness. Check in with clients at least once a year to see if anything has changed.

Assessing the client's exposure to risk exercises your and your client's intuition. Neither of you can see the future, but you and your client must consider the possibilities and the potential financial fallout.

If your client truly trusts you and understands the relevance to your work, then you'll be the keeper of many secrets, which is a humbling burden in this profession. Never break the trust or confidence your clients place in you. You want to be known as the financial advisor with integrity.

Step 2: Educate the client on mitigating risks

Although you can't put a price tag on risk, I like to use a formula to demonstrate the wisdom of allocating some portion of the client's assets to protect against potential losses. Here's the formula I use:

> Present value (PV) of financial loss ≥ PV sum of all premiums + Opportunity cost – PV of cash value accumulations (if applicable)

Where,

>> **PV economic loss** is the present value of some future, possible, and/or probable liability in dollars.

>> *PV* **sum of all premiums paid** is the amount of money paid over time into an insurance policy or contract or other strategy to protect against that specific future liability.

>> **Opportunity cost (if premiums were invested elsewhere)** is the money that could have been made if those insurance premiums were invested somewhere else. (Figure a five to six percent compounding return.)

>> *PV* **of cash value accumulations** is the accessible cash value that has accumulated in the insurance policy contract at some point in the future, if that feature is applicable.

The equation shows that a possible loss would cost your client more than the total cost of having insurance to protect against that loss. If you wanted to get even more fancy, you could try to research the probability of your client experiencing a particular event, like death or disability. There's just one small problem — no one believes it could happen to him, which makes the whole probability exercise futile with clients.

To calculate present value (PV), use the following equation:

$$PV = \frac{FV}{(1+i)^n}$$

where *FV* is future value, *i* is the discount rate, and *n* is the number of years.

Here's a simple example: A 40-year-old household breadwinner earning $200,000 per year and receiving an annual raise of 6 percent adjusted for inflation stands to earn $10,972,902.40, over the next 25 years leading up to retirement at age 65. You can use a lifetime earnings calculator or a spreadsheet to figure that out or do some really long math:

First year: $200,000

Second year: $200,000 x 1.06 = $212,000

Third year: $212,000 x 1.06 = $224,720

Fourth year: $224,720 x 1.06 = $238,203.20

and so on to the 25th year, and then total all annual salaries to arrive at a total lifetime earnings of $10,972,902.40.

Assuming a discount rate of 3 percent for inflation, the present value of $10,972,902.40 is

$$PV = \frac{\$10,972,902.40}{(1+.03)^{25}} = \$5,240,719.30$$

The breadwinner could protect against that loss with a renewable term life insurance policy, paying annual premiums of $5,000 that increase 3 percent annually, which comes to $182,296.30 over the 25-year term. Assuming a discount rate of 3 percent for inflation, the present value of that policy is

$$PV = \frac{\$182,296.30}{(1+.03)^{25}} = \$87,065.74$$

The opportunity cost of not investing that $182,296.30, assuming an annualized return of 6 percent is $274,322.56. Assuming a discount rate of 3 percent for inflation, the present value of that policy is

$$PV = \frac{\$274,322.56}{(1+.03)^{25}} = \$131,017.98$$

Based on these three numbers, you can show the client that the potential loss to the family if he dies without insurance is $5,240,719.30, but he could protect the family from that loss by paying $218,083.72 for a term life policy. Here's the math:

PV of financial loss ≥ PV sum of all premiums + Opportunity cost − PV of cash value accumulations (not applicable, because this is a term policy)

$5,240,719.30 ≥ $87,065.74 + $131,017.98

$5,240,719.30 ≥ $218,083.72

Note that PV of cash accumulations isn't applicable, because this is a term life insurance policy. Using cash value life policies can be a good way to build contract value, which reduces opportunity cost on the capital allocated to such a policy, as well as, the cumulative premiums paid.

Step 3: Decide how much loss the client wants to protect against

Insurance isn't free, so people typically make trade-offs to reduce the cost. For example, Healthcare.gov offers four levels of health insurance — bronze, silver, gold, and platinum. A healthy 25-year-old man would probably opt for the bronze plan, in the belief (and hope) that he doesn't contract a serious illness. Someone who's older and has numerous health issues may be better off with a gold or platinum plan.

REMEMBER

Risk tolerance varies among clients. They don't always need to hedge against a total loss or worst-case scenario.

After you and your client agree on a monetary value of what a potential loss would be, the next step is to ask your client how much of that loss he's willing to risk. The most conservative client will want to protect against 100 percent of the potential loss, whereas a client with much more tolerance and disconnection from risks may be interested in covering only 50 percent of a highly probable liability and opt for no coverage on what he considers a low probability loss. Clients' decisions are influenced by several factors but mostly by how relevant they believe the risk is to them personally.

REMEMBER

You can't read people's minds, so try to get your clients to open up about how they feel regarding the risks and the costs of hedging against those risks. Only then can you offer the rational processes to help them make decisions that are in their long-term best interest.

Step 4: Research insurance products

After you and your client agree on the monetary value of the potential loss and your client indicates the amount of that loss he wants to protect against, you can start shopping for insurance products to meet his needs. As you shop for products, use the following criteria to make your recommendations:

>> **The insurance provider's financial strength:** You can whittle down the list of options by choosing to work only with the best of the best insurance providers. Financial strength is a good indication that the company has great

management, offers great products, and will continue to grow and adapt. Check the insurance company's Comdex rating to gain insight into its financial strength. Most insurance companies list this figure on their website, where they show all financial data. Also, as a licensed insurance broker, you'll have access to this data through your brokerage group's subscription to VitalSigns or EbixLife.

>> **Value:** Compare the cost, coverage, and features of different plans to determine which plans offer the most for the money. *Features* are additional benefits; for example, some life insurance policies waive the premium if the client becomes seriously ill or disabled. Features can make or break an insurance policy, so don't overlook their value.

>> **Flexibility:** If you're shopping for a life insurance policy, consider whether your client will be able to convert the policy or contract to another type of insurance; for example, he could convert a term policy to a permanent policy later.

Find at least one low-cost, mid-range, and high-cost policy, so you can present the options to your client.

If you conclude that a recommendation is worth giving, do so only after conducting your own competitive marketplace product analysis. If your firm favors and promotes a certain insurance carrier, that's fine, but conduct your competitive analysis and recommend products that are truly in your client's best interest.

You can often address your client's needs best with a blend of products. Consider using different types of insurance policies and contracts to produce the desired outcomes.

Step 5: Present the options, reach agreement, and implement the plan

Create a table to illustrate your liability management plan, as shown in Figure 9-1. For each solution you recommend, state your reasons for including that solution as an option and present its pros and cons or its cost, benefits, and features. Let your clients know that you have chosen only the best of the best insurance providers, and explain the importance of choosing products from companies that are in a financial position to back those products.

Type	Pro	Con	Cost	Benefit	Features
Life Insurance	Protects household lifestyle	Poor health rating makes it expensive	$5,000/year level premiums for 20 years	$1,500,000 death benefit	Convertible into permanent policy after one year
Disability Income insurance	Accident prone breadwinner	Certain activities are excluded from coverage	$2,000/year level premiums, paid until age 65	$10,000/month until age 65, plus annual 2% inflation rider	Dividend participating policy, own occupation protected
Annuity	Pays a guaranteed income for life	Given a long life, income loses purchasing power	Total contract expenses are 2.75% of contract value per year	Guaranteed income of 5% starting at age 65, based on a guaranteed roll-up credited interest rate of 7% per year	Can be liquidated for cash value, up to 10% of contract value without back-end sales charge

FIGURE 9-1: A sample illustration of a liability management plan.

WARNING

Don't use emotional coercion to manipulate a client into a product or strategy. Most clients sense when their arms are being twisted, and they're more likely to reject your recommendation than embrace it. You can get your point across in ways that aren't coercive. I prefer presenting the facts objectively to appeal to the sentient beings I want to serve and allow their rational thinking to drive the best choices.

Several insurance-sales coaching programs are available to train advisors in techniques designed to connect clients with the gravity and emotion of potential life disasters, so clients are more receptive to insurance solutions. These approaches are effective because they increase clients' awareness and understanding without being pushy.

Using the income replacement approach

One approach to estimating how much life or disability insurance a client needs is to calculate the income the person would earn over the course of his life.

A general rule in calculating coverage for losing a breadwinner's income is to multiply the person's annual salary by 20 years. If the person earns $150,000 per year, then $150,000 x 20 years = $3 million in today's dollars paid as a lump sum. However, you should adjust for the ages of the surviving spouse and children, if any. With younger survivors, you may want to multiply the annual salary by 40. If the survivors are older, you may go as low as 10 times the salary.

For example, suppose your client is a family of five. Mom's a 32-year-old attorney earning $250,000/year married to a 28-year-old dad who stays at home and raises the kids. In the event of mom's death or physical disability, the family would probably need $250,000 x 40 = $10 million to maintain their lifestyle and achieve their future financial goals.

The family could decide that the premiums on a $10 million insurance policy are too expensive. They figure that in the event of mom's death or disability, dad could get a job to offset the loss of income, they could scale down, and the kids would be able to take care of themselves in 15 years. They figure that they could probably get by on $100,000 per year, so they decide that $100,000 x 20 = $2 million of coverage would be sufficient.

Taking the needs-based approach

With a *needs-based approach* to estimating insurance coverage, you link the benefit payout to a future liability. For example, suppose your client wants to make sure his eight-year-old daughter's college expenses are paid for in the event of his death.

You could use an online calculator or the future value (FV) function in Excel to crunch the numbers and determine that the total cost of a four year college education starting 10 years from now would be about $432,000:

Four year college tuition and expenses now	$200,000
Average inflation rate for college education	8 percent
Time until freshman year	10 years
Four year college tuition and expenses ten years from now	**$432,000**

A simple $500,000 life insurance policy specifically timed to provide that coverage throughout the daughter's college career would suffice here. To be precise, a $500,000 death benefit, 15-year term life policy would do the trick.

Reviewing Insurance Lines and Products

Insurance is available for nearly every risk you take in life, except for most illegal risks and some foolish risks. You won't find insurance to back a client's losses at the local casino or a client's poorly informed purchase decisions, but you'll find insurance products that cover property losses, medical bills, and malpractice lawsuits and that pay out to a beneficiary in the event of a client's death.

In this section, I bring you up to speed on the insurance categories you need to know about.

REMEMBER

The insurance categories presented here aren't an exhaustive list of insurance/liability management products, strategies, or solutions. These categories are the essentials.

Life insurance

Life insurance provides financial benefits to heirs in the event of the insured's death. The three biggies are:

>> **Term life** provides a tax-free death benefit (tax-free) to the named beneficiaries, if the insured dies within the specified time period. The policy has no cash value, so if the client lives past the term, he can't recoup any of the premiums. The good news is that term life policies are relatively inexpensive.

>> **Permanent life** policies provide protection for the insured's entire life, assuming the premiums are paid. These policies also have a cash value — a portion of each premium is held by the company and allowed to grow tax-deferred. Unfortunately, permanent life policies, such as universal life or variable life, may not live up to their name. Stock and bond market returns, company management, and product pricing can all impact the staying power of a particular policy with a constant premium. If you're advising a client to purchase a permanent life policy, read the fine print and make sure the provider is financially strong and well established and that your policy performance assumptions are sound.

>> **Whole life** policies are a type of permanent life policy that locks the premium for the entire life of the policy regardless of changes to the insured's age and health. A whole life policy has a cash value that can grow tax-deferred, and be accessible through policy loans. Most whole life policy providers even pay dividends to policy holders. If you're offering whole life policies, be especially careful to work with a stable carrier, and ones that pay dividends based on nondirect recognition (no adjustment is made to policy dividends when there's an outstanding loan balance)

Life insurance policies often include features that make them stand out, such as the following:

>> Waiver of premium if the policyholder becomes seriously ill or disabled

>> Accelerated death benefit, which pays cash advances if the policyholder is diagnosed with a terminal illness

>> Guaranteed purchase option, which enables the policyholder to purchase additional coverage without having to prove he's in good health

>> Mortgage protection to pay off a mortgage upon the death of the policyholder

Disability insurance

Encourage your working clients to consider disability insurance in the event that an injury or illness prevents them from working. Social security disability pays only $700 to $1,700 per month, and the payments start six months or longer after the date the disability began. Unless your client has a good chunk of change squirreled away, even a short-term disability can be financially devastating.

Your clients who need disability insurance should consider both short-term and long-term disability insurance (see Table 9-1).

TABLE 9-1: **Short-Term and Long-Term Disability Insurance**

Short-term disability insurance	Long-term disability insurance
Typically pays 60 to 70 percent of salary	Typically pays 40 to 60 percent of salary
Provides coverage up to 12 months	Provides coverage until the disability ends, after a certain number of years, or upon retirement
Has a short waiting period, typically a couple weeks or less	Has a longer waiting period, typically 90 days

Disability insurance policies differ in several ways, including the following:

>> **The definition of disabled:** Whether you're unable to work, period, or are able to do a job that's outside your field of expertise. For example, if you're a disabled attorney but can work as a secretary, the policy may not pay.

>> **Partial disability coverage:** Some policies pay a portion of the salary if the insured can work only part time, whereas others pay only if the insured is unable to work at all.

Health insurance

Unexpected medical bills are one of the biggest contributors to personal bankruptcy in the United States, so your clients should have health insurance and the means to cover the deductible. For example, a family with a policy that has a household deductible of $10,000 per year should have at least that much saved in basic FDIC insured bank savings before allocating funds elsewhere.

Even if you decide not to provide health insurance plans, develop a clear understanding of your client's health insurance policy terms and conditions, including deductible amounts and limits. With this understanding you're in a better position to help clients plan their savings and investments, so they have resources to draw on if necessary.

Homeowner's insurance

Although you'll rarely, if ever, encounter a client who owns a home and doesn't have homeowner's insurance, you should review the policy to ensure that the coverage is sufficient. Coverage should include the replacement cost of the home and personal property inside the home, including expensive artwork, jewelry, and collectibles.

For many clients, the home they own is their most valuable asset. Without sufficient insurance coverage, a single tragic event could rapidly deplete the homeowners' net worth.

Auto insurance

Because drivers are required to have auto insurance, most drivers have it, but you should review the policies to ensure that your clients aren't underinsured or paying too much for their policies.

Encourage your clients to get one or two auto insurance quotes from reputable companies. Comparing policies from two or more insurance companies may reveal ways your clients can save money to allocate elsewhere.

Liability insurance

The possibility of a client being sued (especially if he has millions) is a real risk to a family's accumulated assets. Various types of personal or professional liability policies, such as umbrella policies and malpractice insurance, fund the possible settlement and/or judgment from an unlucky personal or professional lawsuit.

Many businesses and professions (including financial advisor) are required to carry error and omissions policies. Policy premiums are typically range from $700 to $1,500 annually for $1 million in protection against unintentional damage to a client.

Annuities

An *annuity* can be a combination of insurance and investment that pays the holder a certain amount of money starting on a certain date and every month for the rest of the holder's life. The idea is to provide a guaranteed income stream, so annuity holders don't outlive their money. The other benefit is that investors in annuities don't have to concern themselves with managing their investments; that job is handled by the annuity manager, although the investor may have some choices.

As much as guaranteed income for life sounds great, annuities have several drawbacks, including the following:

>> When you buy an annuity, you're pretty much stuck with it, or you have to pay a stiff surrender fee to get your money out.

>> Some annuities (like, variable or indexed) are commonly sold by brokers who are paid a commission, sometimes as high as 10 percent or more.

>> Often certain annuities typically charge annual fees of 2 to 3 percent compared to 1 to 1.5 percent for managed mutual funds.

>> When you die, your money stays in the annuity; it's not passed to your heirs. This is the case for life income–only annuities.

Here are the two main versions of annuity contracts:

>> **Single premium immediate *income* annuity:** This old-fashioned annuity is a simple promise to pay the annuity holder a certain amount based on a lump sum deposit. The payment isn't subject to market volatility and is widely regarded as a favorable tool in retirement income planning.

>> **Flexible or multiple premium deferred *accumulation* annuity:** This newfangled annuity adds interest to the deposits, and this interest may be guaranteed for a certain number of years. The promise here is that the annuity will "capture stock market upside without downside capital loss risk." This type of variable or indexed annuity is typically expensive and somewhat complex. Use extra due diligence to figure out how a product really works before recommending it to a client.

WARNING

Do your homework and be prepared to explain the pros and cons to your clients. I've witnessed too many so–called financial advisors who fail to comprehend the finer details in these kinds of annuity contracts. By demonstrating your thorough understanding of the product's pros and cons, your client will have gained tremendous confidence in their plan.

Comparing Revenue/Compensation Models

When you're helping clients select insurance policies, you're essentially working in sales and collecting commissions. This arrangement is prone to conflicts of interest. After all, the more expensive the policy, the more money you make, and there's really no way around it. The only choice you have is between the lesser of two evils:

» Collecting a one-time, up-front commission

» Receiving annual recurring trailing revenue (getting paid in installments)

Which compensation model is more closely aligned with the client's interests is a seemingly simple question that has the entire industry completely ensnared in debate. The National Association of Insurance Commissioners (NAIC) is actively debating a fiduciary, best-interest standard on life insurance sales, but until they set the standard, you need to decide for yourself. In this section, I describe both models and reveal which side of the debate I'm on.

Collecting a one-time, up-front commission

A vast majority of insurance product manufacturers incentivize and compensate their salespeople by paying up-front commissions of anywhere from 50 to 120 percent of the first year's total premiums. Commissions like that can add up to big bucks and make your clients wonder whom you're really working for.

If you choose this compensation model, here are a few ways to ensure that your interests align with those of your clients:

» Present products from more than one product manufacturer.

» Present high-cost, mid-range, and low-cost options, and let your clients choose what's best for them.

» Broaden your service offerings, so you don't come across as just an "insurance salesperson." While I believe that being a risk-management-first advisor is a noble profession, adding asset management and guidance on other financial matters to your service offerings takes some of the focus off insurance sales.

Getting paid in installments

Getting paid in installments (officially known as *annual recurring trail revenue*) involves small payments over a number of years instead of one large, up-front commission. You can still earn the same amount of money, but it's spread over several years. I recommend this arrangement for two reasons:

>> Getting paid over several years projects to your clients that you're committed to their long-term success.

>> Spreading out commission payments typically improves short-term policy cash value accumulation (specifically in the case of whole life cash value policies) because most of the first-year premium payment is being applied to the policy instead of being paid out in commissions.

REMEMBER

Lean toward the smaller, ongoing revenue, whenever possible. Most insurance product manufacturers provide a variety of compensation models.

Embracing transparency

Whichever compensation model you choose, be transparent with your clients. Get ahead of any future regulatory pressure by incorporating commission transparency on all sales today.

I've begun the difficult practice of being consistently transparent, which has been refreshing to my clients. To follow in my footsteps, here's what you need to do:

1. **Reveal the percentage commission that you'll earn when the contract or policy is in force.**

   For example, whether you're receiving 100 percent of the first year premium in the first year or over the course of five years, quote that total.

TIP

   Be general. If you're getting a 55 percent up front plus another 20 percent financing bonus and another 25 bonus, you don't need to break it down. Just tell your client that you'll be getting 100 percent of the total first year premiums.

2. **Educate your client on the competitive marketplace and the industry's predominantly commission-based compensation model.**

Revealing commission compensation to the client has expanded the types of insurance products and structures I offer clients. I can often find insurance products that are better aligned with my client's interests when I expand my search to include products that pay, for example, 10 percent up front and 10 percent over the next nine years.

IN THIS CHAPTER

» **Creating an estate planning checklist**

» **Brushing up on federal and state estate tax laws**

» **Anticipating dysfunction and disagreements**

» **Enabling clients to leave a legacy of giving**

» **Collaborating with other estate-planning professionals**

Chapter **10**

Excelling in Estate Planning

For many people, the word "estate" conjures up images of an estate in the country — a mansion situated on a large expanse of land with servants, cooks, and groundskeepers. Clients often think that estate planning is only for the ultrarich. However, this chapter focuses on a different definition of *estate* — all the money and property owned by a person, however much or little that may be. Under this definition, nearly everyone owns an estate and can benefit from *estate planning* — the process of preparing for the management and distribution of assets to one's heirs or beneficiaries during and after one's life in a way that minimizes taxes, expenses, and disputes.

In this chapter, I provide guidance on how to educate clients and assist them in addressing their legacy and estate planning challenges — from tax matters to family dysfunction — to ensuring that clients transfer not only their wealth but also their values to future generations. I also emphasize the importance of collaborating with your client's attorney and any other relevant professionals to ensure the best outcome for your clients. I don't cover various planning techniques or governing documents; I leave that to your certified financial planner (CFP) courses.

Addressing Estate Planning Essentials

The purpose of an estate plan is to make sure that after someone dies, all his assets (and liabilities) will be managed according to one or more documents completed in advance of death. The most common desired outcomes associated with an estate plan include the following:

>> Making sure the right people receive the right assets.

>> Eliminating or minimizing disruptions in a family-owned business.

>> Choosing the guardians for underage children.

>> Minimizing fighting among family members who are so inclined.

>> Reducing taxes and estate processing expenses.

The following sections examine these points in greater detail.

TIP

For simple estates in probate-easy states, your clients have the option of a low-cost estate planning to create a will that names the heirs and specifies what they are to receive. Clients must also be sure that the beneficiaries named in any of their retirement accounts and life insurance policies are up-to-date, as I explain in the later section "Naming beneficiaries."

DO CLIENTS EVEN NEED ESTATE PLANNING?

With the passage of the Tax Cuts and Jobs Act in late 2017, fewer families will be subject to paying an *estate tax* — a tax levied on the net value of a deceased person's assets prior to asset distribution to heirs. Prior to this new tax bill, heirs would have had to pay 40 percent tax on all inherited assets beyond $5.49 million. The new tax reform bill more than doubles this individual exemption amount to $11.2 million. Married couples can now exclude $22.4 million of their estate property from taxation.

Life insurance policies designed to pay estate tax bills are less likely to be needed. However, with any permanent tax cut, tax regimes change as frequently as both executive and legislative branch leaderships. In addition, even clients who aren't subject to the estate *tax* need estate *planning* to deal with other potential issues, such as transferring closely held business assets.

Naming heirs

One of the most crucial steps in estate planning is to name the *heirs* (typically children and other blood or though marriage related individuals, although not exclusively) and specify how the money and property are to be divvied up among them.

WARNING

If your client dies *intestate* (without a will or other governing document that names the heirs and beneficiaries to the estate), then the state's inheritance laws kick in, which may result in the last people your client wanted to benefit from his estate being the first considered as rightful heirs. And, if the government can't find anyone who has legitimate claim to the estate, then the government gets to keep the assets. I've yet to meet a client who would be happy about either of those possible eventualities.

Naming the heirs and figuring out how to divvy up the estate among them can range from simple to complex. For example, if a husband and wife have a couple of adult children together who are successful, independent professionals and are amicable to one another, setting up their estate may be a simple matter of stating that if either the husband or wife dies, the other is named to the estate, and if they both die, the estate is split 50/50 between the two children.

Naming heirs can become more complicated in various situations; for example, when a client has many different family members across multiple marriages — children, grandchildren, ex-spouses, and so on. Another common example is a client who owns a business that none of the children wants or is qualified to take over, or when two or more want control of the business.

Complications also arise when distributions are or are perceived to be unfair by one or more heirs; for example, when one heir is a professional, earns a good living, and stays in close contact with mom and dad, while the other has been in and out of rehab a few times, drops off the map for months on end, and generally disrupts the family peace. Disinheriting the troublesome offspring may be a no-brainer for some clients, but most parents feel obligated to leave something to every child.

Many times those who've been a pain-in-the-posterior during the parents' life prove to be just that into and after their parents' death. They'll hire attorneys to sue the estate for more than their fair share, costing money and suffering to all survivors.

TIP

Encourage your clients to be proactive in thwarting such strife by being extremely specific in their estate planning documents. For example, your client can stipulate in the family's trust that the problem child will be entitled to ongoing funds, at certain intervals, as long as he doesn't challenge the estate in court. (Most reputable attorneys would advise the problem child to take the funds as provided and back off from filing additional claims unless some new material factor becomes evident.)

Such an arrangement wouldn't resolve the family dysfunction, but it would budget for ongoing support and relieve the more stable heir from having to waste precious time, money, and sanity trying to resolve inheritance issues in court in an effort that ultimately drives the siblings even further apart.

Sibling rivalry isn't the only case in which being proactive helps. Another example is an ex-husband who raised the children and never remarried. Accommodating for his needs in the estate planning documentation can reduce the possibility of having him fighting with his own children over her estate.

The bottom line is that too many households lose tons of money in attorney's fees fighting over what ends up being peanuts after the attorney's fees are deducted.

When naming heirs, make sure your clients factor in their own feelings, as well as those who will be affected by the news. Clients may even hire a family psychologist to provide guidance with the goal of removing their own pain and biases toward heirs or perhaps even come to understand the role they themselves may have played in the family dysfunction. Your clients should also protect their own future interests to ensure that they're properly cared for in the event they can't care for and make decisions for themselves.

Naming beneficiaries

Naming *beneficiaries* (any blood/family related and/or nonrelated individuals, also can include charitable organizations) can be as simple as submitting an updated beneficiary form to the manager of any retirement accounts. Many brokers enable customers to update their named beneficiaries online.

Be sure your client updates the named beneficiaries for all accounts, including all IRS tax-qualified accounts (401K plans, IRAs, SEP IRAs, and so on) and any and all annuity contracts such as fixed, variable, and income. In addition, be sure to review that the heirs named in the estate planning documentation are the same as those named as beneficiaries of those retirement accounts. A named beneficiary who's not referenced in the estate planning documents can spur on a fresh battle when the time comes to settle the estate. A client's trust and will should leave no room for confusion for heirs and beneficiaries, which may include special gifts to beneficiaries through designations made on qualified accounts. This is perfectly legitimate but just requires extra attention.

Planning for business succession or continuity

If you're pursuing small-business owners as clients, great idea! Financial advice tailored to the closely held small business owner (and family) is sadly lacking, especially in the areas of business succession and continuity. Small-business owners are often too busy running the business and raising a family to think about what will happen to the business when they're no longer able or willing to run it. Or they ignore the uncomfortable inevitabilities. I've had clients tell me boldly, "I'll be dead. What do I care what happens to the business?"

REMEMBER

This kind of defensive, reflexive response is pretty common but wholly wrong, and you must leap into the trenches on this one. Clients must understand the great peril that befalls a family or closely held business, especially if other business partners outside the nuclear family are involved. Other business partners will jump at the chance to take advantage of another partner's lack of planning.

Here are a couple ways you can help your small-business clients:

>> If the business is a partnership, advise your client to install a *fully funded cross-purchase, buy-sell agreement* for all partners. With this arrangement, all business owners agree to buy the business interests of any owner who dies or becomes disabled. To ensure funding is available to buy out the departing owner's interest, the business owners obtain life and disability buy-out insurance on the other owners. In the case of an owner's death, funds are paid to the deceased owner's family in exchange for its interest in the business.

REMEMBER

The agreement should require that the owners revalue the business annually (or hire an objective third-party appraiser to do so), so if a trigger event occurs, valuation isn't decided solely by the remaining owners.

>> Advise clients to include in their cross-purchase agreement plans for buying out owners if other trigger events occur, such as retirement, divorce, personal bankruptcy, or the firing of one of the owners.

>> Ask your clients what they plan to do when they retire. Who will run the business? Who's the backup manager? What's the plan B? Often, the owner has someone in mind but hasn't put it in writing. Sometimes the owner hasn't even told the person he has in mind and doesn't know if that person would be interested. The exit strategy needs to be formalized, captured in writing, and communicated to everyone that the plan may ultimately impact.

Keep in mind that unless you're an attorney, you're not the one formalizing the agreements. As financial advisor, you get the ball rolling and perhaps recommend a lawyer and certain insurance policies.

TIP

Get comfortable asking the uncomfortable questions. Ensuring that a business continues to operate after one (perhaps the only) owner withdraws or departs, is a major impact area for financial advisors. Unfortunately, too few financial advisors make this issue a priority and fear being out of their depth or upsetting their clients by calling attention to unsettling prospects. Getting comfortable with the uncomfortable is a great way to differentiate yourself from competing financial advisors.

Accounting for estate taxes

If you have any clients with a net worth more than $11.2 million (or $22.4 million for a married couple), their estate may be subject to a 40 percent federal estate tax at the time of their death. For a married couple's estate valued at $12 million, the federal estate tax would be $4,800,000! In addition, the estate may also have to pay a state estate or inheritance tax.

To protect the estate from a tax hit of this magnitude or greater, strongly encourage your clients to take out a life insurance policy that covers a significant portion of the total estate and inheritance tax bill. When your client dies, the life insurance policy will pay a big tax-free death benefit to the heirs at the same time the IRS comes to collect the taxes, and they only accept cash.

WARNING

Don't forget to plan for any estate or inheritance taxes levied by the states. As of this writing, 15 states and the District of Columbia have an estate tax, and six states have an inheritance tax. In Washington state, the estate tax can be as high as 20 percent. In addition, the net worth threshold that's subject to estate or inheritance tax is much lower than at the federal level. For example, in Oregon, a net worth of anything more than $1 million is subject to estate tax.

The federal estate tax is political football that's kicked back and forth with the regularity of changes in the White House administration. Given the extreme indebtedness of the U.S. government, the federal estate tax is likely to return with a vengeance in the not too distant future — a higher percentage and a lower net worth threshold. Considering a future congressional need to balance the federal budget, a return to the early 2000s when the exclusion amount was $1 million and the tax rate was 55 percent is likely.

REMEMBER

Federal and state governments write the rules and can change them at any time, so keep abreast of both federal and state estate and inheritance tax legislation. More importantly, you and your clients need to think ahead and perhaps even plan for the worst. After all, as your clients age, their life insurance premiums increase dramatically. If a client with a high net worth has a life expectancy of more than 20 years, he is likely to see the return of something like the federal estate tax of the early 2000s. He would probably benefit by locking into a suitable permanent life insurance policy now with much lower premiums than if he were to wait.

Managing estate liquidity (or lack thereof)

Estates heavily invested in real estate or business interests aren't very liquid because such assets aren't easily divested. A need to sell these assets quickly results in what's called a *fire sale*, in which buyers can purchase assets for pennies on the dollar. One of your jobs is to ensure that heirs aren't forced to liquidate in a hurry or into a deeply discounted buyer's market. This challenge is made more difficult by any of the following circumstances:

>> The number of heirs is large and their interests and needs diverse.

>> Market conditions are unfavorable for the sale of the assets.

>> The disposal demands of the trust require or drive the need to sell assets quickly.

>> No funding is in place to cover estate or inheritance taxes, resulting in a need to sell assets to pay the taxes due. (Even a relatively small tax bill can cause a liquidity crisis.)

>> Heirs who have no desire, interest, ability, or inclination to own the assets (for example, if the asset is a business) or who need or want their inheritance quickly.

Here are a few ways you can help your clients' heirs avert a liquidity crisis:

>> Strongly encourage your clients to buy enough life insurance to cover any and all estate and inheritance taxes along with any costs related to the estate settlement.

>> Discuss these liquidity issues with your clients and work together to address the issues proactively. You and your clients may even want to work toward making their estate more liquid as they advance in age.

>> Upon the death of your client, meet with the heirs to discuss their needs and expectations and to explain to them what they stand to lose if they need to liquidate assets in a hurry.

Considering capital market conditions at time of death

When auditing client portfolios, beware of *highly concentrated holdings* (assets that represent more than 25 percent of an estate's value) and bring them to your clients' attention. An example of a concentrated holding is a large position in a publicly traded company; maybe the matriarch worked there for 40 years and never sold those vested shares. Another example would be a commercial office building in the middle of downtown Detroit just before the 2008–09 recession.

Concentrated holdings can make for a colossal headache when the time comes to settle an estate. If the market crashes prior to, during, or shortly after the estate settlement, heirs may be stuck holding the bag with little or nothing in it, especially if they need to sell in a hurry. This is what's known as a "bad *heir* day" — when an expected inheritance is wiped out due to an unanticipated market condition or event. As you may expect, heirs won't be happy. Even worse, if you were the financial advisor who had advised your clients on such investments, you could find yourself on the receiving end of a liability claim.

The moral of this story is to work toward minimizing a client's exposure to risk by diversifying his holdings. See Chapter 7 for details.

Preparing for Estate Settlement Complications

For most families, with the possible exception of couples who have only one child, settling the estate is, to some degree, unsettling. The death of the surviving patriarch or matriarch creates a power vacuum that often results in siblings and sometimes other family members struggling for control and disagreeing over their definitions of "fair" and "equitable."

As you help your client with estate planning, part of your job is to anticipate complications and address them before the time comes to settle the estate. In this section, I introduce two common sources of estate settlement complications and provide guidance on how to address each one.

REMEMBER

As your client's financial advisor, you need to be as much psychologist as financial professional. Complications arise more from human factors than from financial or legal factors. Emotions and perceptions tend to be far more powerful and perilous than the rational distribution of assets.

Handling differences over a closely held business

Family businesses are notorious for breeding bad feelings among family members, and this continues and often intensifies when the last surviving head of the family dies or is no longer in a position to call the shots. Two or more heirs may fight over control of the business. Others may want their fair share, so they can do their own things. One sibling may be deemed heir apparent in the future management of the business and feel disadvantaged as the one who has to shoulder the responsibility, while a sibling gets to play artist at the local art school (always seems to be the case). With such disparity of interests, how can an estate plan be fair to both heirs?

REMEMBER

Ultimately, the family must resolve such issues, but as financial advisor to the head(s) of the family, you can help navigate this minefield by engaging your clients in a discussion of the issues and possibilities. Here are a couple options:

>> Your client, the head of the family, figures out a way to inspire and arrange for the heirs to work together in harmony, each contributing in his own unique way to the business's success and reaping the rewards. Unfortunately, this scenario is highly unlikely. Heirs display their level of interest early on, and disinterested siblings rarely become happy, active participants in the business after the parents pass away.

>> Heirs who are actively engaged in the business inherit the business, and other assets are used to provide for heirs who have little or no interest in the business. Family businesses are managed best by engaged family members who reap the fruits of their labor. Forcing them to share the success of the business with less or nonengaged family members removes some of the performance incentive and often leads to bitter divisions, so leaving the business to the heir most interested and able to manage it is usually best.

If clients express a desire to name two or more heirs as co-CEOs, encourage them to carefully reconsider. Having two CEOs usually leads to further complications down the road. Suggest that one heir own and manage the business while the others who want to participate in the business agree to do so in a different capacity with compensation and equity that align with their respective positions. For example, one heir may be skilled in management and operations, while another is geared more toward marketing and sales. The head(s) of family should encourage each heir to develop those strengths and then should track their contributions to ownership, remuneration, and recognition.

This is another area where a large life insurance policy can do wonders. The benefits from the policy can be used to equalize inheritance on day one of the settlement, while the estate provides for fair equity ownership and/or awards for heirs who want to participate in the business moving forward.

Fair doesn't necessarily mean equal or the same. Defer to your client, the head of the family, who is currently running the business. He is best able to articulate his desire for business succession and continuity, while ensuring that all his children are adequately and fairly provided for.

Anticipating a struggle for control

Detailed instructions in your client's settlement documents remove much of the ambiguity that often stirs conflict among heirs, but clients should still anticipate some struggle for control when the time comes to settle the estate. I've found that heirs don't really know how they feel about their inheritance until a dramatic event stirs their thoughts, such as Mom being rushed to the hospital for chest pains and later learning that she just had a bad case of indigestion. The incident triggers thoughts and concerns that linger long afterward but can mark a good starting point for discussions.

To identify sources of potential future conflicts over the estate, engage your clients in a discussion about the heirs of their estate. Be inquisitive regarding their children's demeanors and behaviors. Ask questions that reveal hidden sentiment or avoidance, such as:

>> Do your children take vacations together? Vacationing together is a good sign that heirs will be less likely to fight over the distribution of assets.

>> Do they see each other away from family holiday gatherings? Again, if siblings spend quality time together, they're less likely to quibble.

>> Is one child more involved in caring for or managing the finances of the parent(s) as they age? A child who provides more care may expect more from the settlement.

These are just a few questions that could help you identify a future possible challenge in the transition of a business or other family assets.

TIP

A family counselor may be able to alleviate some of the discord resulting from family dysfunction. Although families are likely to take issue with an outsider's suggestion that they need family therapy, if you help them understand the potential waste of time, energy, and money due to family in-fighting, they may heed your advice.

Helping Clients Pass along Values, Not Just Wealth

One of the best ways to prevent *affluenza* (the sense of entitlement that often afflicts wealthy young people) is to nurture in children and grandchildren a sense of social responsibility and a culture of giving, beginning around the age of eight years old.

You can help your clients nurture these positive values while leaving a legacy of giving through the use of their estate. In this section, I present several options you may want to present to clients who express a desire to pass along their values to future generations.

Checking out donor-advised funds

Years ago, people had to be extremely wealthy to develop, implement, and manage a charitable strategy. Today, *donor-advised funds (DAFs)* serve as a turn-key solution to creating and managing charitable-giving programs.

DAFs allow donors to make tax-deductible charitable contributions over the course of a given tax year to receive an immediate tax benefit. The donors can then award grants from the fund to IRS-designated charitable organizations whenever they so desire.

Your clients can establish and contribute to a DAF over the course of their lives or even set up a contribution as part of the estate settlement. The DAF can then be passed to one or more heirs of the estate to manage.

Considering private family foundations

If family members want to play a more active role, the family may want to consider setting up a *private family foundation (PFF)* — a charitable foundation established, funded, and run by family members. In addition to providing tax benefits, the PFF can hire (and pay) family members to run it. PFFs can be paired with DAFs to maximize the tax benefits.

TIP

If you have clients who express an interest in starting a PFF, check out the Foundation Source (www.foundationsource.com) for information and resources to facilitate the creation of a PFF for your clients.

Brushing up on CRTs and CLTs

To formalize giving as part of the estate settlement, clients can set up charitable trusts, which serve the following three purposes:

>> Enable the client to give money to charitable organizations.

>> Reduce income, estate, or gift taxes.

>> Provide a limited monetary benefit to the client or to heirs of the estate.

In this section, I introduce two common charitable trusts you may want to present to your clients.

REMEMBER

Enlist the assistance of a qualified lawyer to set up any charitable trust.

Charitable remainder trust (CRT)

With a *charitable remainder trust (CRT)*, the client places an irrevocable gift of an asset, such as a highly appreciated stock, into the CRT. Your clients or the heirs to the estate can then draw an income stream from the asset for a specified number of years, after which the remainder in the account is transferred to the charity.

Charitable lead trust (CLT)

A *charitable lead trust (CLT)* is the inverse of a CRT. Income from the trust flows to the charity for a specified number of years, after which the remainder goes to the beneficiaries. As with CRTs, tax benefits abound with this type of irrevocable gift.

Teaming Up with Estate Planning Attorneys and Family Accountants

When you're engaged in estate planning, active collaboration with your client's other advisors (accountants, lawyers, and so on) is mandatory. I encourage you to take the lead in scheduling, hosting, and conducting estate planning discussions. Invite your client and any other family members your client wants to include along with your client's accountant and estate attorney.

Bringing other advisors to the table provides a smoother decision-making process for the client and eliminates complications that may otherwise arise later. Gathering to discuss options early in the planning process greatly reduces the chances that one advisor will contradict another's recommendation later.

Also, by actively involving other professionals, you showcase your skills and abilities to people who can recommend you to their clients.

IN THIS CHAPTER

» **Resisting the urge to play accountant, unless you're a CPA**

» **Teaming up with tax pros to reduce your clients' tax burden**

» **Grasping the tax implications of different investment types**

» **Reducing taxes by socking away money for education and retirement**

» **Leveraging your clients' generosity to trim their taxes**

Chapter **11**

Tackling Taxation

Your clients will remind you at least once a year how much income tax they pay and how much they hate to pay it. At the same time, they'll want to know what *you* plan to do about it. Reminding clients that a big tax bill is a good sign that they're making lots of money doesn't cut it. They want to know how to slash that tax bill, so they can put more of their hard-earned cash to work for them.

Using tax-deferred retirement accounts, municipal bonds, annuities, 529 plans, health savings accounts, deductions for charitable donations, and more, you can tailor a tax-saving strategy for each client.

In this chapter, I introduce you to numerous tax-advantaged investments and strategies that any successful financial advisor would consider using to meet a client's goals and objectives.

REMEMBER

Be prepared to explain and remind your clients of the different tax implications of the financial products and strategies they've chosen. These tax implications are often difficult to understand and even more difficult to remember.

Reminding Yourself That You're Not an Accountant

WARNING

Unless you're a certified public accountant (CPA) or other credentialed accountant or tax expert, remain fair and balanced in your tax advice and be transparent about your level of tax expertise. Here's a sample disclosure you should get into the habit of sharing (orally or in writing), when presenting financial products or investments that have tax benefits:

> XYZ and its affiliates do not provide tax, legal, or accounting advice. This material has been prepared for informational purposes only, and is not intended to provide, and should not be relied on for tax, legal, or accounting advice. You should consult your own tax, legal, and accounting advisors before engaging in any transaction.

Far too often, clients rely exclusively on conversations with their financial advisor for tax advice only to discover, years later, that the information they received was either poorly explained or grossly misunderstood. Such miscommunications not only upset clients, but they may also result in unexpected and unplanned for tax liabilities and possibly even penalties or other adverse monetary consequences.

One example of a common misunderstanding that causes trouble later relates to an employer's contribution to a Roth IRA. The employee pays into the Roth IRA with money that has been taxed, so distributions from the account based on the employee's contributions are tax-free. However, an employer contributes untaxed (pre-tax) dollars, so distributions related to the employer's contributions *are* subject to tax.

The nuances involved across a wide variety of tax-deferred or tax-exempt strategies require special care and communication. Don't go it alone. Involve your client's tax advisor in your discussions. If your client doesn't have a tax advisor, take the opportunity to engage one from your established or growing referral network of professionals.

REMEMBER

It takes a village to properly steward a client's finances. Take full advantage of the value that another professional can bring to the client's situation, as I explain next. (See Chapter 15 for more about teaming up with other professionals to optimize client outcomes.)

Adding a Tax Advisor to the Team

If your client is paying more than her fair share of taxes, she's leaving money on the table. And if she's leaving money on the table due to insufficient planning, a poorly executed tax-savings strategy, or improper implementation of a financial product, you should be concerned too. Bringing a tax specialist on board to offer guidance is the logical solution and a savvy move for a vast majority of financial advisors.

Unfortunately, many financial advisors view other specialists as threats. They fear that other professionals will steal their clients or sabotage their relationships with clients by questioning recommended products, planning, or strategies.

Lose the fear. Adding a tax advisor to your clients' financial advisory team sends a strong signal to your clients that you're committed to doing what's best for them. This tactic is also a good business move for you, because it gives you an opportunity to showcase your value to another professional — value they may want to bring to their clients. The most successful financial advisors I know leverage this technique to expand their network of professionals and clients.

WARNING

Leave the sales pitch at home. Other professionals earn fixed or project-based consulting fees, not commissions, so they're wary of other professionals, especially financial advisors, who they suspect receive any income from product commissions.

TIP

To prepare for your meeting with your client and her tax advisor, ask yourself the following questions and do your research to try to answer them for yourself because you'll be asking the tax advisor these same questions:

>> Is there a realized capital gains threshold that I should budget annually? Are there losses from other sources that could be used to offset stock portfolio gains? Would my client benefit from tax-loss harvesting? (See the nearby sidebar for more about tax-loss harvesting.)

>> Are taxable or tax-free investments more advantageous for my client? To answer this question, the tax advisor needs to consider several factors, including returns on the various investment options, the tax savings on contributions to different plans or accounts, and the tax rate on distributions when the client starts withdrawing from an account.

REMEMBER

Few investments are completely tax-free. They're usually tax-deferred or subject to less tax than other options. See the later section, "Exploring Tax-Free and Tax-Lighter Investments" for details.

>> Are estate taxes a concern? If so, what can I do now to relieve a future tax burden for the heirs and beneficiaries? (See Chapter 10 for more about estate planning.)

>> Should my clients own or rent their primary home or a second property? Real estate investments could be a great asset diversification strategy and possibly produce future rental income.

>> How could I optimize required minimum distributions (RMDs)? Would a qualified longevity annuity contract (QLAC) be an appropriate allocation? A *required minimum distribution* (*RMD)* is the amount the government requires be withdrawn from a qualified retirement savings plan per year when a person reaches the age of 70 ½. To bypass the RMD, clients can move funds from a retirement account into a QLAC, which doesn't have an RMD.

>> Does my client have a charity to which he or she would want to donate cash or other appreciated securities? Most nonprofits have ability to facilitate all kinds of donations, which could reduce taxable income for those that itemize deductions.

By coming up with your own answers to these questions, you can be more qualified to engage your client's tax advisor in an intelligent and productive discussion. When discussing any of these tax topics, the best approach is to share the results of your own cost-benefit analysis for each option. (See Chapter 8 for a discussion of cost-benefit analysis in terms of evaluating a client's risk profile.)

TIP

If you have a strong sense of what's best for your client, take the lead. Propose what you deem is the best course of action, explain the reasoning behind your recommendation (by sharing your cost-benefit analysis), and ask the client's tax advisor to weigh in. By doing your research and effectively communicating the costs and benefits of each choice, you're likely to reach agreement on the approach that will produce the most favorable outcome for your client. However, keep an open mind; your client's tax advisor may suggest a better approach that addresses factors you may not have considered.

DEFINING TAX-LOSS HARVESTING

Tax-loss harvesting is a technique used to reduce taxes owed on short-term or long-term capital gains — earnings from the sale of capital assets, such as stocks, bonds, real estate and even collectibles.

With tax-loss harvesting, the client sells an asset that has decreased in value to realize the loss (convert that loss to cash), thus offsetting any realized gain from the sale of an asset that has increased in value.

Managing Capital Gains: Don't Let the Tail Wag the Dog

Don't let taxes be the tail that wags the dog of good portfolio management. Time and again, clients freak out when, after years of holding a stock position that has gained tremendous value during a market cycle, I recommend pairing back that position, and they see the tax bill that would result from following my advice. Usually, that's all they see — the tax bill.

To save your clients from themselves, help them understand the wisdom of your advice. Again, it's cost-benefit analysis to the rescue. Do the math and show them the bottom-line impact of the different options in dollars and cents.

For example, suppose your client has a portfolio position that has grown from $100,000 to $200,000 in a decade. She's happy to see that 100 percent return. Then you say, "It's time to take some profits off the table and rebalance the proceeds elsewhere to other investments with better future growth prospects." Your client, knowing that the realized gains from selling the stock would be taxed, sits straight up in her seat and says, "Whoa! I don't want to pay the taxes!"

In this case, paint the following scenario to convince her of the prudence of your advice: If we do nothing and the market cycle ends (more a function of when, not if), then the unrealized capital gains are vulnerable. That $200,000 position could realistically drop 30 percent in a bear market, wiping out $60,000 of gains, leaving a compromised market value of $140,000. However, if we were to sell the whole fund position, realizing $100,000 of long-term capital gains, you'd lose only 15 percent in taxes ($15,000), leaving you with $185,000 to invest elsewhere. (The holding period to qualify for the long-term capital gains tax rate is 366 days, and in 2018 long-term capital gains are taxed at 15 percent for married filing jointly taxpayers with taxable income from $77,400 to $480,050.) The amount of $185,000 is $45,000 more than you'd have if your holding suffered a 30 percent loss.

TIP

Strongly recommend to clients that they pay all tax bills generated by the portfolio from the portfolio itself. Otherwise, a nasty bear market could wipe out the capital gains. By selling at a high price, yes, your client will have to pay a tax, but at least you've secured the portfolio's bottom-line market value.

Prior to recommending a course of action like the one in the example I just presented, consider the following:

>> No financial advisor has a crystal ball. Present the pros and cons and explain the rationale of any recommendation based on its alignment with the agreed-upon portfolio management goals as expressed in your client's Investment Policy Statement. (See Chapter 7 for guidance on preparing a client's Investment Policy Statement.)

>> If your client takes your advice to sell the highly appreciated holding and allocates the money to another investment that doesn't perform as well, your client may understandably be upset. When evaluating new investment opportunities, you may need to wait until the right opportunity is available. Don't rush it.

>> You won't know the wisdom of selling one security and investing in another until you look back in time, but the tax is a known amount. Let this known value and your knowledge of market conditions be your guides.

>> Only experience hones your ability to masterfully rebalance client portfolios, given the present market conditions and tax bills. All the client really cares about in the long run is the bottom line.

TIP

Keep yourself honest by asking yourself how you'd feel if it were your money. How comfortable would you be if you were standing in the client's shoes and had to pay the tax? How would you feel if you sold one investment that was performing well, paid taxes on the gains, and reinvested the remaining cash in an asset that performed worse? Honest answers to these questions guide your recommendation. You may decide that the best course of action for your clients is to rebalance their portfolio, or you may conclude that doing nothing is more prudent.

Using Tax-Deferred Accounts to Maximize Compounding Returns

Clients are often aware of the magic of compounding returns. Over time the value of their well-performing portfolio grows exponentially as they reinvest their earnings. However, clients often overlook the negative impact of taxes on compounding returns. As a result, they underinvest in financial products or account vehicles (such as IRAs) that can enhance compounded returns by eliminating or postponing a tax burden.

TIP

To show clients the benefits of investing in tax-free or tax-deferred options, compare the compound annual growth rate (CAGR) to the client's actual compounded return:

>> *Compound annual growth rate (CAGR),* also known as the *compounded total portfolio return,* is the cumulative effect of gains and losses across a period of years, expressed as an annualized rate.

>> The client's actual compounded return accounts net of taxes. Depending on the taxable income generated from the portfolio in any given tax year, the client's ultimate compounded return may be dramatically less than the CAGR.

For example, suppose your client's portfolio invests in a mutual fund that earns an annualized 6 percent. Assume, on average, 25 percent of that return is in the form of long-term capital gains, another 25 percent is earned through qualified dividends, and 25 percent is through short-term capital gains. Assume long-term capital gains and qualified dividends are taxed at 15 percent, and short-term capital gains are taxed at 28 percent.

Of the 6 percent annualized return, half comes from long-term gains and dividends, so 3 percent of the return (half of 6 percent) is taxed at 15 percent, resulting in an annual return of 2.55 percent. Another quarter of the 6 percent annualized return is taxed at 28 percent, resulting in an annual return of 1.08 percent.

Your client invests $6,500 annually in that portfolio over the next 15 years. Growing inside a tax-deferred vehicle, the compounded return is 6.82 percent compared to a compounded return of 5.13 percent compounded return outside a tax-deferred vehicle. If your client invested that money in a tax-deferred account, she'd have $151,293.80. If she invested it in a taxable account, she'd have $141,640.86, nearly $9,652.94 less.

Exploring Tax-Free and Tax-Lighter Investments

Tax-free and tax-light investments include municipal bonds, U.S. savings bonds, and Treasury Inflation-Protected Securities (TIPS). Those three are the biggies you need to know about. In this section, I bring you up to speed on these options and provide guidance on how to determine whether any of them is a good option to consider for a client.

Buying municipal bonds

Most financial advisors don't realize how significant the U.S. municipal bond market is in size and issuance. According to the Municipal Securities Rulemaking Board (MSRB), nearly half a trillion dollars of new bonds were issued in 2017 alone and $13 billion is traded daily. Most of these securities are tax-exempt — free of federal and state taxes (for residents of the state of a bond they hold).

If you and your client are considering municipal bonds, the big question you need to answer is whether a taxable or tax-free bond is best. To make this comparison, calculate the client's *taxable equivalent yield* — the return required on a taxable bond to match the return of the tax-free bond. To calculate the taxable equivalent yield, take the following steps:

1. **Calculate the client's *effective federal income tax rate* — the taxes she'll owe as a percentage of her taxable income.**

   For example, a married couple earning $500,000 taxable income and filing jointly owes $126,400 in federal income tax, so their effective federal income tax is $126,400 ÷ $500,000 = 25.28 percent.

   TIP

   TaxAct has a calculator you can use to calculate the marginal and effective tax rates. To use the calculator, go to www.taxact.com/tools/tax-bracket-calculator. (See the nearby sidebar for an explanation of the difference between marginal and effective tax rates.)

2. **Calculate the client's effective state income tax rate.**

   (If you can't find an online calculator for a given state, use the numbers from the client's state tax return. Divide the total state tax paid by the client's total taxable income.) In this example, assume an effective state income tax rate of 7 percent.

3. **Go to www.calcxml.com/do/inc11 or find another tax-equivalent yield calculator on the web, plug in the federal and state effective income tax rates, and click the button to see the result.**

   For the couple in this example, the taxable equivalent yield to a 3.5 percent yield to maturity municipal bond would be 5.037 percent. In other words, all other things being equal, the taxable bond would need a yield higher than 5.037 to be a better choice than the tax-free bond.

REMEMBER

Generally speaking, the higher the tax bracket or effective income tax rate, the more likely a client will benefit from municipal bonds, though not always. As with any concentration in asset class, risks can develop in the municipal bond market separate and apart from risks in the corporate bond market.

CLARIFYING MARGINAL AND EFFECTIVE TAX RATES

Marginal tax rate is another term for *tax bracket*. For example, a couple earning $500,000 of taxable income and filing jointly is in the 35 percent tax bracket, so their marginal tax rate is 35 percent.

Effective tax rate is the percentage actually owed, which is less than the marginal tax rate. Why? Because the government doesn't tax *all* of a person's income at the marginal tax rate. For example, a married couple filing jointly pays:

   10 percent on income over $0

   12 percent on income from $19,050 to $77,399

   22 percent on income from $77,400 to $164,999

   24 percent on income from $165,000 to $314,999

. . . and so on. So, although a couple with a taxable income of $300,000 is in the 24 percent tax bracket, they pay 19.59 percent effective federal income tax.

At other times, municipal bonds have much broader appeal and use in client portfolios and not just for ultrahigh income earners.

Investing in tax-exempt securities

Two tax-lighter securities worthy of mention are U.S. savings bonds and Treasury Inflation-Protection Securities (TIPS). Both are designed to protect savings from inflation and are exempt from state and local taxes but not from federal income tax. Table 11-1 highlights key characteristics of the two in terms of marketability, price, earnings, and taxes. (For additional details, visit www.treasurydirect.gov.)

Beyond using U.S. savings bonds as the go-to gift for their grandchildren, your clients probably won't have much use for savings bonds. TIPS, however, can be a valuable addition to a client's portfolio, providing protection against inflation along with state and local income tax relief.

TABLE 11-1: **TIPS versus U.S. Series I Savings Bonds**

Characteristic	TIPS	U.S. Series I Savings Bonds
Marketability	Marketable, can be bought/sold in secondary securities market.	Nonmarketable, registered in owner's name.
Price/earnings	Price and fixed interest rate determined at auction; interest calculations based on principal adjusted semiannually for inflation/deflation.	Priced at face value; rate of return based on fixed rate at time of purchase and variable semiannual inflation rate.
Interest	Semiannual interest payments.	Interest accrues over the life of the bond and is paid upon redemption.
Federal tax	Semiannual interest payments and inflation adjustments that increase principal are subject to federal tax in the year they occur.	Tax reporting of interest can be deferred until redemption, final maturity, or other taxable disposition, whichever occurs first; interest can also be claimed annually.
Lifespan	Term of 5, 10, or 30 years.	Interest earned up to 30 years.
Disposal before maturity	Can be sold in secondary market.	Redeemable after 12 months with 3 months interest penalty; no penalty after five years.

Although I think double-digit inflation is unlikely in the next 20 years, I think inflation will be significantly higher than the recent decade's range of 1 to 2 percent. Adding TIPS to a client's portfolio could make you look smart in years to come.

Slashing Taxes with Retirement, College, and Health Savings Accounts

Clients can take advantage of some of the biggest tax breaks by investing money in tax-deferred retirement accounts, in college, and in health savings accounts (HSAs). In this section, I explain these options, call your attention to factors that clients and financial advisors often overlook, and steer you and your clients clear of common mistakes.

Contributing to a retirement plan

Contributing to a retirement plan is a no-brainer for most clients. I assume you're familiar with the retirement account options, including 401K and 403(b), Solo 401K, SEP IRA, traditional IRA, and Roth IRA, along with their various contribution limits. If you're not familiar with these options, study up on them. Investors can use these retirement accounts to maximize the power of compounding returns (see the earlier section "Using Tax-Deferred Accounts to Maximize Compounding Returns").

The standard advice from many financial professionals is for clients to maximize their contributions to their retirement accounts, which is generally prudent. Certainly, if a client works for a company that offers a 401K and matches the employee's (your client's) contribution, your client should contribute enough to take full advantage of the employer's matching contributions.

WARNING

However, like all generalities, the advice to max out contributions to retirement accounts has its limits. Contributing pre-tax dollars to a retirement account is a great way to build wealth and provide retirement income in the future, but a client can accumulate too much in a tax-deferred account. Imagine a client who's been maxing out her contributions to her 401K for 40 years and contributing nothing to a taxable account. When that client retires, 100 percent of her retirement income will be taxable at ordinary income tax rates, once withdrawals begin to fund retirement income needs. No one knows how high ordinary income tax rates will be in the future. Making sure your client has different tax buckets is prudent. As an example, long-term capital gains tax rates are historically lower than ordinary income rates, and may provide some respite from projected higher ordinary income tax rates.

REMEMBER

Capital gains taxes have been and are now much lower than ordinary income tax rates. Diversifying a client's portfolio to include both tax qualified (for example, retirement accounts) and nonqualified (regular taxable accounts) is a good idea. Roughly half and half is a good place to start: half of your client's supplemental retirement income from tax qualified accounts and half from nonqualified accounts. Then, make adjustments based on your client's employment status and other factors.

Socking away money in college funds

Clients who plan to send their children to college can trim their tax bill and perhaps protect college savings from inflation by contributing after-tax dollars to one of the following 529 plans (earnings aren't taxed):

>> **Prepaid plan:** Your client purchases tuition credits at today's prices, which can then be used in the future. Because college tuition is highly prone to inflation, prepaying could be a great strategy. The downsides are that fewer than a dozen states offer this solution, and parents need to be fairly certain that their child will attend a qualifying college in the state.

>> **Savings plan:** Account holders have the opportunity to grow their deposits based on market performance of the underlying mutual funds. Most 529 savings plans offer a variety of age-based or target-date asset allocation funds that automatically rebalance funds toward fixed income investments as the child (beneficiary) gets closer to college age.

WARNING

Inform your clients of the risks of 529 plans, so they understand what they can and can't pay out of the 529 plan without paying taxes on the distributions. The biggest risk involves accumulating funds in a 529 account for a child who ultimately decides not to go to college. Any nonqualified withdrawals from the account are subject to income tax *and* a 10 percent penalty. (Note that due to changes in the tax law, the funds can now also be used toward any expense from K-12 public or private school as well as higher education.)

Trimming taxes with an HSA

Clients who have high-deductible health insurance policies can take advantage of an additional tax break by contributing pre-tax dollars to a health savings account (HSA) and paying qualified medical expenses out of that account. Any unused money rolls over into the next year. After the age of 65, your client can withdraw the money without a penalty but must pay income tax on any money withdrawn, or she can use it tax-free to cover retiree medical expenses. Any money withdrawn for nonmedical purposes is subject to a 20 percent penalty, if under 65.

Taking a Nibble Out of Taxes with Charitable Contributions

The purpose of charitable contributions isn't to save on taxes; it's to give to the less fortunate or support certain causes. However, the tax advantages of giving may offset the cost of giving or enable your client to give more.

REMEMBER

Clients who claim the standard deduction ($12,000 for singles and $24,000 for married couples) instead of itemizing deductions on their tax returns receive no tax benefit from their charitable gifts. Only if they itemize and their itemized deductions exceed the standard deduction do they benefit.

The good news for your very charitable clients who can benefit from itemizing is that cash donations are now deductible up to 60 percent of adjusted gross income (up from 50 percent). Gifts of stock continue to be deductible up to 30 percent of income.

TIP

Here are a few ways your clients can donate assets that would otherwise be highly taxable:

>> **Gift appreciated assets, such as shares of stocks or other marketable securities.** Donors can deduct the full market value (up to the limits previously stated) and, by doing so, avoid the capital gains tax.

>> **Donate from an IRA (for clients aged 70 ½ or older).** Clients can use contributions up to $100,000 to satisfy their RMD, while excluding the distribution from their taxable income.

>> **Bundle other qualifying expenses into years when they can exceed the standard deduction.** Bundling increases your client's likelihood of being able to itemize her expenses.

Chapter **12**

Getting Up to Speed on Behavioral Finance

To find true success as a financial advisor, you must be able to guide your clients through the labyrinth of their own emotional decision-making process. Millions of years of evolution haven't been able to erase the fight, flight, or freeze mechanism hardwired into the human brain. Although this mechanism has been a key to human survival in nature by protecting against physical threats, it's often counterproductive when applied to relationship and investment decisions. In the world of personal finance, when markets are rising, clients get aggressive and want to jump in; the instinct to fight drives their greed. When markets drop, clients panic and look for the exits; fear drives their instinct to flee.

In this chapter, I introduce you to the topic of *behavior finance* — the study of the role that human psychology plays in investor decisions and hence market movements. Here you develop an understanding of the emotional and irrational factors that often influence client behavior, and you discover practical techniques to help your clients think and behave more rationally.

REMEMBER

During times of great market volatility, the phrase, "I'm running into a burning building" will become your daily mantra. However, with the understanding and techniques you develop in this chapter to help your clients, you'll have the mindset needed to calmly enter that building and start rescuing your clients.

Recognizing Irrational Factors That Drive Thinking and Behaviors

More than twenty years ago, at Boston College, I became fascinated with the topic of behavioral finance as the secret key to maximizing success in the capital markets. After all, people drive the global capital markets system, and these people not only think, but they also *feel*. Plenty of software is available to take the emotion out of investing, including the latest machine learning algorithms that drive artificial intelligence. Their purpose is to churn out actionable data void of bias, although even algorithms are susceptible to bias and variance, and human emotion continues to drive the markets.

As a financial advisor, you're in an ideal position to help clients think and act more rationally, but first, you must recognize and understand the sources of irrational thinking and behavior. In this section, I identify and explain several of the more common sources of skewed thinking, all of which sprout from the same root — irrationality.

REMEMBER

A big part of your job is keep your client on the financial path set forth in his Investment Policy Statement (see Chapter 7). This responsibility is equally important to that of designing the best performing portfolio strategy to meet your client's goals. To maintain client compliance with the plan, you must control your own emotions and maintain a rock solid conviction. If you waver in your conviction, seek additional training and credentialing. Unwavering in the face of blind passion is a critical element to your client's success and ultimately to your success.

Myopic loss aversion

Myopic loss aversion occurs when investors overreact to short-term losses at the expense of potential long-term gains. It's based on the fact that people hate to lose more than they love to win. A sudden and significant drop in the market often triggers the reaction to bail out.

People who suffer from myopic loss aversion tend to overlook the fact that the stock markets are volatile. In recent years, the frequency of daily +/− 1 percent market volatility on the S&P 500 has increased dramatically. Investors who are accustomed to such volatility are less prone to get rattled by it.

Confirmation bias

Confirmation bias is the tendency to gravitate toward or interpret evidence as validation of one's own beliefs or feelings. For example, many people subconsciously watch news channels or read newspapers and magazines that express opinions that align with their own beliefs.

TIP

You and your clients can reduce confirmation bias by becoming aware of it and seeking out different perspectives. For example, I watch a variety of news channels, some of which lean toward the left and others that lean toward the right in an attempt to get a more balanced view of what's really going on. I don't want to live in an echo chamber, because I don't want my judgment and the advice I give to my clients tainted by confirmation bias. Clients benefit most from rational and balanced analyses of all facts, insights, and opinions.

Mental accounting

Mental accounting is the practice of conceptually separating money into different accounts base on subjective criteria, such as how a client got the money or what he plans to spend it on. Clients have a different attitude toward the funds in each account.

This haphazard categorization of money leads to trouble. For example, a client may accumulate considerable cash over the course of many years and believe that cash is always king.

To counter mental accounting, identify and explore any feelings and beliefs that are driving this behavior and challenge them with facts and rational argument.

Illusion of control

Illusion of control is the belief that a person has more control over events or outcomes than he really has. If you've ever pressed a button at a crosswalk more than once to get the traffic lights to change, you've succumbed to the illusion of control, thinking the more times you pressed the button, the faster the lights would change.

Having an illusion of control causes some clients to trade more actively or be overconfident in a belief they have when it's based on insufficient knowledge and understanding. For example, an investor who has the illusion of control is more likely to fall victim to a get-rich-quick investment opportunity, thinking he has the inside track and that his investment has a huge upside and no downside.

TIP

Remind clients who are susceptible to the illusion of control that markets are inherently volatile. The only sure thing is that higher risk holds the potential for higher returns. If a client expects big earnings and is unaware of the risks, he needs to be informed of those risks. Ultimately, other factors beyond your client's control determine the outcome.

Recent extrapolation bias

When a stock is hitting new highs day after day, people get excited. They want in. They're lured by returns, and their greed gets the better of them. They've succumbed to *recent extrapolation bias* — the belief that recent performance is a sign of future results. This bias runs counter to the traditional wise warning that's presented in nearly every prospectus: "Past performance is not indicative of future results."

Extrapolation bias is common in any soaring investment. Just look at Bitcoin. I don't know how many times clients have asked about it over the past year (2017–2018), but every time it's with great desire. As I write this, the price has collapsed 70 percent from its highs. Those same clients don't say, "Thank you" when I conduct their quarterly review. As soon as it's down, they forget it even exists.

Hindsight bias

Hindsight bias, often referred to as "I told you so" bias, is the tendency of a person to overestimate his ability to predict the future by using as evidence an instance in which he happened to guess an event or outcome that was impossible to predict.

I've had a few prospective clients boast about how much money they made as investors. That's great, but unfortunately it's rarely true. An audit of the masterful investor's portfolio invariably reveals mediocre performance, usually because the one great investment has already been sold and the money reinvested into something the investor conveniently failed to mention performed poorly.

Herd mentality

As with cows, sheep, and lemmings, *herd mentality* drives people to move en masse in a certain direction. Safety in numbers is the supposed reason behind this behavioral bias, but like the urban myth of herds of lemmings stampeding off cliffs to their certain death, investors often get caught up in stampedes that lead to massive losses.

When people are irrational, all sense flies out the window, and something else takes over. That something else is the remnant of the Neanderthal brain. I'm not being flippant about the paleo brain here. Extensive studies trace these irrational human behavioral responses to the *limbic system* (the paleomammalian cortex), and more specifically to the amygdala, which controls basic emotions, including fear, pleasure, and anger.

The only way to combat herd mentality is to create a plan and stick to it. The plan works like blinders on a horse to focus your client on moving forward instead of being drawn off course by the distractions of what other investors are doing.

Muting Irrational Thoughts and Behaviors

To win the battle against the paleo brain, you need an arsenal of techniques to mute instinctive and often irrational thoughts and behaviors. Start with the following tried-and-true methods:

>> **Schedule an in-person meeting in a nonbusiness setting.** Instead of meeting in your office, choose a neutral location, such as a restaurant, coffee shop, or your social club. A shift in setting often triggers a shift in a client's thinking.

>> **Share established research.** Don't use complicated charts or white-paper articles, unless you're planning to spend time doing a lot of hand-holding. You can find plenty of research charts that highlight established market facts in support of operating according to a carefully crafted financial plan. Big mutual fund companies publish numerous client-friendly articles and graphs specifically for this purpose. Here are a few links to check out:

- www.americanfunds.com/individual/planning/investing-fundamentals/time-not-timing-is-what-matters.html

- lplresearch.com/2017/09/13/what-happens-if-you-miss-the-10-worst-days-of-the-year/

- www.aaii.com/journal/article/missing-the-markets-worst-and-best-months.touch

- ritholtz.com/2011/04/missing-best-worst-days-in-markets/

- www.putnam.com/literature/pdf/II508.pdf

- blogs.cfainstitute.org/investor/2016/07/07/missing-the-best-weeks-a-mistake-investors-should-fear/

- www.invesco.com/pdf/RR10-BRO-1.pdf

>> **Remind your clients that their asset management is just one piece of the plan.** As I reveal in Chapters 7 and 8, asset and liability management go hand-in-hand. Failure to plan for a liability can result in a considerable loss of asset value. Insurance products can alleviate fear and prevent panic, but when clients forget why those products are in place and when greed strikes, they'll fight you over the cost. Being able to articulate the value of the balanced approach can keep your client from making a potentially costly miscalculation.

Appealing to the Rational Side of Your Client's Brain

I've successfully led clients through the Great Recession using the rational-mind concept, which I attribute to my firm's business partner, Jonas Lee, who, after 35 years in the financial advisory business, has picked up a thing or two. I've been fortunate to work with great advisors over the course of my career. As a proven method, this approach warrants its own section. Here, I walk you through the process.

REMEMBER

The most delicate situation you have with a client is when he calls in a panic due to a stock market sell-off. What you say in those first few seconds matters most. Don't trivialize your client's feelings, don't tell him not to worry (too late for that!), and, whatever you do, keep your cool.

Step 1: Acknowledge your client's fear

You won't get far in the conversation unless you level with your client right out of the gate. You're competing with 24/7 news media, which is only interested in keeping eyeballs glued to the set during tumultuous times in order to drive ad revenue. Admit to your client that the sell-off appears scary, but explain that's what the media want everyone to believe. It's like watching an accident — people can't look away. Acknowledge that it *looks* scary but is just business as usual, as proven through the history of the markets.

Step 2: Tell your client to take a deep, cleansing breath and smile

Okay, I know I live in Los Angeles, and we're all yogis out here, but I wouldn't include this advice unless it was absolutely effective. Before you can introduce rational or logical thought into a client's mind, you have to secure a stable space to work within. Through deep breaths and smiling, the mind-body union is engaged, producing a grounding effect that naturally extends to encompass both you and your client.

REMEMBER

Smiling after taking a deep breath triggers endorphins. Try it when you're stressed out. Smiling, even when you don't feel like doing so, brings forth calm and serenity from within.

Step 3: Introduce a rational argument

When you feel as though your client has backed away from the cliff's edge, he's ready to receive your rational argument. This technique is both popular and effective in quickly arresting the disorienting effects of a stock market meltdown.

TIP

Let your client know that you're happy to sell all the holdings, *but* as with any portfolio management strategy, together you'll need to also define the buy strategy. After all, selling to sit in cash is a portfolio action that wreaks more havoc on long-term portfolio total returns than any other investing decision. So, you need to proceed prudently. If you're going to sell, when are you going to buy back in? What price or index thresholds do you reference to trigger this buying action?

This is your appeal to rational thought. The assumption is that markets will eventually stabilize, and when they do, when are you buying back in? Are you buying back in when the markets have recovered 5 percent from current levels? 10 percent, 20 percent? If you're buying back into the positions after they've corrected 20 percent, then you've permanently lost that 20 percent gain, which is a permanent capital loss.

WARNING

Permanent capital loss is the most dangerous risk around, but most investors subject themselves to it actively and routinely, even though it's completely avoidable. All the investor needs to do to avoid permanent capital loss is to sit on his hands, look away, garden, or take a walk around the block.

Step 4: Have your client explain the strategy back to you

Having clients explain the strategy they're requesting back to you is the best way to engage them in rational thought. I've had clients begin to explain the strategy of selling their positions and then buying back in when those positions have recovered 20 percent from current prices. When they're done, I say something like, "Oh, is that what you really what?" and they don't even know what they just said. It hasn't quite clicked for them. And then, as if struck by a lightning bolt to the brain, they say, "No! Wait! I don't want that!" Finally, eureka, they've got it, and the rational brain wins another battle over the paleo brain.

Riding Out Market Cycles: Balancing Fear and Greed

For many investors, fear and greed drive their decisions and often drive their portfolios into the ground. By calming your clients' emotions, you can help them ride the wild swings in the market to outperform the portfolios of less disciplined investors. These sections how to calm those fears and reign in greed.

Calming common fears

During market meltdowns, clients often assume that their portfolios are directly correlated to the events they're watching in the nightly news. If you've done your job properly, each client's portfolio has much more diversification than what is reflected in the Dow Jones Industrial Average Index (DJIA), the Standard & Poor's 500 Index (S&P 500), or the National Association of Securities Dealers Automated Quotations (NASDAQ) exchange. However, those three indexes are the ones highlighted every night on every new channel. If any or all of those indexes have tanked, your clients will feel the fear course through their veins.

To calm your clients' fears, highlight portfolio holdings that have risen in value or, at the very least, have held their value when other markets are crashing. Don't just talk about it. Show them on their statement or have them log in to their account so they can see for themselves. Nothing takes the place of hand-holding to reveal their exposure to risk — not the nightly news, not their friends' portfolios — just what they hold in their account and how it has weathered the storm.

REMEMBER

Your clients aren't thinking about how their portfolios are constructed to handle market volatility. That's your job, especially when times get tough. Jump into the deep end and wrap your life-saving arms around your clients. Show them what you see, and share with them what you know.

Reining in greed

The old saying "Pigs get fat, hogs get slaughtered" is always true in the financial markets. I've talked to many prospective clients over the years who've insisted that some private placement offering memorandum promising 12 percent annual returns with no risk is where they want to allocate significant portions of their investment savings. Who wouldn't?

The truth is that risk and reward always meet in the battlefield of the global capital markets. There's no free lunch, just lots of pretenders and con artists hoping that a sucker will forget all the rules and throw some cash their way. You have to protect your clients from these predators who live off the fact that people are prone to being greedy.

TIP

Greed is also found in the mundane. Portfolio positions held for many years during a bull market are hard to let go for most clients. Encourage clients to reconsider in the context of the big picture. Rebalancing their portfolio or offsetting profits with charitable contributions may be the more prudent course of action.

3
Providing Superior, Personalized Service

Screen and onboard new clients, so you and your clients both know what you're getting into and are on the same page.

Create a personalized financial road map for each client and review it annually to stay on track or shift course, as needed.

Collaborate with other professionals to form a dream team for managing your client's financial health and wellbeing.

Allocate time and resources to clients according to their return on your investment, so you get what you need from the relationship.

Conduct a performance review on yourself to identify your strengths and weaknesses in order to identify the value you bring to the table.

Chapter **13**

Formalizing Your Client Due Diligence Process

How do you decide whether to work with a particular person, household, or business *and* in which capacity (broker or advisor) will you serve them to maximize value? I know plenty of advisors who say they want to work with high-net-worth clients or business owners. However, determining a client market characteristic isn't the same as developing a repeatable client acquisition process. The most successful financial advisors are those who seek opportunities that enable them to deliver real economic value to the client or consumer, regardless of potential revenues to be earned from fees or commissions.

REMEMBER

A *consumer* is someone who shops for and buys products, whereas a *client* is someone who seeks guidance or wants to outsource more of the decision-making to a specialist.

In this chapter, I explain the difference between acquiring a new consumer versus a new client and how to make sure you're prioritizing *their* needs and agenda, *not* yours. At the chapter's end, I present a standardized framework called "The Four A's of Due Diligence" that you can use to successfully acquire and serve clients over the long term, which is the best way to ensure your own long-term success.

Deciding Whether You Want Clients or Consumers

The decision of whether to look for clients or consumers depends largely on where you're at in your career; for example, whether you're new to the business or just finished your tenth year. Ultimately, your time in the business drives the level of interaction you're likely to have with the client or consumer, and that determines your role:

>> **Broker/agent:** As a broker/agent, you sell financial products (investments, insurance, and so on) to consumers. You're an agent between manufacturer and consumer.

>> **Financial advisor:** As a financial advisor, you have an ongoing relationship with your clients, helping them set financial goals and offering insight and guidance on how best to achieve their goals.

REMEMBER

Clients *and* consumers both can be great revenue sources, but clients are a more consistent revenue source and a stronger referral source.

Serving consumers as a broker/agent

An agent or broker is typically paid a *commission* — usually up front and based on the amount of money being deposited or paid into the product. Serving consumers as a broker/agent isn't necessarily a bad thing, because it requires less time, and you can deliver value to consumers by explaining product features and benefits.

WARNING

What you don't want is for a consumer to relegate you to a certain product class; you don't want to be "insurance go-to" or the "investment broker." You want to be known for selling a wide range of quality products across both asset management and liability carriers.

REMEMBER

Characteristically, a consumer:

>> Likes to shop the market for the best product.

>> Acts as the ultimate decision-maker, after conducting his own thorough product due diligence. Consumers aren't interested in outsourcing decision-making.

>> Typically accumulates products over years of buying them from agents or brokers.

>> Takes responsibility for his own financial well-being.

>> Accepts the assistance of an agent or broker to transact more complicated products and perhaps to explain product features and benefits.

>> Knows that *caveat emptor* (buyer beware) is the only way to find the best solution.

TIP

Use your first transaction with consumers as a way to bring them into the fold, and then begin to educate them on the bigger financial planning picture. Offer and welcome them to reach out to you whenever a financial question arises in their household. Over time, you'll be encouraged by how many consumers eventually become clients.

Serving clients as a fiduciary financial advisor

A *fiduciary financial advisor* is required to give advice that is in the client's financial best interest. As a fiduciary financial advisor, you can charge an hourly rate or annual fee for advice or a percentage of the investment portfolio you manage for your client (called *asset-based fees*). You're not prohibited from collecting a commission on products you sell, but doing so is generally considered a conflict of interest. (See Chapter 4 for more about compensation models.)

REMEMBER

As a fiduciary financial advisor, your success is tied to the success of your clients. The more money they make, the more money you earn (in the case of asset-based fees).

Clients are quite different from consumers in that clients seek competent professional advice. Characteristically, clients:

>> Don't like to shop. They know that products may play a role in a solution, but they don't want to mire themselves in the details — that's what the professional is for.

>> Are interested in listening to professional advisors who care about them and their objectives. Clients want advisory relationships to span many years, even a lifetime.

>> Are looking for fiduciary financial advisors. Clients want to work with a financial advisor who can assess their current situation and then offer recommendations or a course of action that's in their best interest.

>> Don't want to be responsible for making a decision. They prefer to have a professional give them recommendations that serve their best interest.

>> Don't buy products, but pay a fee for a service. They want to be able to clearly identify the value that the advisor has added into their life. This value can be explicit or implicit, but it must be something that can be articulated.

WARNING

Don't sell clients. Straying into agent/broker behavior is a surefire way to disconnect from a client.

>> Are loyal and, when satisfied, are better sources of new client introductions.

WARNING

Don't try to pigeonhole a potential new client or consumer. Let the discovery process unfold using The Four A's Due Diligence Process at this chapter's end. If you experience some resistance to the assessment phase, then you know you're most likely interacting with a prospective consumer, not a future client.

Considering the Factors That Really Matter

Whether you're serving consumers or clients, focus on factors that really matter to them. In other words, yield priority to what they want to focus on. For example, if you're meeting with a prospect and she shares with you certain issues that keep her up at night, don't force your own agenda.

Brokers/agents tend to struggle more in this area, because they typically don't have a large quiver from which they can draw products to solve every imaginable prospect concern or worry. Often this limitation is due to being inadequately licensed and therefore unable to transact in an area that's of particular interest to the consumer.

If you find yourself in this position, you have only two choices:

>> Tell the client or consumer that you hear his issues of highest priority, but those aren't in your wheelhouse, and move on.

>> Refer another professional who could make further progress given his level of expertise or licensing.

Obviously, the second choice is superior. If you bring another advisor into the mix properly, you have an opportunity to experience that business line. Use this technique to gain more skills, especially early in your career.

Assuming you're a fully licensed financial advisor, your express duty is to listen closely to your clients, recognize and acknowledge their priorities, and then adjust your agenda accordingly. You don't like when people don't listen to you, so don't be one of those advisors who just grinds ahead with his or her own agenda. Doing so is a surefire way to lose the transaction, or end the relationship, and start earning a reputation as the financial advisor who doesn't listen.

TIP

Adapt your agenda and presentation to prioritize what you've heard the prospect say. Repeat key words or phrases that stood out to you, demonstrating that you actually have been listening.

REMEMBER

Your listening skill is the most valuable tool you'll ever have in the financial advisory professional. You can't attain success as a financial advisor without proactively subverting your own agenda for that of your prospect's.

If you're a broker, earning a living on commissions, this challenge is especially difficult when your consumer's needs conflict with your own. When your agenda is to sell a high-commission product and your consumer would be best served with a low- or no-commission product, overcoming bias can be extremely difficult.

ADDRESS THE ELEPHANT IN THE ROOM, SITTING ON THE PROSPECT'S CHEST

A new prospect accepts your invitation to have a meeting to review financial services for his household. In this meeting, the client mentions having an old 401K plan and is concerned that those assets haven't had ongoing supervision.

In your briefcase, you have an illustration for a high-commission financial product that you're convinced the client will love. You're eager to pluck it from your briefcase and start reviewing in detail all the features and benefits that this miracle solution provides. Like the siren's call, it beckons your attention, now driving an impervious wedge between you and your client. You may as well leave, you think, because no sale is happening today.

That's the wrong approach. The right approach is to toss your agenda and tune in to what the client is saying. Don't get me wrong; I love presenting great solutions to clients. It's just that when your prospect tells you what's at the top of his mind and gives you a road map to where you can add immediate, articulated value, you'd be a fool not to deliver.

You must drop your mental agenda, immediately, and take the path toward what your client perceives is the highest value add. Certainly, clients often identify, or are worried about, financial issues that are insignificant in the context of their overall financial well-being, but that doesn't matter. Unless you address the elephant in the room sitting on their chest, you'll never be able to add more value later.

Of course, if you're at later stages in your career, you may want to assess your ongoing involvement with this particular client and appropriately refer the case to a junior advisor who's ready, willing, and able to get into the weeds on this client's IRA rollover.

Mastering the Four As of Due Diligence

When you're bringing a new consumer or client on board, you need a clearly defined, repeatable process for evaluating the person's financial situation and needs. Any time you get into a more formal process, you're more likely to be working with a client (not a consumer), but the process you follow should be able to help you distinguish between clients and consumers, as well.

Years ago, I developed a consultative framework to guide my own practice called The Four As of Due Diligence:

>> **A**ssessment: Ask big questions.

>> **A**udit: Dig into the details on current products/solutions.

>> **A**ction: Close the gap from what's in place versus what the client actually needs.

>> **A**lignment: Monitor changes to maintain alignment with products and the household's situation.

This formalized client due–diligence process delivers the following benefits:

>> Provides a format to broaden and deepen your existing consumer or client relationship.

>> Is independent of any specific financial planning software or tools, so you can adapt it any way you like.

>> Bakes into the process a professional accountability and feedback loop, leaving you no escape from the commitment made to your client.

>> Is easy to remember. Clients and advisors can follow the process in a paint-by-numbers' approach.

Even though aspects of financial and estate planning can get very complicated, the framework doesn't have to be. The ultimate purpose of this formalized process is to keep you accountable to adding value to your client's financial life at every stage of interaction.

Assessment

Assessment is all about understanding the consumer's or client's big picture. What are the household's financial goals and objectives? If you find that question too obtuse, ask more pointed questions such as the following:

- » What are you dreams for a fulfilling life?

- » What does retirement (if any) look like to you?

- » How much is enough to leave to your heirs (if any)?

- » What keeps you up at night?

- » What are you passionate about (for example, social causes, charitable organizations, volunteering, sports, new business ventures)?

- » What would you hope a relationship with a financial advisor would accomplish for you?

TIP

These are only few of the many questions you could ask. Be genuine and get real. Ask what you'd want people to know about you if they were asking you to put your financial future in their hands.

WARNING

As you engage in discussion with prospects, consumers, or clients, try to get a feel for behavioral factors that may impact your ability to serve them. Often, your ability to optimize their financial outcomes is directly related to the level of engagement and openness of the household members. For example, a family matriarch who refuses to discuss the family's fortune or think about how the family business will thrive in the hands of her heirs when she's gone is a tremendously difficult environment to add value. Be vigilant of these situations in advance and use the assessment phase to discover whether anyone you'll need cooperation from has a closed behavioral mindset. (See Chapter 12 for more about behavioral finance.)

When you have a solid sense of who the client (or consumer) is and why she's interested in the services you provide, the next step is to find out more about the current collection of financial products and how they're being managed. To elicit this information, ask these sample questions:

- » What's been your experience (if any) in working with a financial advisor?

- » Do you prefer to be the ultimate decision-maker, or would you be comfortable delegating decision-making to a fiduciary financial advisor?

- » How's your current financial plan (if any) being stewarded?

- » What are the qualifications of your current broker or financial advisor to warrant your trust?

- » Is a personal friendship with your broker or current advisor a substantial enough quality to determine the fate of your financial future?

The main objective of these questions is to understand the motive, mode, and beliefs that have driven the consumer or client to choose the current products and the person she's been trusting to help her achieve her financial goals. You want her to honestly evaluate the nature of any current advisory relationship to which she's become accustomed.

After this initial assessment phase, you should have a clear idea of what to prioritize in in her financial plan, how the current plan is being tended to (for example, frequency of reviews), and where the client or consumer may benefit from a more formal and structured approach to managing a vital area of her life.

Audit

An *audit* is a deeper dive into the client's finances. The first step is for the client or consumer to gather and deliver all relevant financial information you need to conduct a thorough audit. Ask your client for copies of the following documentation divided into personal finance and business documents.

Use this checklist for personal financial planning documents:

1. ❑ Recent investment portfolio and bank statements (including household checking, 401K plans, IRAs, and nonqualified individual or joint accounts)

2. ❑ Life, long-term care, and healthcare insurance policies (including in-force policy illustrations and annual premium notice)

3. ❑ Household financial statements (a budget showing income and expenses and a balance sheet showing asset and liability itemization)

4. ❑ Trust agreements (family, irrevocable, separate property, and so on)

5. ❑ Wills

6. ❑ Disability income policies (through employment or individual policy)

7. ❑ Income tax returns (past two years)

8. ❑ Prenuptial agreement

9. ❑ Gift tax returns

10. ❑ Total household budget (income and expenses)

This checklist includes the business documents you need:

1. ❑ Balance sheet

2. ❑ Profit and loss (P&L) statement (two years)

3. ❑ Corporate tax returns (two years)

4. ❑ Business-owned life insurance (for example, key person)

5. ❑ Cross purchase buy-sell agreements

6. ❏ Qualified plan document

7. ❏ Summary plan description

8. ❏ Form 5500 C

9. ❏ Employee census

10. ❏ Additional employee benefits

11. ❏ Group life and/or disability insurance

12. ❏ Property and casualty insurance policies

REMEMBER

Most people don't scan and store their financial documentation in the cloud. They can't just email you a link to click to download the documents. This phase can take anywhere from a week to months to even years. The more factors, players, and dynamics, the longer it takes your consumers and clients to get the information to you and the longer it takes for you to complete a full audit.

After you've received the information required, you're ready to begin the audit. The goal of an audit is to determine how well (or not so well) the current plan is optimizing the client's finances and helping the client achieve her financial goals. To conduct a thorough audit, you must closely analyze five areas of the client's existing financial plan:

>> Asset management (see Chapter 7)

>> Liability management (see Chapter 8)

>> Budget (see Chapter 9)

>> Estate plan or lack thereof (see Chapter 10)

>> Taxation (see Chapter 11)

You'll can use various software applications and other audit tools to help with the technical evaluations on current products and solutions.

Action

The *action* phase involves closing the gap between what your consumers or clients currently have and need to have in their plan in order to achieve their desired financial goals. Put another way, your audit results expose shortfalls, whereas your recommended corrective action plan seeks to minimize those shortfalls.

For example, as part of your audit, you conduct a simple needs-based analysis (as explained in Chapter 8), and you discover that the household's primary breadwinner should have a life insurance policy equal to 20 times the current death benefit amount. In the action phase, you want to correct that shortfall, so you shop the marketplace for the highest quality policy that provides the greatest benefit for the lowest cost.

For each shortfall you identify in your audit, recommend a corrective action. Base each corrective action you recommend on a clearly articulated cost–benefit analysis:

>> **Costs (of current or missing products):**

- Direct and indirect fees, expenses, or costs (for example, commissions on investment products)

- Intangible costs such as anxiety over not having enough money to retire

- *Opportunity costs* — the loss of potential gain (for example, losing out on profits from a high-performance mutual fund by having money in a low-performance fund)

- Cost of potential risks that aren't being managed (for example, the potential cost of medical bills from not having sufficient health insurance if the client becomes seriously ill)

>> **Benefits:**

- Direct benefits such as increased cash flow

- Indirect benefits such as peace of mind that comes from financial security

Cost–benefit analysis relies on both financial analysis, intuition/prediction, and a sense of the client's preferences, so it rarely (perhaps never) results in a perfect solution. For example, a client may choose to invest in certain stocks or mutual funds with lower earnings because the companies are more aligned with her beliefs.

You can harness the power of some professional strength tools and references to crunch the numbers and make well-informed decisions, but you also need to look to your experience and intuition for guidance.

As you conduct your cost–benefit analyses, keep in mind that sometimes doing nothing is the best course of action for the situation. Recommending that a consumer or client do nothing (not changing anything) can be of great value to her. If you're a fee-only advisor (as described in Chapter 4), you're likely to be less prone to ferreting out a solution to a problem that doesn't need solving.

Alignment

Alignment is a key factor in business success. A business sets a goal, develops a strategy for achieving that goal, and attempts to align all of its business activities with that goal to achieve maximum impact. A similar approach is effective in financial planning. All financial products and services should align with the client's financial goals.

REMEMBER

The financial advisory profession has two main care standards:

>> **Suitability:** Offering recommendations that fit within an average advisor's belief of what's appropriate to meet the consumer's or client's needs.

>> **Fiduciary:** Monitoring life changes, market changes, and behavioral changes and adjusting the client's financial plan to maintain alignment.

Both standards are important aspects of the ongoing alignment phase of due diligence. In short, you have two responsibilities: achieve and maintain alignment. After achieving alignment, you need to challenge yourself routinely by asking the question of whether the client's plan is still best for meeting the client's financial goals, which are also subject to change.

REMEMBER

Financial management isn't something you can just set and forget. Monitoring the implemented plan requires ongoing rigor and candor along with a healthy dose of humility. It means that you have to be prepared to share with consumers or clients that a product or solution that seemed perfectly suitable for their needs a few years ago may no longer be.

During the alignment phase (an ongoing phase), you must remain vigilant and prepared to adjust the plan in response to the following:

>> **Marketplace changes:** Products change, industries evolve, and new technologies are constantly being developed. Technology can improve data collection and financial conditions within financial firms, yielding greater efficiencies and greater profits, which may shift the balance of product offerings in the marketplace. To keep up on marketplace changes, monitor the following:

- Capital markets conditions (for example, crashes, bubbles, and interest rates)

- Financial product/solution changes (for example, bankruptcies, mergers, better offers, better products/solutions)

>> **Life changes:** Households change, too. New members join (children, grandchildren) while others depart. Children graduate and set out to seek their own fortunes. Family members may be diagnosed with serious illnesses. Businesses fail. At least once a year, you should touch base to see what's changed in their lives, such as:

- Life events (for example, marriages, divorces, and graduations)

- Health issues (for example, mortality or morbidity challenges, diseases, and major longevity)

- Changes in income (for example, promotion at work, job loss/change, or change in the success of a business)

» **Behavioral changes:** As clients age, their situations change, they develop different perspectives, and their financial attitudes and behaviors change. Monitor these changes:

- Pre- versus post-retirement life purpose and outlook

- Pre- versus post-business sale

- Pre- versus post-children or grandchildren

Monitor market changes, life changes, and behavioral changes throughout the year. Once a year meet with your clients for a formal review. Include updated audits on their products and solutions and offer recommended adjustments to keep them on track better than if they were to do nothing.

Here are a few examples of common adjustments along with a possible rationale for each:

» **Change portfolio asset allocation:** Moving more to a cash allocation to fund midterm income needs in order to create more psychological cushion of safety and lifestyle maintenance due to fear of an impending economic recession.

» **Modify risk coverage:** Less net worth means a low or nonexistent tax bill. Combined with changes in estate tax legislation consumers or clients may not need the same level of death benefits. Maybe the kids have become financially independent and the parents no longer need life insurance.

» **Monitor changes to family governing documents:** Divorce, remarriage, birth or adoption of a child, or a premature death of a family member are all samples of triggering events that would necessitate revisiting the family's trusts and wills. Review other formal documents, such as medical healthcare directives. Collaborating with the client's attorney in these matters is best. (See Chapter 15 to find out about the benefits of engaging in multilateral cross-industry advisor collaboration.)

REMEMBER

An ideal client due diligence process means that you're optimizing her specific asset management solution so that she's maximized a positive *net* financial impact in the light of any probable (not simply possible) future liability.

IN THIS CHAPTER

» **Taking your client's input into consideration**

» **Mastering the three Cs of financial planning**

» **Making sure you cover the key areas**

» **Harnessing the power of financial planning tools**

» **Reviewing and revising the plan routinely**

Chapter **14**

Developing a Personalized Financial Plan

Your client's financial plan is the cornerstone of his financial future and one of the few tangible products you're solely responsible for delivering to him. The plan must be a comprehensive and holistic assessment of the client's goals and objectives, so it places him on the best path toward the financial outcomes he desires most.

In this chapter, you discover how to understand your client's priorities and concerns, create a financial plan that places the client on a path to achieve the agreed-upon goals, and review and modify plan to keep your client's finances on the right path or to shift course when life doesn't cooperate with the plan. I also recommend a variety of professional financial planning tools that can make your job much easier while enabling you to present the client with a polished product. As an added bonus, I include my own *Three Cs* philosophy to personal financial planning.

One of the benefits of developing and implementing a comprehensive, holistic plan for each client is that you don't need as many clients because you're providing for all their financial needs. Financial advisors who deal exclusively in investments or insurance or other niches have to spend much more time in client acquisition.

Obtaining Your Client's Input

A solid financial plan begins with client input. You must have a clear picture of his current finances, goals, concerns, and any potential threats or issues that could impact his finances.

Start by gathering copies of your client's household budget, bank statements, loan statements, credit card balances, investment statements, insurance policies, and family governing documents (such as a will or estate plan). Gathering this documentation is part of the client due diligence process that I explain in Chapter 13.

Documentation provides a solid base for developing a financial plan, but dig deeper to evaluate your client's mindset and financial attitudes, behaviors, goals, and concerns. Here are a few open-ended questions that can help reveal more about what makes your client tick:

>> What keeps you up at night? What concerns do you have about money?

>> What experience do you have working with a financial advisor, if any?

>> How would you describe what your life looks like in five years, ten years, and twenty years from now?

>> What concerns do you have that are unrelated to money?

>> How would you describe a successful financial advisory relationship?

These questions loosen up clients to provide you with much more relevant input than merely what appears in their financial documentation. Even better, the answers to these questions and the resulting discussion provide a context for understanding the details in the financial documents. Only by talking with your clients do you begin to understand any frustrations they face with their current financial situation and any encounters they've had in the past with other financial advisors. You may also gain insight into the client's mindset and behaviors that have contributed to these frustrations.

Listen not only to what your clients say, but also be aware of what they're *not* telling you. Often, I've found that clients reveal more in what they omit from the narrative of their financial life than what they disclose. Sharing past financial decisions and mistakes is much more personal for clients than sharing intimate details about their health with a doctor. Even though most health issues arise due to poor diet and lifestyle decisions, patients often withhold that information, either because they're embarrassed about it or because they don't want to be told to make difficult changes.

The same is true of clients working with their financial advisors. When someone optimistically and enthusiastically invests in a stock that subsequently loses all its value, a client has a funny way of erasing that experience from his memory banks, a symptom of the behavioral aversion to loss. If the client eventually discloses the mistake, he's likely to express his embarrassment by saying something like "*I should've known better!*". (Actually, he shouldn't have known better, because the ability to know better comes from acquiring professional knowledge and experience.)

Invite clients to share with you all their financial experiences — the good, the bad, and the ugly. Full disclosure provides the most valuable input when developing a client's financial plan.

Going Deep and Broad with Every Client

Because each client's financial life has so many different facets, even when the individual isn't a high-net-worth client, I developed a useful guide to organize a financial advisor's thinking. I call it The Three Cs of a Holistic Financial Plan.

Imagine a Venn diagram (Figure 14-1) with three intersecting circles:

» Copy

» Capital

» Consequences

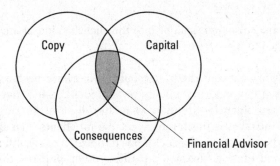

FIGURE 14-1:
The Three C's
of a holistic
financial plan.

The area of overlap is where you, the financial advisor, operate when you're developing a holistic financial plan. Each area requires specific care and attention, not only in terms of making client assessments, but also with regard to uncovering the levels of uncertainty that a client may be comfortable living with.

In the following sections, I explain each area in detail.

Copy

Copy (words on a page) refers to all the written documentation or family governance paperwork that's been drawn up (usually by an attorney) to spell out what the family's intentions are for their assets. In most cases, these documents are family trusts or wills, medical directives, powers of attorney, and other related documentation that dictate how the family is to act and who in the family will be in control when a patriarch or matriarch is no longer able to make decisions regarding their household matters.

Triggering events could be as varied as early onset dementia, Alzheimer's disease, or any other mentally or physically debilitating disease. More often than not, families must handle some level of deterioration in health of a parent or other loved one before death occurs. Making sure that all matters have someone who can step in, and be in charge, is extremely important.

Your role in respect to the copy aspect of a financial plan is to be sure that your client has received legal counsel in these areas and has the documentation to ensure that the directives are carried out.

TIP

Consider providing your clients with a document or a folder that contains all of the following information and documents that their loved ones will need in the event of your client's death or inability to make decisions. Include the following:

>> Your name and contact information

>> A list of income sources, including pension plans, IRAs, 401Ks

- ➤ A list of banks and account numbers

- ➤ Any Social Security or Medicare/Medicaid information

- ➤ Insurance information, including all policy providers, policy numbers, agent names, and contact information

- ➤ A copy of the client's most recent tax returns

- ➤ A copy of the client's will

- ➤ A copy of the client's living will (advanced medical directive)

- ➤ A copy of any power of attorney your client has signed

- ➤ A list of liabilities, such as mortgage loan, car loan, and property tax, including what's owned to whom and when payments are due

- ➤ The location of any mortgage documents, such as the deed of trust for a home the client owns

- ➤ The location of car title(s) and registration(s)

- ➤ The location of any safe deposit box(es) and key(s)

You may want to include this package as part of your service or charge a separate fee for preparing it. Having all of this information in one place makes it easy for authorized relatives or friends to take over when necessary. In the event that it's needed and used, the relatives or friends in charge will greatly appreciate it and likely sing your praises to everyone they know.

Capital

Capital (any asset or investment holding) refers to all allocations of household money, including all claims (or demands) on those assets. For example, in most U.S. households, the largest family asset is the primary home/residence. In other families, the most valuable asset is the family-owned business. These assets typically have some kind of debt associated with them, such as a mortgage for a home or a line of credit for a business.

All the various components of capital are constantly changing. Fluctuating stock and bond markets, real estate markets, the business environment, economic expansion or recessions, and so on all dictate the market value of these myriad holdings on any given day. Market valuations plus the liabilities associated with these assets affect the household's net worth. Unknown liabilities (such as those that blindside a family — disabilities, death, job loss, and so forth) can wreak even greater havoc on a household's net worth.

THE THREE CS IN ACTION

One of my clients, a business owner in his 60s with a net worth of $20 million, was on his third marriage and had six children. As with any blended family, getting the family governing documents (*copy*) up-to-date was essential for the family to avoid any ugly surprises down the road. In this client's case, I made introductions to a couple local estate planning attorneys and let the client meet with both and make the choice.

Getting the *copy* part completed took nearly a year due to various circumstances, including vacations, family events, and good old-fashioned need-to-think-about-it time delays. As a financial advisor, your job is to steward this process, which means gentle and timely prodding to move the process along. You never know what may lurk around the corner in terms of life events, so you want to wrap up the estate planning as quickly as possible.

At the same time, I worked with the client to align his *capital* with his *copy* to proactively address any unforeseen *consequences*. The *capital* part of his financial plan included one-time gifts, liquidity from life insurance policies, and market liquidity from his investment portfolio. I structured capital in a way to avoid any illiquid investments that could have caused extra stress or concern to the family in the event of any major family crisis, especially one that would impact my client's ability to shepherd his family through the crisis.

Within two years, my client was diagnosed with a serious illness and started treatment. Knowing that the *copy* was in place and that it aligned with the *capital* was a great personal relief to me and provided the family with the assurance and financial support they needed to make it through this challenging period in their lives. It allowed the family to focus on getting their primary breadwinner back to health instead of having to worry about unintended (but well-planned-for) *consequences*. Having the client's wishes clearly documented also assuaged the fears of family members, which often leads family members into contentious power struggles when they fear that their needs won't be met. Everyone understood that the planning had been done.

The key to this client's success was having a detailed financial plan in place that covered the three Cs of financial planning well in advance of any subsequent life event.

As you develop your client's financial plan, you must account for all the capital assets and liabilities and review the plan regularly to ensure that the household's net worth is on track and address any and all potential threats to that net worth.

Consequences

Consequences refers to the various scenarios that your client wants to avoid, such as the following:

>> A difficult family dynamic or dysfunction that persists for decades and becomes a major threat to the family's capital at a point in time when most families achieve a heightened awareness of the desire to maintain their lifestyle.

>> The panic that often ensues after the stock market plummets, which can drive clients to liquidate their holdings at the worst possible moment. Doing so creates a long-lasting consequence, which isn't easily rectified.

>> Naming a trustee or executor within the family documents who has a contentious relationship with family members or siblings, which can create terrible long-term financial and emotional consequences.

All of these situations (and others) are avoidable with the proper planning and proactive approach, and all of them are part of your responsibility as your client's financial advisor. By addressing any and all scenarios that could place your client's capital at risk, you give your client the best opportunity for success.

Outlining a Client's Financial Plan

Often, the most difficult part of a project is getting started. To simplify the process, begin with an outline that covers the six key components of personal finance success:

>> Cash flow

>> Investments

>> Taxes

>> Insurance (home, auto, life, and health)

>> Estate planning

>> Business succession

REMEMBER

Each of these components is within the capital section of "The Three Cs of a Holistic Financial Plan," presented in the previous section. In the following sections, I explain each of these areas in greater detail, so you know what to include in the client's financial plan.

Focusing on cash flow

The first order of business in financial planning is to document the client's cash flow. You should have all the information you need to complete this section after working with the client on budgeting (see Chapter 9). The financial plan needs to contain a personalized cash flow statement similar to what businesses use to gauge their solvency. Divide this part of the financial plan into three sections:

» **Income:** Salary, bonuses, self-employment income, government benefits, child support/alimony, investment/retirement income, interest income, and so on.

» **Expenses:** You can divide this section into fixed and variable expenses.

  • **Fixed expenses:** Mortgage/rent, car payments, insurance premiums, property taxes, alimony/child support, and so on.

  • **Variable expenses:** Groceries, utilities, medical bills, entertainment, dining, home/auto maintenance, spending money, and so on.

» **Net cash flow:** Subtract expenses from income to determine monthly and annual net cash flow.

Cash flow can be a positive or negative number based on numerous factors, such as the client's stage of life and how well the client is managing the family's finances. A negative value isn't necessarily bad; for example, if an older client's expenses exceed his income, he may be enjoying the fruits of his labor, which is great. However, if a younger client who's not independently wealthy has negative cash flow, that's a problem to address.

REMEMBER

Getting a clear picture of a client's baseline income and expenditure is fundamental to making any kind of financial plan. Of course, unexpected income and expense events can change cash flow dramatically, but the financial plan tries to minimize those risks by addressing insurance needs, as I explain in the later section "Addressing insurance needs."

Considering savings and investment goals

In the investment goals section of the financial plan, list the client's financial goals along with details on how the client's capital will be invested to meet those goals. Common investment goals include the following:

» **Retirement:** Generally, clients need 70 to 80 percent of their pre-tax income to maintain a comfortable lifestyle in their golden years. The plan should include the retirement savings goal and details on how the client will meet the agreed-upon goal, including income from Social Security, investments, and other assets (such as selling a home to downsize). (See Chapter 7 for more about retirement planning and other asset management topics.)

>> **Education:** If your client plans to pay for a child's or grandchild's education, include the projected amount needed and the amount of money to be invested monthly to achieve that goal along with the expected rate of return.

>> **Emergency reserves:** Every client should have the equivalent of 3 to 12 months of basic household expenses (excluding discretionary spending) in a liquid account, such as a savings or money market account. Include the amount and how much your client needs to set aside each month to meet that goal. (See Chapter 9 for details.)

>> **Starting or growing a business:** If your client is planning to break free of the corporate grind to start or grow his own business, the personal financial plan should contain a business plan with details for starting the business. (Creating a business plan is beyond the scope of this book. Check out *Creating a Business Plan For Dummies,* by Veechi Curtis (John Wiley & Sons, Inc.) for details.)

>> **Income:** If your client plans to invest in vehicles that generate additional monthly income, include this as part of the plan.

WARNING

Don't let clients limit their financial plans to savings and investments. Clients may seek your advice solely for good investment recommendations, but plotting the course to get them from here to there (their financial goals) is much more involved than just buying a good mutual fund or stock, socking away a certain amount of money routinely, and hoping for the best. Without other considerations that surround a client's life, any great investment plan can be undone by a number of unforeseen money events or behaviors.

Accounting for taxes

Taxes are a fact of life, but part of your job is to ensure that your clients aren't paying more taxes than necessary, so they can put more of their hard-earned capital to work for themselves. When creating a financial plan, include a plan for minimizing their tax burden.

TIP

Team up with your client's accountant to identify ways to reduce a client's tax burden, which may include the following:

>> If your client routinely receives a large tax refund at the end of the year, review his tax withholding and advise him to have less tax withheld from his paycheck, which can improve cash flow and provide opportunities to use that money in other ways to reduce taxes.

>> Maximize the amount your client invests in tax-deferred retirement accounts, such as a 401K or individual retirement account (IRA).

>> If future taxes are a concern, your client may want to sock away additional money with a Roth IRA or 401K. If tax rates are expected to rise considerably in the future, your client may also benefit by shifting money from a regular IRA or 401K to a Roth IRA or 401K, although your client must pay income tax at the current rate on any amount converted.

>> If your client has a high-deductible health insurance policy, have him set up a health savings account (HSA) to pay for medical bills with pre-taxed dollars.

>> Make sure that when your client files taxes, he maximizes the allowable deduction by taking the standard deduction or itemizing deductions. (Here's where a tax-savvy accountant has the best opportunity to reduce your client's tax burden.)

>> As possible, consider the timing of events, such as a marriage, the purchase or sale of a primary residence, and the purchase and sale of investments to take advantage of any relevant tax breaks provided by the government.

>> If your client plans to support charitable organizations, include contributions (and the timing of those contributions) as part of the tax-savings plan.

Dozens of tax-saving strategies and techniques are available. See Chapter 11 for additional details.

REMEMBER

Taxes, including federal, state, and local income taxes; property taxes; and capital gains taxes, can reduce a client's disposable income by up to 50 percent depending on the client's effective tax rate. That percentage represents a good chunk of money to leave on the table. The tax portion of your client's financial plan could save your client enough in taxes to more than cover your advisory fees. This savings in itself can be a key value-add to your clients.

Addressing insurance needs

Every financial plan needs a section devoted exclusively to insurance. This section should include the insurance types, cost, and coverage. Be sure to include the following insurance types, some of which depend on your client's situation, such as whether he owns a business:

>> Life

>> Health and supplemental insurance

>> Disability

» Homeowner or rental insurance

» Auto

» Business, including personal liability, property, workers' compensation, home-based business, product liability, and business interruption insurance

Refer to Chapter 8 for additional details on keeping your client's properly insured.

Don't focus exclusively on delivering asset management, even if that's your area of focus. If you're primarily an investment manager, you still need to make sure your clients are properly insured, even if that means partnering with an insurance expert. If your client experiences an unexpected life event he's not insured against, it could wipe out a significant chunk of his accumulated assets, leaving you with that much less to manage. A temporary disability or financial hardship may not have a huge impact, but long-term disability, illness, or death could be devastating for the family's finances. Every solid financial plan makes allowances for managing possible and probable risks.

Connecting the financial plan to the estate plan

Your client's estate plan is separate from his overall financial plan, but this section of the financial plan provides an opportunity to make sure that your client has an estate plan in place. Think of it as a checkbox on the financial plan. Check the box if the client has an estate plan in place, and leave it unchecked if that's something you need to prepare for your client. Chapter 10 discusses estate planning in greater detail.

In simple estates with few assets and no family contention or dysfunction, estate planning doesn't require much more than some basic family governing documents, including a will and a living will. However, many households have some degree of family dysfunction that requires further attention and proactive discussion. Also, if the client's estate exceeds certain market value thresholds due to sizeable accumulated assets (including, a family-owned business value), then the IRS is going to come knocking when that asset is being transitioned to the next generation's ownership, and a plan must be in place to deal with that.

Connecting the financial plan to the client's business succession plan

If your client owns a business, a *succession plan* is part of the overall financial plan. However, on the financial plan itself, this section is more of a checkbox that indicates whether the client has a business succession plan in place. You may want to include a few additional details from the business succession plan in this section of the financial plan, such as:

>> A list of trigger events the activate the business succession plan

>> The current business valuation

>> The name of the person who's going to run the business if your client is unable to do so temporarily or permanently

>> How the client or the client's family will draw compensation from the business if a trigger event occurs

The actual business succession plan should contain additional details and be prepared by the family's lawyer. (See Chapter 10 for details.)

REMEMBER

Assisting your business-owner clients in creating a solid business succession plan is a great value-add for any financial advisor. By providing this service, you differentiate yourself from a majority of the financial advisors practicing today. Of course, you'll have to team up with a lawyer to get it done.

Making Your Job Easier with Tools and Guides

A financial plan requires a considerable amount of math to figure out cash flow and perform projections related to financial goals. Fortunately, numerous financial planning software packages are available to make the job much easier and construct a plan that is and looks professional.

When you're in the market for financial planning software for your advisory business, make the following considerations:

>> **Whether the software is based on goals, cash flow, or both:** Your choice depends on your approach to financial planning. If you're big on budgeting and want to track every dollar spent, look for more of a cash-flow product. If you primarily encourage clients to set financial goals and allocate a certain amount of money periodically to meet those goals, look at products that are more goals based.

REMEMBER

The trend in this market is to provide feature-rich products that cater to both cash-flow and goals-based financial advisors, but some products still favor one over the other.

>> **Comprehensiveness:** Some financial planning software is dedicated solely to investment management. If you do as I recommend and function as a full-service advisor, you want a product that can handle various insurance types, Social Security benefits, retirement distributions, college savings, stock options, and more.

>> **Ease of use:** Consider how easy (or difficult) the software is to use, including ease of input and the ability to change values and make other adjustments.

>> **Projection features:** Many financial planning tools include projections based on historical data and market expectations to predict financial results. Look at how the software formulates projections. Some packages use a straight-line method based on an estimated projection, such as a 5 or 6 percent return. Others use a Monte Carlo simulation that models the probability of different outcomes based on random variables. And still others feature what-if analyses, so you can play with the numbers to explore different outcomes, such as a best- and worst-case scenario.

>> **Reports and interactive tools:** All financial planning software can generate reports based on the numbers you enter. However, some include interactive tools, such as a dashboard with sliders that enable you to play with numbers and gain immediate feedback on how changes to inputs affect the outputs. These graphical, interactive financial planning programs are great if you like to sit down with clients and explore the outcomes of different financial decisions. They're also useful if you just want to conduct in-depth analyses yourself.

>> **An online client portal:** If your clients want to be more involved in the financial planning process and be able to monitor their financial performance more closely, having an online client portal can be a big plus. More and more financial planning software developers are moving in this direction, because more and more clients are demanding it.

You can find plenty of templates and software (for free and for cost) by searching online. Just search for "professional financial planning tools," and you'll find dozens of links.

Based on established products and market share, here are the top three financial planning software packages:

>> **eMoney Advisor (emoneyadvisor.com/products):** This product serves as a virtual lockbox, giving you the ability to house the various aspects of a client's financial life in one place. It features a client portal, screen sharing, account aggregation, an interactive estate planner, an advisor dashboard, a mobile web app, a goal planner, and much more. The ability to aggregate accounts, whether or not you have custody of the assets, is a big selling point.

- » **MoneyGuide Pro** (`www.moneyguidepro.com/ifa`): This software includes a planning portal that encourages clients to focus on long-term goals and discourages reactive behavior; what-if scenarios that enable you to show clients the impact of market corrections, early death, and unexpected expenses; streamlined data gathering; a Play Zone, where clients can see the impact of adjusting variables; a Social Security planner for maximizing benefits; and more.

- » **Naviplan** (`www.advicentsolutions.com/products/naviplan`): This software focuses on cash flow planning with an option to produce quick, goal-based assessments. It features comprehensive planning centered on detailed tax analysis, advanced estate planning, models to test alternative planning scenarios, and an optional client portal. Many advisors access this software through their broker/dealer's licensing agreement and don't pay for it separately.

Reviewing the Plan Regularly

Even the best laid financial plans can fail, either because the client doesn't stick to the plan or because life throws your client a curve ball. Stay proactive by meeting with your client quarterly, semiannually, or annually to review the plan and any changes in your client's life that may call for adjustments.

TIP

During your review, always explain the rationale behind the plan. When clients understand the plan and the strategy you've painstakingly developed for them, they're more likely to adhere to it and less likely to get spooked by unexpected events. Be methodical in your due diligence process, as I explain in Chapter 13. Making sure your clients understand how the different pieces of their plan function relative to each other is probably one of the most important and challenging aspects of this profession.

Chapter **15**

Offering Collaborative Value-Added Advice

Although it may take a village to raise a child, it takes only a small group of talented and dedicated professionals working together to manage a client's finances. The problem that many prospective clients have, even though few are aware it's a problem, is that they've siloed the various products and services they use for financial security and wealth-building. They may do their own bookkeeping and hire an accountant to do their taxes. They have a lawyer prepare their wills and business documents, but they probably don't have an estate plan. They have insurance policies purchased from one or more brokers. And have various types of investments cobbled together as part of their retirement "plan" and wealth-building "strategy."

This haphazard approach to financial management poses two problems:

» **Lack of alignment and balance:** For optimum performance, a client needs to set goals and align all elements of her financial life with those goals, just as a business must align its daily operations with its short-term objectives and its objectives with its long-term goals. For example, a client may have too much money in savings and not enough in stocks and bonds, limiting potential earnings.

>> **Gaps:** A solid financial plan covers everything that can impact a client's finances, including budget, savings, investments, insurance, legal, and tax issues. Without professional guidance, a client can easily overlook a key area. For example, if a client invests heavily in building a successful business and overlooks disability and liability insurance or having clear policies in place to ensure compliance with government regulations, she places that investment at risk.

Having a team in place and carefully coordinating their efforts and expertise eliminates gaps in the client's financial plan and aligns all elements of the plan for optimal efficiency and performance. In addition, it provides checks and balances to hold everyone on the team accountable, and it provides you with different perspectives, so you don't overlook important considerations.

REMEMBER

You should be eager to have your ideas and recommendations vetted by other professional advisors representing your client. More opinions and evaluations across disciplines can sometimes be chaotic and induce analysis paralysis, but when managed properly, this interdisciplinary collaboration delivers optimal results.

In this chapter, I explain how to take a consultative, collaborative approach when engaging other advisors to deliver superior service to your clients.

Recognizing the Benefits of a Collaborative Approach

If you've been a financial advisor for a while, you may already have had positive or negative experiences with other client advisors, such as accountants and lawyers. Other advisors can not only shoot down one or more of your recommendations, but they can also go so far as to tell their client (your client) to fire you. Whenever you bring other advisors into the mix, those risks are always present, but they're not sufficient reason to avoid or hide from these other advisors. Avoidance puts you at a disadvantage by closing off you and your clients from the expertise that other professionals offer.

TIP

Send your clients a clear message of inclusion by expressing your desire to work with their other advisors. This approach clearly differentiates you from other financial advisors who are reluctant to do so, and it builds instant trust by showing that you're confident enough in your advice and the services you provide to open your recommendations to the scrutiny of other professionals. In addition, this approach promises to save your clients the time and bother of coordinating their advisors' activities. Most clients are busy and have limited in-depth knowledge regarding detailed financial planning discussions. Volunteering to discuss your ideas directly with their other trusted advisors takes team management off your client's plate.

Collaborating with your client's other professional advisors is a great opportunity to share the planning discussions that you and they have had with your client up to that point. Through these discussions, you're likely to discover important facts about your client's planning and about elements that are already in place that your client never thought to mention. The more information and insight you have about your client's mindset, family and business dynamics, tax profile, and other aspects of your client's life, the better your financial plan design and the resulting client outcome.

Aligning your compensation model with that of other professional advisors

The so-called financial advisors who clash with other professional advisors are usually those who sell investment and insurance products and receive up-front commissions. Other advisors rightly question the motivation of these "financial advisors," because they wonder whether these advisors are serving their clients or their own best interests. Most practitioners who consider themselves financial advisors typically engage in positioning an investment or insurance product and not proposing a broader financial advisory solution or relationship.

TIP

Position yourself as a true fiduciary advisor and embrace a compensation model that's better aligned with the way these other professionals are paid. For example, if your client's other advisors charge fees for services rendered, consider doing the same. This approach places you in a category that's familiar to the other advisors and usually makes them feel as though they can collaborate with you more freely without the overarching concern of a compensation conflict. If you're charging commissions, you'll experience an immediate disconnect when you start working with these other professionals. (See Chapter 4 for details about compensation models that are more conducive to collaboration among fiduciary advisors.)

Delivering optimal results

Obviously, a team of specialists is better suited than an individual who tries to be a Jack-or Jill-of-all-trades to serve a client's diverse financial and legal needs. Equally obvious is that engaging in active dialog with these specialists will yield superior financial outcomes for your clients. Keep in mind that these various specialties are all connected — taxes, legal issues, and asset management all have the potential of impacting one another. A failure in one area can cause a domino effect that seriously undermines your client's ability to achieve her financial goals.

In this section, I present a couple examples that demonstrate the importance of coordinating the efforts of your client's advisors.

Collaborating on a family trust

After a family trust has been established and executed, your client's lawyer usually tells her to contact all of her account and policy holders to change the account title or owner registration on each account/policy to reflect the new trust. Changing account registrations is a big deal. If the client forgets to do so, puts it off indefinitely, or overlooks the registration for one or more assets, all of the estate's assets, including the family home, could end up in probate. Going to court is a time-consuming and expensive process, and it's totally avoidable, assuming the client has set up a trust *and* registered all assets accordingly.

As part of your normal due diligence process (see Chapter 13), ask prospective clients about any trusts or wills that have been drafted *and* executed. If they don't have one drafted and have assets and beneficiaries they want to be directing those assets toward, make a referral to a trusted lawyer in your network. If your clients have a trust already, ask to verify that all their assets and holdings have been listed in their trust appendix or exhibit and that each account has been registered accordingly. Doing so will save your clients from an ugly surprise should something unexpected happen.

Collaborating to reduce your client's tax burden

Through close collaboration with your client's accountant, you can lower your client's tax bill, thus freeing up more money to achieve her financial goals. Unlike legal issues that revolve around trust and estate law, tax law and rates change routinely, usually when a new administration steps into the White House and gets around to pushing its new tax plan through Congress. For this reason, consult with your client's accountant regularly or at least whenever new tax legislation is enacted.

Be proactive. Your client's accountant may not inform all of her clients about changes in tax legislation or recommend specific actions to take. By keeping abreast of tax changes and considering the changes during your periodic review with clients, you can provide a valuable service to your clients, something they'll certainly remember.

For example, as you prepare or review your client's financial plan, consider the tax implications of any investments you recommend, so you can optimize your client's returns. Start by looking at your client's effective tax rate. (The *effective tax rate* is the client's total tax bill divided by her household taxable income. It's lower than the client's tax bracket. See Chapter 11 for details.) You can have your client obtain this rate from her accountant or, better yet, ask your client to put you in touch with her accountant and give permission to exchange data, so you can ask for it yourself. Asking your client's accountant for the client's effective tax rate is a great way to introduce yourself and launch ongoing discussion in your mutual client's best interests.

Understanding where your client falls in tax expense plays a key role in portfolio allocation decisions. For example, qualified stock dividends, which are taxed at lower rates than capital gains, may not provide a real benefit if your client's effective tax rate is already quite low. Also, depending on market conditions, buying certain kinds of tax-exempt securities (such as municipal bonds) may provide little tax benefit to outweigh potential concerns about that asset class.

REMEMBER

Ultimately, taxes shouldn't be the tail that wags the dog of good portfolio management decision-making (see Chapter 11), but you should consider taxes as one factor. Engaging your client's accountant in these discussions is a great way to improve your client's portfolio performance while gaining the appreciation of both your client and your fellow advisor.

Creating a system of checks and balances

If you're operating in a silo and not subjecting your ideas and recommendations to challenge or critique, then you're not growing in experience and knowledge. In my own practice, ongoing dialog with professional advisors for the benefit of mutual clients has been a great source of education, as well as new prospects. By working within a network of professionals who trust and respect one another, you create your own system of checks and balances that holds everyone accountable for their advice.

REMEMBER

Any professional could be wrong in his or her recommendations. By engaging in open conversation about a recommended client strategy — whether it's proposed by the client's accountant, lawyer, or you — educated professionals have the opportunity to weigh in on it from different perspectives. Although each professional has different education and work experience, they all have a common client experience and know that every strategy has its pros and cons. A good client advisory team recognizes that the best strategy is that which delivers the most value to the client, so ideas generally don't get shot down unless they deserve to be.

Leveraging the power of specialization

Many professions, including law and accounting, have general practitioners and specialists. Typically, the more complicated and sophisticated the situation is, the greater the need for a specialist. If your client has complex financial needs and is relying on a general practitioner to meet those needs, consider recommending that a specialist be added to the team.

A classic example of when a specialist needs to be called in is when a client owns a family business. In this situation, the client would be well served by having two lawyers — a corporate and an estate lawyer, who collaborate to develop the optimal business transition plan. The business plan and the family's estate plan are intimately connected through family members who are functioning in the business as employees (often as key employees), and both plans need to reflect that.

Also, at some point in the future, the family business will face a transition of leadership and ownership, which may be anticipated or unexpected (as in an owner's untimely death). Coordinating the family trusts with the business succession and ownership plan is a Herculean task best handled through the collaboration of specialists.

Your job initially is to make sure that your client has the right people on the team to address her unique needs. Then, your responsibilities shift to ensuring that the assigned tasks are completed and providing information and insight as requested by the specialists.

Accounting has several specialties that may benefit certain clients depending on their situations:

>> **Bookkeeping:** Businesses and some families use bookkeepers to record and manage their day-to-day finances. A client who's struggling with budgeting and financial record keeping could benefit (especially if she owns a business) by having a bookkeeper.

>> **Business accounting:** Clients who are struggling to grow their business could benefit from the services of a business accountant. Although business accountants typically spend a good deal of their time on bookkeeping chores, they also create and review reports and provide insight into how a business can run more efficiently.

>> **Tax accounting:** Clients who have complex tax situations are wise to consult an accountant who specializes in taxes. In fact, all of your clients would be wise to consult a tax accountant. A tax accountant does much more than merely prepare tax returns; she can offer valuable insight on how to take advantage of all qualified federal, state, and local tax breaks for businesses and individuals.

A tax accountant should also be on the corporate and estate lawyer team when they're planning a client's estate. The tax specialist can make sure that the tax expense of moving a business from one generation to another is done without the IRS showing up at the client's business after the estate tax filing.

>> **Forensic accounting:** If you have a client who's entangled in a messy divorce and suspects her soon-to-be ex of hiding money or other assets, you may want to recommend a forensic accountant. Forensic accounting is like a special ops SEALs team being tasked with a targeted mission — in this case to uncover shady business or money activity the results of which can be used to support a case in litigation.

Collaborating to Serve Your Clients Better

As your client's financial advisor, you play a key role on the advisory team, as I explain in the later section "Taking on the Role of Your Team's Quarterback." As such, you must collaborate with everyone on the team — client, lawyers, accountants, and any other relevant professionals.

In this section, I explain how to communicate and collaborate with different advisory team members, including your client.

TIP

Cross-industry professional collaboration is a key differentiator among financial advisors. You'll find little competition in the marketplace for financial advisors who routinely coordinate their activities with other professionals on behalf of their clients. Leverage the power of this key differentiator by letting clients and prospects know that you're dedicated to partnering with others on their advisory team to optimize their financial success.

Teaming up with your client

As with any partnership or good relationship, communication is key. Touching base with your clients regularly — on an ongoing basis — is the only way to ensure you're getting the whole picture. Remind your clients that you and they both want the same thing — a great financial outcome over the course of their and their loved ones' lives.

REMEMBER

Tell clients what they *need* to hear, not what you think they *want* to hear. The fact is that most clients *want* to be told what they *need* to hear. That's what they're paying you for. Just be sure to present it without judgment or sarcasm. If you're telling clients what you think they want to hear instead of what they need to hear, you're enabling bad habits. Your job is to lead your clients in the direction of financially healthier decisions and behaviors.

Your client has hired you because she can't see the forest for the trees, and you can. If she knows that you're in partnership together to achieve the same agreed-upon goals, then teamwork will come naturally. Your client will be more open, responsive, and engaged. She'll understand that she's better off working with you than trying to manage her finances by herself or with another financial advisor who's less committed to teamwork.

REMEMBER

As with any partnership or team, your relationship with a client may encounter some friction and frustration. Even the closest teammates and partners can butt heads and engage in heated debates over what's best. Usually, they have the same goal; they just disagree over the best way to achieve it. Not only are disagreements completely normal, but they're also to be expected and can be quite productive. With every disagreement, you and your client glean more about each other, which ideally leads to a deeper relationship with greater understanding.

Partnering with your client's lawyer

The easiest way to connect with your client's lawyer is to have your client introduce you via email. This also serves as a written notice, which lawyers like to have to ensure they have permission to discuss client-specific information with another party.

To simplify the task for your client, write the introduction yourself and email it to your client to use. Figure 15-1 is a sample introductory email that your client can send to her lawyer:

Hi John,

I'd like to introduce you to my financial advisor, Ivan Illan. We're developing a financial plan and considering all the different components. He asked to have a chance to touch base with you. He said that the more engaged all our advisors are with one another, the more likely we'll have a better outcome.

Ivan also asked that you avail yourself of up to one hour of discussion as a professional courtesy. It's possible that we'll end up needing you to make some minor changes or adjustments.

Please let me know if you have any questions. Otherwise, please welcome Ivan's call. You have my permission to share any information he requests or answer any questions he may ask.

Thank you,
Susan Smith

FIGURE 15-1: A sample introductory email.

Working with your client's accountant

Your client's accountant can be helpful in the area of tax planning (see Chapter 11) by providing you with your client's effective tax rate along with an overview of your client's income and any ideas on how the two of you can work together to ease your mutual client's tax burden.

I've found that accountants are less formal to deal with than lawyers, but you should still ask your client to introduce you via email and provide permission to share information and answer questions.

TIP

I recommend hosting a brainstorming session with your client's accountant to freely discuss ideas or strategies that she may have leveraged with other clients.

In general, business owners have more complicated tax planning concerns than do salaried employees, so if your client owns a business, having a tax advisor on the team is a big plus. During your initial conversation with your client's tax accountant, here are a few tax-savings strategies for business owners that you may want to discuss to get the ball rolling:

>> **Changing the client's business structure:** Business structure (sole proprietorship, C-corporation, S-corporation, LLC) impacts the way the business owner gets paid, which can affect income taxes and the amount of self-employment tax (FICA) your client pays.

>> **Establishing a profit-sharing retirement plan:** *Profit sharing retirement plans* enable businesses to contribute a portion of the business's profits into an employee retirement account that grows tax-free. In addition, contributions made by the business aren't included in the business's taxable income. In a family business, this can be a great way to build wealth for family members who work in the business.

>> **Using fringe benefit plans for employees:** *Fringe benefits* include group life, health, and disability insurance; dependent care; and tuition reimbursement. They're a great way for employers to improve employee recruitment and retention by adding compensation that provides tax breaks for the business. For example, employee health insurance premiums paid by the business are generally tax-deductible.

>> **Using an accountable plan:** An *accountable plan* governs how a business reimburses employees for business expenses. Under such a plan, reimbursements to an employee or business owner aren't included as part of the employee or owner's income, but the business can take a deduction for these amounts.

These methods of allocating capital toward corporate benefits and other business continuity or succession planning items can reduce the business's taxable income, while enhancing its overall value and efficiency.

Working on your follow-through

Nothing is more embarrassing than going through all the time and effort to collaborate with other advisors for a client's benefit only to lose track of who's doing what next. To avoid such embarrassments, get organized and follow through on whatever the team discussed.

TIP

Set deadlines in your communications with other advisors and your clients. Create reminders in your customer relationship management (CRM) software or whatever scheduling tool you use. Collaborations can take considerable time to come to fruition, and everyone can easily lose track when they get busy with other things. I've had projects go on for a year or two before we finally proceeded to implement the plan.

The more complicated the client's needs and the more advisors are involved on a project, the longer the process takes. Don't be discouraged; it's a natural side effect of going up-market in your client acquisition.

Taking on the Role of Your Team's Quarterback

When you're collaborating with other professional advisors for the benefit of your mutual client, you take the field as the advisory team's quarterback. You're the point person. Whenever your client needs the team's assistance, you call a huddle and work with the other advisors to figure out the next play.

In this section, I explain how to fill the role of financial advisor on your client's advisory team.

Acting as the central point of contact

As the team's financial advisor, your number should be on speed dial for your client. You should be the first or second person your client calls when life-changing events occur that are likely to impact her finances or when she's thinking of making an investment decision or changing the financial plan. It's okay to be the second call if your client is changing beneficiaries to her estate, which her lawyer would need to do, but then you need to be notified to update beneficiary designations on all qualified accounts.

REMEMBER

Remind your client to call you for advice whenever she's about to make even relatively small decisions, such as refinancing a home mortgage, buying a vacation home, buying or leasing a car, investing in a business venture, bank-rolling a down-and-out relative or friend, and so on. You can help in these matters, as well, and your clients should know they can count on you for unbiased advice. In some instances, you may want to consult with other advisors on your client's team, just to make sure you're not missing any salient point from a legal or tax perspective.

Maintaining separation among advisors base on their roles

Although everyone on the advisory team should collaborate to optimize the client's outcome, each advisor has a unique role to play:

>> **Financial advisor:** You're in charge of allocating the client's capital and reallocating it to take advantage of new opportunities, limit the client's exposure to risk, and adapt to changes in the client's situation. You add value through favorable allocations that either *build* or *protect* accumulated wealth.

REMEMBER

You must be the calm captain on the stormy seas. Much of the value you bring your clients involves talking them off the cliff in the midst of wild market swings and listening to them when family discord leads them to consider changing beneficiaries. In these situations, your client is much more likely to call on you instead of her lawyer or accountant.

>> **Lawyer(s):** Your client's lawyer is generally in charge of ensuring that the control/disposition of assets is handled according to the client's wishes *after* the capital has been allocated. A lawyer can also add value by drafting wills and estate plans and helping the client establish a business entity and structuring it in the best way possible.

>> **Accountant(s):** Your client's accountant is primarily in charge of recording and managing profits and losses and advising on tax-saving strategies. An accountant can also help advise on estate planning gifting techniques.

Unlike other professionals, a financial advisor holds the power to provide lifetime income to a retiree, make sure funding is available to put all the kids through college, and deliver a check to a surviving loved one in the event of an untimely death of a household breadwinner. These are heavy responsibilities. Dropping the ball can have serious consequences on par with a person's world ending, which is why you must take the lead on the advisory team.

In contrast, lawyers and accountants are mostly project-based advisors, who have limited interaction with the client throughout the year and face less serious consequences if they drop the ball. If the client's accountant overlooks a tax break, it's not the end of the world, just an opportunity to optimize. Likewise, if a lawyer omits a provision in the estate plan, it may cause a huge headache, but again it's not the end of days.

Shopping solutions

A key role as advisory team quarterback is to shop solutions that most effectively meet your client's needs, whether you or someone else on the team is recommending that the client obtain a certain product or service. Being able to shop the market effectively builds confidence in you among the other professionals on the team as well as the client.

Ideally, you have access to an independent, nonproprietary product suite that allows you to fulfill a variety of potential needs — something commonly referred to these days as an *open-architecture solution platform*. If you work for a company that manufactures high-quality products, using those products is fine as long as they pass the cost-benefit smell test. If you're at a firm where you're pressured to sell certain products, the best approach is to give your employer's proprietary products the *right of first refusal* (if they give the best offer based on cost-benefit analysis, then they win the business). If the manufacturer can offer a great product at a great cost that's at least as good as the other options on the market, then you agree to recommend the product, but if you find something better, that's what you recommend. To do otherwise betrays your client's and other advisors' confidence.

TIP

A side benefit of shopping the market for solutions is that the broader your marketplace, the more referrals you're likely to develop from your professional network.

Chapter **16**

Adjusting Your Service Level to Different Clients

After you've started to build your book of business, you'd be wise to begin tiering your client service levels. Trying to be everything to everyone is difficult, not to mention inefficient. Some clients don't need or expect or even want to meet with you frequently, whereas others can waste your time with pointless meetings, phone calls, and indecision, if you let them. By scoring a client's value to your practice and governing the time and energy you allocate accordingly, you can eliminate or at least reduce inefficiencies and avoid having your motivation sapped by overly demanding clients.

REMEMBER

A client's value to your business is not only a matter of revenue, but it's also a mosaic of factors that contribute to your practice growth and enjoyment. You want to spend more time with clients who leave you feeling energized and enjoying your work and are disciples to your efforts in manifesting great financial outcomes for people, and less time and focus on the rest while continuing to serve their needs.

In this chapter, I describe the various traits that characterize client value and explain how to use those traits to categorize and score clients. I also provide a few examples of how to make the most of lunch meetings and special events used to engage your best clients.

Building a Tiered Client Service Model

The first order of business to establishing a tiered client service model is to create the tiers or brackets to which you assign clients. Whether you use an A-B-C-D model or precious metals model (Platinum, Gold, Silver, Bronze), you need brackets to separate client groups based on their value to your practice.

In this section, I present the tier model I use and then provide some guidance on how to deliver the best service to your best clients.

Scaling services to different clients

Financial advisors and other service professionals commonly rank clients using an A-B-C-D system. "A" clients are best, whereas "D" are those who represent limited revenue or referral opportunities, waste your time, or rue the day you entered the profession.

I recommend using a precious metals model, such as the one presented in Table 16-1, simply because I don't like the idea of giving clients a "C" or a "D" as if they're average or below average clients. After all, if a client found out he was given a "D," he would understandably be upset. With the precious metals model, a client would be less likely to be upset finding out that he was in the bronze bracket. He would probably even expect it given his level of engagement. (The platinum metals model also supports the whole financial motif.)

In Table 16-1, the column on the left lists the services and perks, while subsequent columns present the various service levels: Platinum, Gold, Silver, and Bronze.

REMEMBER

All clients deserve quality service, but that service doesn't need to come from you as financial advisor or firm owner. It can come from an associate or assistant. For example, I spend most of my time working with clients in the Platinum and Gold brackets, whereas associates at my firm spend more of their time servicing clients in the Silver and Bronze brackets. Clients can move up or down in the brackets. For example, if one of our associates uncovers a diamond in the rough, he escalates it to my attention for collaboration.

A unique service item is our charity support benefit, which ties the values of our firm to that of our clients. We make charitable contributions to the different non-profits that our clients support. The contributions come from a pool of funds allocated to the client tier. The more engagement and understanding we have from our clients of what causes they care about, the more gifts we're able to make.

TABLE 16-1:   **Service Level Brackets in the Metals Model**

Services and Perks	Platinum	Gold	Silver	Bronze
Client connect	Quarterly	Semiannually	Annually	As needed/reactive
In-person check-in/checkup	Ivan	Ivan and/or associate	Associate	As needed with associate
Mini email review	Quarterly	Quarterly	Semiannually	Annually
Birthday card	Handwritten	Signed	Auto	Auto
Dinner/lunch	1–2 per year per client	0–1 per year per client	N/A	N/A
Year-end gift basket	1	1	N/A	N/A
Holiday cards	Handwritten	Yes	Yes	Yes
Associate reconnect	One time as necessary	As needed in process	As needed in process	Annually
Summer kickoff event	Invite	Invite	Consider	N/A
Charity support (donations to the client's chosen cause)	$5,000 pool annually	$3,000 pool annually	$1,500 pool annually	$500 pool annually

TIP

If you're running your practice as a lone wolf, you have only your own time to leverage when conducting client service work. Although this approach is common practice, it's a highly inefficient and costly use of your time and expertise as a financial advisor. Consider allocating specific upgraded client service work (in-person check-in or checkup) to a full-time associate (recommended) or a part-time assistant. Only developing a service offering for your Platinum clients is good enough to gain some strategic efficiency. At least you won't be running around like a chicken with its head cut off, trying to deliver great service to all clients all the time.

Giving your best clients concierge care

You've probably heard of white glove or concierge services, usually in reference to service at a luxury hotel or a fine dining establishment, but financial advisors should also deliver this level of service to their Platinum clients. Your concierge care needs to include higher levels of service in the following areas:

>> **Time:** The most valuable commodity anyone has is time, so the most valuable component in your concierge care offering is the quality time you spend with clients. Whether it's reviewing a client's portfolio in a face-to-face quarterly meeting, discussing the family's estate plan, or sharing a leisurely meal, the interaction demonstrates your time commitment to your best clients.

>> **Attention:** The close attention you pay to all aspects of a client's financial planning and management shows that you care. Listening attentively to their concerns and proactively addressing issues instead of waiting for clients to call are both ways to pay increased attention to your best clients' financial matters.

>> **Appreciation:** Taking your client out to lunch or dinner, sending handwritten birthday and holiday cards, checking in with clients regularly, and giving tokens of your appreciation, such as an annual gift basket, are all ways to show your appreciation to clients.

>> **Problem-solving:** When clients come to you with problems you can't solve in your capacity as their financial advisor, consider making a referral to someone who can help. Through your interactions with people in a wide variety of professions, you probably have clients who've encountered and overcome a similar challenge or are experts who can help.

WARNING

The challenge with promising a higher level of service is that you had better deliver; otherwise, the empty promise will backfire. Instead of developing deeper client relationships, you'll send your clients running into the arms of another financial advisor.

Scoring Your Clients

Using a points system, you can categorize your clients more objectively. In this section, I present a scoring system that ranks clients on both their demographic *and* psychographic traits. (*Psychographic* is a fancy term that refers to a method of quantifying a client's psychological attributes.)

A client's score ranges from 10 to 50 based on five demographic and five psychographic traits (ten total traits), which each trait receiving a score of 1–5.

The demographic areas are

>> Annual revenue

>> Marital status and family complexity

>> Profession

>> Net worth

>> Multiple solutions sets

The psychographic areas are

>> Willingness to refer

>> Values advisor relationship

>> Social network/contacts

>> Quality of relationship

>> Philanthropic mindset

In the following sections, I lead you through the scoring process and then present a table that shows how to assign clients to different service level brackets based on their scores.

Considering demographics

Demographics are statistical data relating to the clientele you serve. Table 16-2 provides some general guidelines for scoring clients in five different categories: annual revenue, marital status, profession, net worth, and multiple solution sets. In the sections that follow, I describe each category.

TABLE 16-2: **Scoring Clients Demographically**

	1	2	3	4	5
Annual revenue	<$500	$501–$7,500	$7,501–$12,500	$12,501–$19,999	$20k+
Marital status	Single	Newly married	Married	Married/blended	Unique family complexity
Profession	Employed	Employed + (climbing the corporate ladder)	Professional	Executive	Entrepreneur
Net worth	<$500k	$500,001–$2.99M	$3M–$4.99M	$5M–$9.99M	>$10M
Multiple solutions sets	1		2		3+

REMEMBER

Feel free to adjust the numbers to more accurately reflect the demographics of your targeted clientele.

Annual revenue

Annual revenue is *your* income from the client relationship. Obviously, a client who directly generates more revenue for you is going to rank higher in terms of demanding your time and attention.

REMEMBER

Just because a client is a big source of revenue to your practice doesn't mean that he falls automatically into the Platinum bracket. In fact, annual revenue is just one line item out of several and accounts for only a maximum of 5 points out of a possible 50.

Marital status

The more complicated, blended, or dysfunctional a family has become, the more value you have to them and they have to your practice. Guiding families through challenging waters and in collaboration with the family attorney(s) and accountant(s) provides excellent word-of-mouth referrals and access to professionals around those families.

REMEMBER

All other aspects being equal, a single client generally requires less time and attention. However, that can be misleading, because single clients often just need time and attention in different areas. Still, marital status and family complexity is only one factor of ten, so a single client may still qualify for the Platinum bracket based on his other scores.

Profession

Working as a routine company employee, versus an executive or manager, versus an entrepreneur or business owner plays heavily into your client's value. Opportunities to add value at higher levels of impact — such as companywide or business succession planning — offer significant revenue potential. In addition, clients who have leadership roles at work tend to be more active influencers and thus a better source for referrals.

Net worth

The higher your client's net worth, the greater the possibility for complexities that require more of your time and expertise and the products and solutions you offer. Whether the client has large investment portfolios or sizeable, illiquid investments, such as real estate, a high-net-worth household is likely to need greater protection of its assets.

REMEMBER

The higher the net worth, the greater the vulnerability to changing market or financial conditions or life events (such as illness, disability, or death), particularly when it comes to lifestyle maintenance. Having to submit assets to a fire sale or inopportune liquidation to fund an unexpected liability means solid planning is required.

Multiple solution sets

Clients who've leveraged your advice across different financial planning services, such as asset management, insurance products, or financial consulting fees, are more engaged and valuable. Not only do they get to benefit from a more comprehensive solution set, but they're also more likely to become disciples of your practice.

Weighing psychographics

Scoring clients psychographically enables you to size them up based on their attitudes, values, the expanse of their social and professional networks, and their willingness to refer people they know to you. Table 16-3 provides some general guidelines for scoring clients in five psychographic categories. In the sections that follow, I describe each category.

TABLE 16-3: ## Scoring Clients Psychographically

Points	1	2	3	4	5
Willingness to refer	No	Occasional	Provides intros when asked	Unsolicited referrals	Disciple
Values advisor relationship	Self-advisor	Focused on fees/costs	Family/friend as advisor	Professional advisor	High value on advice; you manage all their assets
Social network/contacts	No connections	Newly affiliated	Follower	Influencer	Connector
Quality of relationship	No personal relationship	Responsive	You spend some personal time together	Trust, friendship, frequent social contact	Intimate friend
Philanthropic mindset	None	Sporadic donors	Consistent donors	Part of charity (board member, for example)	Family foundations

Willingness to refer

Some clients want to keep you for themselves; others freely share you with their network, especially if you've asked them to do so. I call the best clients in this category "disciples," because they're always sharing with members of their networks how good you make them feel about their financial security and future.

Values advisor relationship

Some clients value your services much more than others. Those who value your services most are more engaged and appreciative, easier to work with, and energizing. Because they respect you as a professional and value what you do, you're more eager to help them, and they're more receptive to your recommendations, which warrants a higher score.

Social network/contacts

Clients who have an extensive network of family, friends, and colleagues and who proactively connect you to people in their network score best, whereas hermits aren't highly prized.

TIP

Folks who are followers or influencers can grow into connectors, so make sure to revisit this assessment annually.

Quality of relationship

Frequently clients can become your best friends. I often hear successful financial advisors say that their best friend happens to also be their best client. As a financial advisor, you spend so much time with your clients, especially your best clients, so naturally you'll develop relationships with certain clients who are intimate, caring, and even loving.

Philanthropic mindset

Clients who have causes or charitable interests need additional planning and collaboration with other professionals. This broader scope circulates you among their tax advisors and estate planning attorneys. It also provides you an entry point to specific nonprofits that are always interested in learning ways to increase donor engagement. Such elevated sophistication is a great method to up-market your practice and business revenues. It's a great example of doing well by doing good.

Assigning clients to service level brackets

Table 16-4 shows the total score ranges that apply to each service level bracket. After tallying a client's score, simply use this table to find out which service level the client qualifies for.

TABLE 16-4:

Clients to Service Levels Based on Score

Client Tier	Client Score
Platinum	45–50
Gold	40–44
Silver	30–39
Bronze	0–29

REMEMBER

Don't be surprised if a client you considered Silver is actually Platinum. Clients I naturally assumed were at least Gold sometimes showed up as Silver, and some Silver clients turned out to be Platinum. The weightings for each factor are all equal, so strengths in some areas can make up for weaknesses in other areas. For example, a client who may not be a big direct revenue generator for you, could still be a Platinum-tiered client, deserving that elevated service level because he scores highly in other critical areas, such as being a connector and disciple to your efforts.

Rewarding Quality Clients

Although you're always rewarding clients by providing quality service, you should do a little extra for your quality clients. In this section, I provide suggestions for three ways to reward your best clients, along with some tips on getting the most bang for your time and expense in delivering the rewards.

WARNING

Always check with your broker/dealer before giving gifts or rewards of any kind to your clients. The Federal Industry Regulatory Agency (FINRA) has many specific rules and compliance guidelines that vary from firm to firm. Usually, you're expected to log and submit all client-related gift and entertainment expenses and adhere to nonreportable threshold amounts. Even if these regulations weren't in place, you should limit your gift giving; you don't want to come across as someone who's buying a client's business. Besides, clients may wonder where you got all that money to wine and dine clientele.

Hosting special events

TIP

Consider hosting a special event once a year that's open to all clients and their families and friends. You provide the food, soft drinks, and entertainment. Make the event a no-sales zone, so clients and prospects and their families and friends can focus on getting to know you on a personal level. Dress casually, and leave the business agenda at the office. The most business-y thing you can do at the event is to have people sign a registry to provide their contact information (with your promise not to share that information). You may even want to have a prize drawing to make the registration more festive.

After the event, send follow-up cards to all clients and anyone who registered at the event. Make the card consistent in appearance and tone with the original invitation. Thank the recipients for coming and invite them to schedule an office visit at a later date, so you can find out how to add value to their financial lives.

Inviting clients to breakfast or lunch

Working lunches or business lunches (or breakfasts) are wonderful ways to meet with prospective or existing clients. Reserve dinners for only your top-tier client relationships. Follow these guidelines for taking a client or a prospect to lunch:

>> **Ask questions and listen.** Use this time together to find out more about your client's mindset and concerns instead of flooding his brains with information that'll only spoil the meal.

>> **Don't use printed materials at the table.** Trying to show illustrations, graphs, tables, and other material ends up being clumsy and awkward, especially when the server comes by to take orders, deliver food, and the like.

A NO-SELL ZONE BEACH PARTY

In Southern California, where my practice has been based for more than 20 years, the beginning of summer is a festive and celebrated event. Having lived my first 20 years on the East Coast, I'm impressed that SoCal summer excites residents because they have such great weather the majority of the year already. Termed "Opening Day," festivities occur at the local beach, yacht, and other social clubs — usually near the coastline.

One year, we invited all our clients (regardless of relationship size or revenue threshold) to come and bring their children, relatives, and friends who may also enjoy the day. Such a low-key celebration, which included electric boat rides, paddle boarding, and other activities, provided a great way for our clients to see us in something other than business suits (swim suits mostly that day), and no business agenda to discuss.

For the new faces in attendance, this was a chance to introduce ourselves, thank them for attending, and get to know a little about them. No sales and no pitching of any kind was allowed. This was a sales-free zone. We wanted folks to meet and interact with our team in a fun, authentic environment. That's how people get a *feel* for us, which is hard to do in sterile, orchestrated business meetings.

>> **If you must use materials, prepare a folder ahead of time containing the items you want to share but hold onto it until you're done eating and the table is cleared.** During your mealtime conversation, convey the gist of whatever you're meeting to tell the client about. After the table is cleared, share the folder and let your client know that you'll follow up to schedule time to review the enclosed items and answer any questions he may have before moving forward. The meal conversation conveys the general concept, and the folder provides the details.

WARNING

Don't order dessert, because it prolongs the process of sharing some closing discussion items in printed form.

>> **Allow only one lunch per prospective client.** Don't get into the habit of spending money taking the same person out to lunch time and again, hoping for business to materialize. The point of the lunch meeting is to connect away from an office environment and have more of a discussion and conversation, during which you find out more about the client's needs and desired outcomes. You don't need more than one meeting to achieve this objective.

>> **Allow only one lunch per existing client per year.** If this client is segmented into a dinner-eligible client, then you can justify two or even three lunches per year in place of an annual dinner.

TIP

The big trend lately is to dress down in a business setting, but I still wear a suit and tie every day and to every client meeting for two reasons: First, putting on a suit and tie functions like putting on my armor. It prepares me mentally for the day ahead and the challenges I'll face whether from the market or from my clients' concerns, worries, or rejections. Second, business attire signifies to your client or prospect that you're a professional. Wearing jeans and a blazer, though it's acceptable (and here in SoCal seems to be a uniform), doesn't bring the same gravitas to your meetings or interactions. Business attire still carries a visual cue that important and critical work is in the works, whether you're in the office or at a formal or semiformal social function such as a dinner or event.

Recognizing the need to budget your time

As is the situation in my practice, my best clients spend time with me personally. Conducting regular in-person portfolio and financial planning meetings, usually over lunch, works best. In my commuting situation, one client lunch a day means I'm away from the office for more than three or four hours: 1.5 hours for lunch plus 1.5 to 2.5 hours in round-trip travel in Southern California traffic. This time expense is all the more reason to reserve it for those Platinum clients who value your advice and share you regularly with others.

SPENDING MORE TIME IN LEGACY PLANNING

One of my clients is a charitable widow in her 80s with no children and an active travel schedule. We meet quarterly to review her portfolio, which consists of multiple accounts (qualified and nonqualified), life insurance, charitable gift annuities, commercial income annuities, and other nonmanaged, nonmarketable securities and assets (for example, real estate and collectibles). Our meetings take place at her favorite lunch spot. It's not a casual environment, although other diners may be dressed in Hawaiian shirts.

A folder prepared with portfolio details sits quietly on the booth seat next to me, as I share from memory all the commentary that I know she's routinely interested in hearing. After she orders her favorite dish, we turn the conversation back to her and where she's at regarding legacy planning. We take our time. Trying to rush a conversation about what the meaning of her life has been and what she wants to leave behind as her lasting mark would be dangerous.

Legacy planning is best when clients have the time to breathe, think, and reflect. No protocol governs the amount of time you spend discussing legacy matters with a client, but the time commitment must make sense financially. A client who represents at least 3 percent of your recurring annual revenues is well worth your time in this area. If your *total* annual income from all clients is $100,000 in the form of recurring fee-based revenue, a client making you $3,000 per year deserves your time and focus. You're rewarded for going deeper into the other financial planning areas such as charity or legacy planning. Expanded revenue may come from the client or from a referral to a friend or family member who she's inspired to introduce you.

Chapter **17**

Benchmarking Performance

G iven that this book is called *Success as a Financial Advisor For Dummies*, it should contain some way to measure success. What's the metric? Is it the number of clients you have? Your annual income? The average return on your clients' portfolios? Or is it something else?

Throughout this book, I encourage you to tie your success to that of your clients, but choosing a client success metric isn't easy either. You can be successful with one client by growing her portfolio by an average of 8 percent year over year and another by having a life insurance policy in place when the family's major bread-winner passes away, saving the client's family from financial ruin. In other professions, success and failure are fairly obvious, such as winning or losing court cases or performing life-saving surgeries on patients. In this profession, success and failure can take many forms.

Yet, accountability is a key factor to keeping you on your toes and figuring out where you need to work on improving your game. Benchmarking performance is also a great way to communicate your value to clients and prospects. As a result, you need to have some way to determine how successful you are that's tied to your clients' success.

In this chapter, I explain how to benchmark your performance *for each client* and educate your clients on their progress or failure toward their financial objectives (short term) and goals (longer term). This approach includes popular portfolio benchmarking (along with an explanation of its limitations), as well as an alternative personal benchmarking method that may make more sense for your practice.

Measuring Portfolio Success Against a Chosen Index

No doubt about it, a big part of your success, at least from your clients' perspective is tied to their portfolio performance. If their portfolios aren't performing as well as their stock market index of choice, they may start to question the value you're delivering. If their portfolios are outperforming that index, you're their hero.

Although I prefer not to measure my success solely based on the performance of each client's portfolio, that performance indicator is certainly one factor in my overall success with any client, and it's a major focus for most clients. The challenge is to figure out how to use those stock market indexes in a way that provides a more accurate measure of success while educating clients to do the same.

In this section, I explain how to tune into the client's mindset and recognize the limitations of the leading stock market indexes, present the pros and cons of blended benchmarks, and provide a method for using indexes as performance benchmarks that provides a more accurate indication of a portfolio's performance in a way that most clients understand.

Tuning in to the clients' mindset

If you ask clients what they expect from you, most reply, "To make money, of course!" Your new clients are unlikely to have the same formal approach to allocating capital that you have (see Chapter 7 for details about asset management). More than likely, a client-made investment portfolio looks like a collection of favorite tchotchkes accumulated over time. Their measure of success is that they have more money today than they did yesterday or a year ago or ten years ago.

More sophisticated novices use one of the market indexes, such as the Dow Jones Industrial Average (DJIA) or the Standard & Poor's 500 (S&P 500). They keep an eye on their portfolio's performance and see how the stock market is doing by watching the nightly news or checking their favorite stock market news website to see how the Dow, S&P 500, and Nasdaq have performed. As long as their portfolio is performing as well or better than their chosen index, they claim victory.

Similarly, a German-based investor who looks at the Deutscher Aktienindex (DAX) and then compares it to her portfolio would most likely come to the same assessment. If the index is up, and my portfolio is keeping pace, then all is good (or "alles ist gut" in the case of the German investor).

Recognizing the limitations of stock market indexes

Whether they're tracking indexes in the U.S., Germany, China, Japan, or somewhere else, investors, who share the goal to make money, are using rough guides to judge their success or failure. The DJIA reflects the performance of only 30 blue chip companies in the United States, weighted by share price; the S&P 500 reflects the performance of the only the top 500 companies in the United States, weighted by market capitalization; and the DAX reflects the performance of only the top 30 blue chip German companies.

To measure success more accurately, you'd have to analyze the composition of the investor's portfolio. Assuming a client invests exclusively in blue chip companies or those with large capitalizations in the country of the index's origin, the client's chosen index may be a fairly accurate benchmark for her portfolio's performance. This is especially true if the client invests in an index mutual fund or exchange traded fund (ETF). However, considering that most investors diversify to some extent, any given index is likely to be a poor choice for an overall portfolio benchmark. After all, according to Morgan Stanley Capital International (MSCI) research, the world has 23 developed markets, each with numerous sectors and many companies with a wide range of share prices and market capitalizations.

According to the MSCI World Index, the United States represents 52 percent of the world's stock market capitalization, which means 48 percent of the value of the world's stock markets is outside of the U.S. More sophisticated investors, such as financial advisors, understand that there's a world of opportunity when it comes to capital allocation. For example, according to the Callan Periodic Table of Investment Returns, the U.S. stock market has outperformed the rest of the developed world less than half, 45 percent of the time, from 1998 through 2017. For clients who invest any part of their portfolio in foreign markets, using a U.S. market index as their benchmark makes little sense.

Using a blended benchmark

Many performance-reporting programs today use blended benchmarks. A *blended benchmark* is a combination of market indexes that are weighted to match a portfolio's asset allocation. For example, if a client's portfolio comprises 60 percent U.S. stocks, 20 percent non-U.S. stocks, and 20 bonds, then a blended benchmark may comprise 60 percent S&P 500 index, 20 percent MSCI EAFE (Europe, Austral-asia, and Far East) index, and 20 percent Bloomberg Barclays Aggregate Bond Index. However, depending on the sub-asset allocation within U.S., non-U.S., and bonds, these indexes may or may not be relevant comparisons. For example, if the U.S. stocks are concentrated 20/20/20 across large/mid/small cap stocks, then only 20 percent of the U.S. stocks are a fair comparison to the S&P 500. Likewise, if 20 percent of the portfolio allocation is in country-specific ETFs in the United Kingdom, South Africa, and China, then the MSCI EAFE is a poor benchmark for that portion of the portfolio's allocation.

Through the discussion presented in this and the previous section, you begin to realize the potential messiness of benchmarking portfolio performance. In an effort to try to simplify the benchmarking of portfolio performance, the industry has provided too much detail that's mostly irrelevant to investor's overarching need — to know whether she's getting the performance she needs to achieve her financial goals.

Keeping it simple with your clients

Any benchmark you use to evaluate your client's portfolio performance should be:

>> *Understandable* to you and your client

>> *Relevant* to the client's goals and objectives

After years of reviewing performance reports with clients and attempting to explain the not quite tailored benchmarking system, I've found that simple comparisons are best. If most U.S. investors use the S&P 500, DJIA, or Nasdaq as their yardstick for assessing their portfolio performance, why fight it? A better option is to translate these indexes in a way that deepens the client's understanding, so she can more easily grasp complicated concepts, such as risk-adjusted returns.

For example, a great way to explain risk-adjusted returns is to use *up-market* and *down-market capture ratios*. These ratios are the percentage of the portfolio's returns as compared to the chosen index's returns for the same up or down period as reflected by the index:

$$\text{Up/Down-Market Ratio} = \frac{\text{Portfolio's Returns}}{\text{Index's Returns}} \times 100$$

As long as the up-market ratio is higher than the down-market ratio, your client shouldn't be concerned because the portfolio value is outperforming the index.

For example, if you're managing a client portfolio that has an aggressive growth risk profile, you can highlight the percentage of U.S. large cap stocks in the client's portfolio. Suppose it's 30 percent. You tell your client that you're going to use the DJIA as the portfolio's benchmark. Forget about all the other market allocations. They don't matter. All your client wants is a portfolio that goes up when DJIA rises and goes down *less* when the market crashes. Suppose the client's portfolio value is $200,000:

>> In a period when the DJIA rises 10 percent from 24,000 to 26,400, a gain of 2,400, the portfolio gains only 8 percent or $16,000 and is now at $216,000.

>> In a subsequent period when the DJIA drops 10 percent from 26,400 to 23,760, the portfolio loses only 6 percent or $12,960, going from $216,000 down to $203,040.

In this example, the DJIA *lost* 1 percent of its value (from 24,000 at the start to 23,760 at the end), whereas the portfolio *gained* 1.52 percent value (from 200,000 at the start to $203,040 at the end). In this context, the fact that the portfolio gained only 80 percent of the DJIA return during the up period (8 percent as compared to the 10 percent rise in the DJIA), the risk-adjusted portfolio outperformed the DJIA overall.

Admittedly, this approach to leading a client to an understanding of risk-adjusted returns is extremely simplified. What's important is that the client understands the trade-offs between risks and returns and the necessity to achieve a balance by limiting exposure to high-return investments that carry equally high risks. If you can deliver the message and the result, you'll always be seen as a successful advisor in your client's eyes.

REMEMBER

Given how messy and complicated traditional portfolio benchmarking can be, the industry has seen a rise in alternative forms of measuring success, as the next section discusses. However, regardless of the benchmark you choose, make sure it complies with these two rules: you and your client understand the benchmark, and it's relevant to your client's goals.

Riding the Personal Benchmark Trend

The *personal benchmark* is a measure of a client's portfolio performance that reflects whether the client is on track to achieve the agreed-upon goals and objectives. You figure out how much money the client needs to meet a goal and then calculate the contribution amounts and required rate of return to achieve that goal. *Required rate of return (RRR)* is the minimum percentage an investor will accept from an investment given the investment's level of risk.

In this section, I explain how to calculate RRR and why clients are often receptive to this benchmark. I also reveal the risk of using this approach and how to lessen that risk.

Establishing the client's personal benchmark

Calculating a client's personal benchmark RRR is a form of reverse engineering. You figure out how much the client needs to fund a particular goal, such as retirement or sending a child to college, and you work back from there. Several methods are available to calculate RRR. Here's a simple method:

1. **Determine the amount of money needed to fund the client's financial goal.**

   The method for determining this amount depends on the goal. For example, if the client decides she needs 80 percent of her current income to retire comfortably, you must figure out how much money needs to be in her retirement account at the age at which she plans to retire based on her projected monthly distributions and how long she plans to live. (See Chapter 7 for details.)

2. **Assist the client in deciding how much money she can afford to invest (usually monthly) toward that goal.**

   This amount depends on the client's income, savings, and desire and ability to sacrifice. Start with a ballpark figure and then tweak it in Step 4.

3. **Choose a reasonable rate of return on the amount invested, such as 4 to 6 percent.**

   This is guesswork; you'll hone in on a more precise and realistic percentage in Step 4.

4. **Work with the client to play with the values from Steps 2 and 3 to achieve the agreed-upon goal from Step 1.**

   You may even need to change the goal in Step 1 if that goal is unreasonably aggressive.

For example, after reviewing a client's current household expenses, you know she'll need $100,000 per year in retirement, which is 25 years away, in addition to her Social Security income. That $100,000 needs to be adjusted at a 3 percent annual inflation rate. Using your trusty calculator, you find that she'll need $209,377 per year in the first year of retirement to maintain her lifestyle.

TIP

If you need a refresher on how to use your analyst calculator's *time value of money function*, check out this YouTube video: www.youtube.com/watch?v=nScQsMmohZ0.

Assuming a portfolio withdrawal rate of 5 percent starting her first year of retirement, she'll have to accumulate $4,187,540 by that time. Meanwhile, she'll be able to invest $20,000 per year starting now through year 25. With these numbers, her RRR is 14.03 percent to achieve her goal. Unfortunately, such a high required rate of return would be significantly challenging to achieve, so she'll have to save more to reduce the required rate.

If she doubled her savings to $40,000 per year, the RRR drops to 9.73 percent per year. You can continue to edit the inputs (from Steps 2 and 3) and possibly the post-retirement income goal (from Step 1) until you find the sweet spot, which should be in the 5 to 7 percent return range, and she'd have to accept a high risk account profile to achieve that target.

This example doesn't include additional details, such as the fact that the client's retirement income will need to be adjusted for inflation. It also doesn't account for whether she plans to leave a legacy payment to her beneficiaries or have the final check sent to the undertaker. These two scenarios have different ongoing required rates of return when withdrawals begin.

REMEMBER

The personal benchmark is attractive primarily due to its simplicity and practical application. It quantifies the financial plan while connecting it to the client's goals and objectives, and it shifts the client's focus from the wild swings of stock market indexes to a steady-as-she-goes metric.

Using the personal benchmark to keep calm a client's nerves

The big drawback of the personal benchmark is that significant portfolio under-performance relative to the benchmark, even in the short term, can cause clients to be concerned, which is certainly understandable. If your client feels that he is way off track, he feel pressured to take even greater risks to score a bigger return to make up the difference. Or, if they're nearing retirement or already in retirement, they feel the urge to cut their losses out of fear that unless they do so, they'll lose everything.

TIP

One way to keep yourself and your clients calm during market swings is to maintain focus on the personal benchmark with the understanding that a client's risk tolerance generally shifts significantly before and after retirement. These periods are often referred to as phases:

>> **Accumulation phase:** The period during which a client is building her retirement nest egg, she should be less concerned about market fluctuations, as long as the *average* annual return hits the target (the RRR).

>> **Withdrawal phase:** The period during which a client is taking distributions, she focuses more on the portfolio's value. A significant drop in value causes concern or even panic. Withdrawing money from a portfolio when it's going through a rough patch is like adding insult to injury. The portfolio will be more negatively impacted when withdrawing on an already reduced market value.

The good news is that during the accumulation phase, the sequence of investment returns doesn't matter. Although most clients don't understand this phenomenon, believing that fluctuating portfolio returns once a withdrawal phase has begun is the same as when she's accumulating portfolio assets. The math shows how different these two portfolio realities are.

During the withdrawal phase (as in retirement), the sequence of investment returns matters *more* than the returns themselves, as shown in Table 17-1. In this table, both portfolios 1 and 2 have the same average annualized return of 9.94 percent and were invested in the S&P 500 index. The difference is that I flipped the sequence of returns for portfolio 2, so it's opposite of portfolio 1. Even though the same amount was withdrawn over the course of those 11 years (assuming a 5 percent initial annual withdrawal rate, adjusted 3 percent each year for inflation), portfolio 2 has nearly $500,000 more value at the end of the term.

This isn't magic, just simple math. If your client experiences big negatives at the beginning of her withdrawal cycle, then she's going to have a big challenge getting back to par. In both cases these portfolios have more than the $1,000,000 by the end of the period (in 2017), even having gone through the second worst recession in U.S. history (2007–2008 and multiple market corrections along the way). However, in 2008, portfolio 1 worked its way down to $581,587 compared to portfolio 2's $1,256,528. Managing to keep the client invested in portfolio 1 would be an extremely challenging project.

TABLE 17-1:   ## Sequence of Returns during the Withdrawal Phase

	Portfolio 1			Portfolio 2		
Year	Return	Withdrawal	Balance	Return	Withdrawal	Balance
2007	5.49%	$50,000.00	$1,004,900.00	21.83%	$50,000.00	$1,168,300.00
2008	-37.00%	$51,500.00	$581,587.00	11.96%	$51,500.00	$1,256,528.68
2009	26.47%	$53,045.00	$682,488.08	1.38%	$53,045.00	$1,220,823.78
2010	15.06%	$54,636.35	$730,634.43	13.69%	$54,636.35	$1,333,318.20
2011	2.11%	$56,275.44	$689,775.38	32.39%	$56,275.44	$1,708,904.53
2012	16.00%	$57,963.70	$742,175.74	16.00%	$57,963.70	$1,924,365.55
2013	32.39%	$59,702.61	$922,863.84	2.11%	$59,702.61	$1,905,267.04
2014	13.69%	$61,493.69	$987,710.21	15.06%	$61,493.69	$2,130,706.57
2015	1.38%	$63,338.50	$938,002.11	26.47%	$63,338.50	$2,631,366.09
2016	11.96%	$65,238.66	$984,948.50	-37.00%	$65,238.66	$1,592,521.98
2017	21.83%	$67,195.82	$1,132,766.94	5.49%	$67,195.82	$1,612,755.62
	9.94%	**$640,389.78**	**$1,132,766.94**	**9.94%**	**$640,389.78**	**$1,612,755.62**

What this means for most clients entering into retirement, a time when they depend on their investment portfolio to provide sustainable, lifetime supplemental income, is that moving from the accumulation phase to the withdrawal phase can be disorienting and nerve-wracking.

A high-risk-profile client who's been socking away money into her 401K plan over the course of a decade or more and owning all stock funds doesn't care about the sequence of returns as much as the average annualized return until retirement. . . when all the math changes. In retirement, in the aftermath of a market crash when your client sees a significant drop in portfolio value, she's likely to get spooked and start looking for the exits, even though remaining invested is the best way for her to keep pace with inflation. Had the owner of portfolio 1 shifted to cash in 2008 and continued withdrawing the designated amounts, she would have been nearly broke by 2017 with $42,697.23 remaining in her account. By staying invested, she has $1,132,766.94, which is $127,866.94 more than she started with.

Through the use of the personal benchmark and one or more tables like Table 17-1, you can calm your clients' fears during both the accumulation and withdrawal phases to convince them to stick with the plan.

TIP

For clients who worry about having enough income to live on in their retirement years, consider purchasing income annuities or building cash values in whole life policies, to cover half or all of the client's nondiscretionary household living expenses. Just keep in mind that income annuities don't adjust with inflation, so the client probably still needs a certain amount of growth-oriented investments in her portfolio to keep pace with inflation. Regardless, she can diversify away risk from bear markets during the withdrawal phase by relieving the burden of income delivery solely from her portfolio.

Using both relative and absolute benchmarks

I recommend keeping clients informed about portfolio performance through both relative and absolute benchmarks:

>> **Relative benchmarks** are useful for showcasing how the portfolio is performing as compared to an index or blended index.

>> **Absolute benchmarks** (such as the personal benchmark) target a specific rate of return and are useful for ensuring that the client is on track to meet agreed-upon goals.

THE PROMISE OF CONSISTENTLY POSITIVE RETURNS

Mutual fund developers have come up with a bunch of new products that are marketed to financial advisors offering investment portfolios that target positive returns, each and every year, regardless of market conditions. Most of these retail funds came into existence after 2008, showing up too late for many investors who needed those a year prior.

Absolute return funds hold a variety of assets, including large cash positions, stocks, commodities, derivatives, and fixed income. During bull markets they tend to underperform significantly, which frustrates investors, but they can be useful for certain clients and applications.

Tailoring Performance to Each Client's Needs

Performing well for clients is about performing well for *each* client individually according to her unique needs. Your value to a client may be tied primarily to the performance of her investment portfolio, but it may depend on something else entirely, such as your ability to provide a holistic solution that both builds and protects wealth, your knack for talking clients out of making foolish financial decisions, your ability to calm clients when other investors are in a panic, your receptiveness to a client's ideas and suggestions, or your personal and professional integrity.

For example, one of my clients is a nonprofit administrator, a good saver, single, has no children, and is a few years away from retirement. Like most people without children, she didn't have heirs or beneficiaries weighing heavy on her mind in terms of financial planning.

This client's scenario, single without children, pushed other questions and concerns to the forefront, such as the following:

>> Who will make sure I'm taken care of when I no longer can do so for myself?

>> Will I be able to afford long-term care should I need it?

>> Who will look after my finances and pay my bills?

>> Should I give my remaining assets to extended family or is it better to leave it charity?

In terms of her portfolio, she needed to achieve a superior risk-adjusted return, but that alone didn't cut to the core of what concerned her most. She had bigger concerns on her plate about what her life would look like if she were no longer able to care for herself, because as she said, "there would be no one who'll be checking up on me regularly."

For this client, the use of an independent institutional or corporate trustee, regulated by the Office of the Comptroller of the Currency (OCC), a division of the U.S. Treasury Department, could solve several of her issues. Conducting due diligence on various trustees — fees, flexibility, and services — played an integral role in delivering value — her overall peace of mind.

In this case, my job extended far beyond portfolio management. I had to make sure that the governing documents for her estate were complete, which took more than four years, due mostly to my client's hesitation to make specific medical directive or powers of attorney decisions. Taking time to steward this process was well worth it to deliver the desired outcomes.

Ultimately, as she ages and has other life events, her mind may change, and that's fine. Documents can be amended to reflect any changes in her sentiments or situation. The bottom line is that she now has a plan in place to address the issues that were keeping her up at night. She didn't really need superior portfolio performance.

REMEMBER

The moral of this extended example is that *your* performance is directly related to your ability to listen and address each client's concerns regardless of whether they're related to portfolio performance.

Own It! Don't Make Excuses for Poor Performance

A benchmark is like a grade on a test. It indicates whether an investment, solution, or strategy is working as planned. If something you're doing or recommending falls short of the benchmark, it's not something you need to beat yourself up over or make excuses for. It's merely an indication that you need to take a closer look at what's going on and perhaps make adjustments.

TIP

The best way to avoid having to make excuses for the poor performance of a product or solution is to do your homework before recommending it. For example, if you're not familiar with the inner workings of a product, start by conducting your own analysis using a tool like Morningstar. Then, get on the phone with the money manager or solution wholesaler and start asking questions until you fully understand the risk-reward trade-off and have confidence in the company and manager offering the product or solution.

Whenever a certain course of action isn't delivering the targeted outcome, take action. Here are a few suggestions:

>> If you're managing your client's assets (see Chapter 7) and are unable to achieve the targeted returns, consider switching to a turnkey asset management program (TAMP), many of which are available in today's marketplace. Most of these have basic index model portfolios, which deliver no-frills-portfolio returns. Outsourcing portfolio management is better than grossly underperforming a return target year-after-year.

>> If an investment solution you recommended isn't performing as expected, let your client know that you're on top of it and will closely monitor the situation over the next quarter for any signs of improvement or further deterioration. Don't wait for your client to come to you.

>> Communicate to your client the specific issues that are contributing to the poor performance, whether it's a bad stock pick or just that the broader stock market happens to be going through it's normal cycle. This distinction is vital to keeping clients on track.

REMEMBER

The bottom line: Don't make excuses for your recommended solution's bad performance. Excuses only make matters worse, and you'll end up losing a client and, even worse, your confidence in providing service to clients.

4

Building Your Clientele

Prove to your clients that you're well worth the investment they're making in your services.

Increase demand for your services through savvy marketing and networking, so you can charge top dollar and always have more than enough clients.

Network and team up with other relevant professionals to improve your level of service, develop new skills, and drum up more business.

Chapter **18**

Earning Clients and Making a Career for a Lifetime

I use the word "earning" in the chapter's title deliberately. Too often, I hear financial professionals talk about winning, closing, or selling clients in relation to client acquisition and building their business. Earning clients is what you should be doing, because it's the sincerest of intentions. You don't need to fake it to make it. In addition to being the best way to attract and retain clients, earning clients provides the satisfaction of having shared your knowledge and experience to help clients achieve their life goals.

When you're earning new clients — earning the honor to serve the financial needs and goals of your clients — you soon discover that it's a secure lifetime career. Like the family doctor and family lawyer, a family's financial advisor plays an integral role in the family's overall success and wellbeing, which is a rewarding role to play.

One of the benefits of earning your clients' trust and appreciation is that you don't have to worry about winning or selling clients. You don't even have to ask clients for referrals. Word of your value spreads, and new prospects come banging at your door.

Financial advisors don't arrive at this point by accident. They have to earn it. In this chapter, I show you how.

Adding Value before Asking for Referrals

One of the biggest mistakes I see many financial investors make is asking for referrals too soon, sometimes as soon as after the first meeting. If that doesn't scream sales, I don't know what does. Asking new clients for referrals is more likely to drive them away than attract new ones. You may lose a prospect and end up with a stack of fake names and phony phone numbers.

REMEMBER

When you're working with clients, focus solely on earning their business first by following this five-step approach (a process you may follow over one or more sessions depending on the client):

1. **Assess the client's needs.**

   She talks. You ask questions and listen.

2. **Make sure you understand what your client is telling you.**

   Repeat back what you heard her say during Step 1, just to be sure you understand. This opportunity allows you to correct any misunderstanding and clarify your client's goals.

3. **Share solutions and your rationale behind them.**

   Be transparent. The more you obscure, the less authentic you'll sound, which will short-circuit your goal of earning your client's trust.

4. **Review what you proposed and gather feedback from your client.**

   Find out what your client thinks about your recommendations.

5. **Agree on the solutions, terms of engagement, and relationship expectations.**

The amount of time spent on each step and the total duration of this process vary from client to client. A client may require five separate meetings over the course of several weeks, or you may be able to wrap it up in a single session. The pace and duration depend a great deal on how ready the client is to start the journey.

Making a choice: Sales or consulting

Financial advisors are often torn between two business models — sales and consulting. The choice is reflected in the two primary compensation models — commissions and fees. Whether you should be asking for referrals early in your relationship with a customer or client depends in large part whether you want to operate as a salesperson or a financial advisor. You just need to decide how you want to practice, because you're unlikely to be successful trying to do both:

>> **Salesperson:** If you want to operate as a salesperson, then asking customers for referrals is fine. Your customers know you're in sales, so they won't be put off by an obvious sales tactic.

>> **Advisor:** If you want to operate as an advisor, avoid any perception of selling or asking clients to sell for you, which is essentially what you're doing if you're asking them for leads.

Personally, I've never felt easy asking for referrals, mostly because I've never put myself in a 100 percent "living off what I kill" commissioned compensation structure. Though the vast majority of financial advisors entering the profession do need to fend for themselves, I don't believe that they're necessarily destined for sales.

REMEMBER

The world is trending toward the do-it-yourself, self-service model, which threatens the profitability of the sales model. The Internet offers efficient methods for households to buy all sorts of financial products. More and more investors are using online brokers, so they can place $4.95 trades and get streaming portfolio updates. If you decide to operate as a salesperson, you'll be competing against all that. The reason people hire a financial advisor is that they know a financial professional adds more value than they get from $4.95 trades, which makes advising more sustainable than selling. Just something to think about as you choose a business model.

Differentiating yourself as a trusted advisor

Client acquisition is a fragile area. You want new clients who are excited and motivated to see that their finances and planning are in good order. However, more often than not, clients don't have an experience of getting good guidance and advice in this area, so many are just sold to; they've been treated like customers, not clients.

FEELING GOOD ABOUT IT

The best financial advisors I know want to make a good living, but even more important is that they want to feel good about what they're doing. Schlepping product doesn't feel good to them. They're constantly asking themselves where and how they add value to people's lives, which becomes their focus.

If you're finding yourself leaning toward sales instead of advising, I suggest you flip your script and start thinking about ways to deliver value to your clients. Your goal should be to deliver a comprehensive solution and an experience that you and your client both find rewarding.

The unique value you offer is your secret weapon to earning clients and having prospects line up down the street waiting to meet with you.

The fact that many clients are sold to provides you with a golden opportunity to differentiate yourself simply by doing the opposite — treating prospects as clients. Take your time. Be methodical. Make recommendations only when you feel confident that they're in your client's best interests. By understanding who your client is, how he thinks, and what the motivations are behind his decisions, you not only earn a new client, but you also earn an advocate who will sing your praises.

Speaking to Clients in Plain English

One way to earn clients is to speak with them in plain English . . . or in plain whatever language the two of you speak. Tossing around financial jargon may convey the sense that you know what you're talking about, but it brings negative value to clients who can't benefit from it. Save the jargon for shop talk with colleagues or when you're networking with other financial professionals to grow your network.

The ultimate goal of communicating clearly to clients is so they can understand the value that you're proposing to bring to them. As a bonus, if they clearly understand what you're saying, they'll be better equipped to articulate your value to others.

TIP

Here are a few suggestions for more effectively connecting and communicating with clients:

>> **Define your terms.** When introducing a financial term, assume your clients have zero understanding of it, but introduce the term and define it without being condescending. For example, you may say something like, "You're probably aware of the difference between investment income and distributions, but I've found too often it's not totally understood."

>> **Explain what it means and how it works.** Near the end of an intense meeting, new clients of mine often say, "Wow, feels like I just went to a college class. Thank you, Professor Ivan!" The first few times I heard this I wondered whether I'd been too technical and too thorough, and my clients were needling me about it. But, as the years went on, I realized more and more that clients were happy that I was taking the time to explain not only what something means, but also, and more importantly, how something works.

Clients are likely to feel uncomfortable if you're recommending something they don't understand, so make sure they understand.

REMEMBER

>> **When describing a financial product, use simple terminology along with appropriate metaphors.** A common description of a portfolio includes many technical terms, such as "strategic and tactical asset allocation." The terminology sounds sophisticated, but you need to explain it in a way that clients understand the practical implications — the effect that a certain course of action (or doing nothing) will have on them. When you bring clients a new level of understanding, they're reminded of why they're working with you. (See the example in the nearby sidebar.)

>> **Ask clients to explain the terminology they use.** When a client asks a sophisticated question or one that sounds sophisticated or challenging, don't be put off or go on the defensive. Instead, ask where he learned about that topic, so you know your client's understanding of the topic before offering your own explanation. Assuming you're speaking in plain English and clearly explaining yourself, you can hold your clients to the same standard.

>> **Take time to respond.** For example, if a client asks about a certain product or strategy, you may want to start your response with something along the lines of "Well, that can be complicated and have good and bad aspects to it, which would need to be considered before putting any money toward it." Every option has pros and cons. By starting your response in this way, you give yourself additional time to respond and a segue to lead the client through the process of considering the options.

>> **Keep it short and sweet.** This is my version of the helpful presentation acronym, KISS. The mark of a successful financial advisor is the use of few words to present complex concepts or strategies. However, don't simplify by omitting the potentially negative aspects of a strategy or option. Give the pros and cons equal coverage, and keep the explanation of each short and sweet.

EXPLAINING STRATEGIC AND TACTICAL ASSET MANAGEMENT

Getting new clients to understand the concepts of strategic and tactical asset management and the difference between the two can go a long way toward earning their trust and getting their buy-in on whatever investment strategy you recommend.

Strategic asset allocation is often described as the only free lunch available in investing. I define it as the practice of "having enough different investments in the account, so that they all zig-and-zag in different ways at different times." I want them to understand that the main benefit to portfolio asset diversification is that when you get it right, profit naturally appears. When various holdings show price movements that differ a little or a lot from each other is when strategic asset allocation delivers the greatest financial benefit.

Adding *tactical asset allocation* is then just figuring out which holdings you want to focus on at different times. Maybe you want to exclude entire sectors or put more money toward a part of the market. Those decisions can add or subtract big value, depending on whether you're right or wrong.

Showcasing Your Value Proposition

A *value proposition* is a product or service that makes a business attractive to customers. Financial advisors and other business professionals often stress the importance of creating a value proposition and presenting it to customers, but few of these same professionals follow this advice. I recommend that you become one of the few financial advisors who showcases his value proposition in both words and practice.

After all, if you're not showcasing your value proposition during a meeting with a prospective or existing client, then you may as well not have the meeting. Like a patient going to the doctor for diagnosis and treatment or a client seeking counsel from an attorney, your clients step into your office wanting something of value. They didn't show up just for the free pen, the refrigerator magnet, or the glitzy presentation. They want to know where and why they're allocating capital in the manner you recommend.

REMEMBER

Your value is your expertise and the outcomes you're able to deliver through the use of that expertise. Clients choose you based on the knowledge and skills you have to benefit them financially. Everyone assumes that a skilled professional is using the latest and greatest tools, so don't hide behind product illustrations, graphs, charts, or portfolio proposals. Focus instead on what *you*, as a financial professional, can do for your client.

Make sure your clients understand your value proposition. Use the following techniques to be sure nothing gets lost in translation.

Ask clients about their past experiences

Question prospective clients about their experience with other financial advisors, brokers, and other financial services professionals. Pay close attention to what they tell you. These are some of the most important words your soon-to-be client will ever speak to you. Letting you know what they think of financial advisors, based on prior interaction, is a tremendous advantage in knowing how you can elevate their experience:

>> Do they think all financial advisors are product-schlepping reps looking to make a quick buck?

>> Do they think all financial advisors are brokers who are simply shopping the financial product market based on their specific expressed financial goals?

>> Do they believe financial advisors are the most important family and business advisor, having been mentored and trained over years on how to make financial decisions that are in their clients' best interest?

A client's experience with financial professionals and attitude toward them tell you a great deal about what was missing in those previous experiences and what your client values. Make sure your value proposition meets the unique needs of the client.

Write your elevator pitch

Write an *elevator pitch* (a 30-second story — the time it takes you to ride an elevator to your office or apartment's floor) that describes your value proposition. I've used many different elevator pitches over the years. Here are a few examples:

>> I deliver clients' their desired financial outcomes.

>> Clients leverage my knowledge and experience to their own greater financial benefit.

>> Clients view me as their financial quarterback to make sure their financial plans are constantly being optimized.

TIP

Paint the big picture in broad strokes. If your statement is too complex, too long, or too detailed, your clients probably won't get it.

Your value proposition, as expressed in your elevator pitch, is your promise to clients. Your clients will hold you accountable for delivering on the promise. You can't tell someone that clients leverage your knowledge and experience and then just sell him some financial product, collect your commission, and move on to the next prospect. You have to deliberate carefully over every recommendation. If you're not doing that, then you're not bringing value.

Quantify your value and qualify your expectations

Every business has key *performance indicators (KPIs)* — quantifiable measures to evaluate success of the business or a specific business activity or initiative. These measures of success ensure that planned activities produce the desired results, and they indicate when adjustments may be necessary to improve progress toward the desired results. You and your clients can take the same approach by setting specific performance goals or expectations. For example, you may design a portfolio for a client that results in an account balance of a certain amount by a given date or delivers a certain net annualized return after fees over the next five years.

WARNING

Present expectations or projections, but don't promise a specific outcome by a specific date. You may design the ideal portfolio for a client only to have a bad bear market come along and completely dash your expectations (and those of your client). You want to prepare your clients for potential short-term setbacks and educate them on the importance of staying the course regardless of bull and bear market cycles. You also want to avoid any lawsuits claiming that you failed to deliver on promised returns.

Following are a few tips to communicate expectations to clients effectively without making explicit promises:

>> Support your projections with research and statistics to show that you and your client can be reasonably confident that your plan will achieve the desired outcome. For additional support, back up your projections with your experience (if you've been in the field for some time) or your knowledge (if you're relatively new).

>> Qualify the expectation you present by pointing out that volatility in the markets can result in some nasty surprises and that part of your value is in steering the ship through stormy seas.

>> Present your expectation (KPI) more as a checkpoint than as a promise. Explain that you'll meet regularly to check progress toward the desired result and make any necessary corrections to stay on course.

The more specific and rational the metrics you use to evaluate your contribution to your client's financial life, the more real your value proposition becomes to you client.

Being Humble and Honored to Serve Your Clients

A big part of earning clients involves adopting an attitude of humble servitude. When people decide to make you their financial advisor, they're entrusting you not only with their financial futures but also, to a large extent, with their lives. You should feel honored and humble at the opportunity to serve them. Assuming you do genuinely feel honored and humble, that feeling and attitude show through, and people respond accordingly. They can sense that you recognize the gravity of your responsibility and your commitment to handling their finances with great care.

To remind yourself of the critical role you play in your clients' lives, imagine the surviving family members of a breadwinner gone too soon or the retiree who worked hard all her life and is now able to travel to her heart's delight. If you've been a financial advisor for some time, you don't have to imagine, because rewards like these are your reality. These are the moments of authentic confirmation that being a financial advisor is one of the few professions that has such a deep and direct impact on people's lives:

>> Doctors are entrusted with their patients' lives.

>> Lawyers are often entrusted with their clients' freedom or protection against financial loss.

>> Financial advisors are entrusted with their clients' financial future and freedom.

Humility comes from the daily realization that people have placed their faith and trust in you, and from the realization that your recommendations and decisions can have a profound positive or negative impact on individuals and their families. When surgeons operate on a patient, they face the real possibility of the patient dying on the operating table — a tragic experience in that profession. For financial advisors, the worry is that they'll lose all of a client's accumulated wealth through a poor investment decision or product implementation. Just one such occurrence can lead to a lifetime of haunting guilt.

Being honored and humble to serve clients also comes from realizing that your clients are allowing you entry into an intimate part of their lives. As financial advisor, you play a role in the intimate relationship between your clients and their money. Just think about how easily many people share their health or medical issues or even their personal relationship issues at social engagements. When it comes to personal finances, however, people often steer the conversation in another direction.

I attribute the reluctance of people to discuss their personal finances to the stigma associated with poor money management. People openly discuss their physical ailments even when those ailments could have been prevented through healthy diet and lifestyle choices, but they don't want anyone knowing about the family finances that have suffered from years of unhealthy financial choices. Money is supremely intimate, and the attitudes around it are as diverse and diseased as people's physical overindulgences.

Whenever you step into an existing relationship between a client and his money, you're taking on the role of trusted confidante, promising to be by his side in good times and bad. You're also placing yourself in the position of being the one person who can challenge your client (for his own good) on financial matters when he isn't seeing what you see and doesn't know what you know. Often, your due diligence and dedication hold the key to success and, as a matter of consequence, to your own, as well.

Chapter **19**

Raising Your Profile with Networking and Marketing

I used to hate seeing the words "marketing," "networking," and "sales," used in the context of attracting and acquiring clients, because they all imply self-promotion, a term that carries the connotation of being pushy, arrogant, and insincere, as in the phrase "shameless self-promotion." To me, these words convey a sense that a person is only in pursuit of the all-mighty dollar and is void of any underlying passion for their profession.

However, I've since discovered that all professionals, especially those who are self-employed, must promote themselves at times, especially when they're just getting started. As long as you're passionate about what you do and are deeply and personally connected to your profession and devoted to your clients, there is no shame in self-promotion. You just need to figure out how to self-promote sincerely and without being pushy. Even better, you may discover ways to promote yourself that give prospective clients a small taste of the unique brand of value you offer.

In this chapter, I introduce you to the mechanics of self-promotion, so you know how to network and how to market yourself online and in the real world. Along the way, I provide suggestions on how to credibly elevate your marketplace visibility while sowing the seeds for future business opportunities in ways that align with your core values.

Establishing an Online Presence

When people are in the market for a financial advisor, they rarely reach for the phonebook. Instead, they fire up their web browser, go to their favorite search engine, and search for "financial advisor" or "wealth manager" followed by the city and state in which they live. Then, they skim through the search results for a promising candidate. You want to be on that list, preferably on the first page of the search results, and you want your listing to be positive. To get there, you need to establish a strong positive online presence. In this section, I explain the basics of marketing yourself online.

WARNING

If you're employed by a firm, carefully read and comply with any policies regarding online activities and social media. If you work for a big investment bank, such as Morgan Stanley, Merrill Lynch, or UBS, for example, you're limited in what you can post online about your work. However, you should still start to establish an online presence as a financial advisor, because you never know what the future has in store for your career. You just need to be sure to comply with your employer's online policy and with any applicable regulations.

Creating a website as your home base

Having an online presence begins with a website. Your website serves as your hub or home base. Everything else you do to market yourself online will point back to your website, so that search engines can begin to recognize that your website is your official online location. When people search for you by name followed by something like "financial advisor" or "wealth manager," the link to your site will appear near the top of the search results.

Whether you work for a firm, own your own firm, or operate as an independent contractor, you (or your firm) should have your own website and unique domain name. For example, I'm a partner at Aligne Wealth, and our website's domain name is www.alignewealth.com. I also own the domain IvanIllan.com, but if you try to go there, you'll end up at www.alignewealth.com because I set up a redirect from my domain to the firm's domain. Even if you work for a firm, you should have a website that you own, so you have a place online where people can always find you. In addition, when you own the domain name, you can have a branded email address — for example, `ivan@ivanillan.com`.

You may have options other than owning your own domain name and hosting your own website. For example, if you belong to any professional organizations, such as the organization that holds your FINRA securities licenses, you can probably create your own member page through the organization's website. If you work for a firm, the firm is likely to provide you with your own page or an option for creating one, so customers can read your bio and perhaps check out a photograph of you. However, I still encourage you (if your firm permits it) to have your own branded website that's yours to keep regardless of where your career leads you.

At the very least, your website should contain the following:

>> About page(s) that introduce you and anyone else on your team (along with photos, bios, certifications, and so on), state your mission, and present your financial management philosophy or process.

>> Page(s) about the services you provide, such as health insurance, life insurance, wealth management, risk management, tax planning, and so on.

>> Basic information, such as your firm's address, phone number, and hours of operation.

>> Testimonials from your delighted clients. Remember to check with your compliance officer about the firm's rules regarding accepting testimonials. Typically if you're an Investment Adviser Representative (IAR) registered through the SEC, you can't share testimonials.

>> Contact form that visitors can fill out to get in touch with you (a contact form keeps your email address hidden, so spammers have a hard time getting it).

If you're experienced and have a team, you can populate your website with additional content, including articles and videos on a wide variety of financial topics, answers to frequently asked questions, and perhaps even financial calculators. Valuable content is likely to boost your site's search engine ranking, draw more visitors, and reinforce your credibility.

Many independent financial advisors enable their clients to log in for additional features, such as accessing account balances and exchanging documents. However, managing client logins and providing the requisite security comes at a premium price.

TIP

To get some ideas for your website, search online for "financial advisor" or "wealth management" followed by your city and state and check out some of the more popular financial advisor websites in your area. If want a high-class website and don't have the time, talent, or desire to build one, google "financial advisor websites" and check out some of the sponsored listings. Numerous web design companies cater to financial advisors, providing a platform to easily build and maintain a professional-looking, secure, and compliant website that has all the features a financial advisor needs to be competitive.

Direct your clients to your website as part of your onboarding routine (see Chapter 13 regarding the Four As of client due diligence). In your first meeting, you may even want to walk clients through the site, showing them where they can find resources, market data, and calculators.

Hosting your own blog

Most websites these days run on a content management system (CMS), such as WordPress, that enables you to add a blog to your website (or host a blog without a website). A blog typically involves the creator posting regular articles on topics relevant to the topic and allowing visitors to comment on those posts. If you're an independent contractor — a Registered Investment Adviser (RIA) or independent broker/dealer affiliate — you should be blogging in your areas of expertise, because search engines love websites that provide fresh, relevant content. In addition, blogging enables you to benefit from content you don't have to spend the time and effort creating — user-generated content. As people comment on your blog post, they create more of that fresh content that search engines love.

WARNING

If you're working for a firm, you'll probably be discouraged or flat-out prohibited from publishing any job-related content due to the firm's concerns over compliance. Read and follow your firm's online policies and check with your firm's legal department if you're uncertain about any of the firm's online policies.

When composing blog posts, follow these recommendations:

>> Write original posts in your area(s) of expertise.

>> Keep it short and sweet (KISS), no more than 750 words per post.

>> Don't bore your audience. Use clever, catchy titles and write posts that would be fun to read on the large video billboards in Times Square.

>> Encourage interaction. Write posts that are likely to generate lively discussion, ask questions, take a poll. Respond when someone posts a comment or question.

>> Break it up with headings and lists. (Avoid long paragraphs.)

>> Have someone with a good editorial eye review and edit your writing before posting anything.

Becoming active on LinkedIn

LinkedIn is a great place to network with professionals and build your street cred by posting and commenting in relevant discussion forums. It's also a great place to ruin your reputation by engaging in shameless self-promotion or posting about topics you know little or nothing about.

To leverage the power of LinkedIn without tarnishing your reputation, follow these do's and don'ts:

>> Don't use LinkedIn or any social media platform as an obvious sales platform. For example, don't post something like "Please contact me to learn more about our services" or "Here's an article that speaks to the importance of this product that we sell and get big commissions to sell you." Okay, so maybe you wouldn't use those exact words exactly, but if you're trying to sell on LinkedIn, most sophisticated users will interpret your soft sales pitch that way.

>> Do engage in intelligent discussions over relevant topics you're genuinely curious about or have something of value to add. Posting a congratulations or "Great post!" comment is okay, but something more thoughtful and personal will resonate more with the community.

When posting anything online, be sure it complies with any relevant regulations. This means avoid posting items that are beyond the selection list of your firm's approved posting system (for example, Hearsay Social). If it's outside the bounds set by your broker/dealer's system, then avoid anything that contains a product-specific endorsement or product education.

>> Do include your website address in your profile. Having your profile link to your website is a great way to boost your website's search engine ranking and enable people on LinkedIn to find your official website.

>> Don't connect with people you haven't met in-person or have a legitimate desire to network with in an exchange of intellectual or professional value.

>> Do post personal experiences, pictures, and other memorabilia that capture or showcase your spirit or personality. You may get some haters, but that's fine. See the nearby sidebar for an example.

>> Don't self-promote on LinkedIn or any social media site. Doing so is offensive and counterproductive. Instead of attracting business, it drives business away because the perpetrator gets labeled as *that guy* or *that gal* in a community of professionals. Having consulted with many financial advisors and their firms over the years, I've taken note mostly of what *not* to do when networking online. The one that takes the cake is when people ask you to introduce them to your connections, so they can start selling through your network. The depravity of such a technique makes my blood boil and skin crawl, but it's best to be polite, so if you choose to reply to a request for your network contacts, a simple, "Uh, no" should do the trick.

>> Do share articles (compliance-approved ones, of course) that you find interesting and always include your accompanying comments. Reach out to your connections directly through the messenger, and share links to things that you either think they'd find interesting or that you can illicit their thoughts and opinions. Join and participate in relevant discussion groups.

The main purpose of social media is to connect with people and enrich one another's lives. It's about community and service, not self-service. Somehow, this core purpose got completely lost, as the barrage of salespeople flooded into the community hawking their wares. If you really want to get noticed, be personal and authentic, and be specific in your connections.

Creating a Facebook page for your practice

Facebook is a great place to gain exposure and visibility into the marketplace while driving Facebook traffic to your website. However, Facebook is primarily a social venue, so conduct business on Facebook accordingly:

>> Create a Facebook page for your financial advisor business, so you can post content to your professional page instead of your personal account.

>> Link your Facebook page to your website or blog by editing your page's business profile.

>> Whenever you post new content to your blog, share a link to it on your Facebook page. Don't merely repost the content to your Facebook page; you want to create links back to your website to boost its search engine ranking.

>> Whenever you post unique content to your Facebook page, make sure it's valuable and engaging content. Look to enrich the lives of Facebook members with your knowledge and insight. The content you post and the links you share are all subtle reminders to your Facebook friends that you're a financial advisor without your engaging in any heavy-handed sales.

TIP

Consistency is key. Use similar language whenever you post content to your website, blog, and LinkedIn and Facebook accounts. When you're building an online presence, you're actually building a brand — You, Inc. — so all of your online properties should have a similar look and feel.

Claiming your business in online directories

Take advantage of any online business directories, especially those that cater to financial advisors. Many professional organizations provide members with a page they can customize to add themselves to the directory, and you can usually link to your website from your page. Here are a few places to go to get started:

>> BrightScope at www.brightscope.com

>> FINRA's BrokerCheck at brokercheck.finra.org

>> Yelp at www.yelp.com

REMEMBER

By claiming your business profile in online directories, you have more control over what people see when they access your profile. Your directory listing may also provide an option to link it to your website or blog, which raises your profile when people search for financial advisors in your area.

Making the most of your certifications

During your professional development, you pursue education and expertise, which bestows upon you certifications and credentials. These professional certifications are your calling card and a great way to market your skills and techniques. Use them on your website, blog, social media properties, and business listings to establish your credibility as a financial advisor.

WARNING

Don't overdo it with certifications and credentials. Newer, obscure certifications may hurt you more than help. At a networking event, I've heard many an advisor look at the business card of another advisor and ask something like, "What are all these certification acronyms? It's just an alphabet soup!" I recommend sticking to the core certifications that I present in Chapter 6.

Getting Connected in the Real World

Many professionals become so obsessed with online marketing that they overlook the wonderful real-world opportunities and challenges that surround them. The truth is that you're probably going to attract and acquire far more clients by pressing the flesh than by blogging or by posting to your Facebook page. When people get to know you personally, they're much more likely to trust you with their money.

In this section, I encourage you to step away from your desk, put down your smartphone, and get connected in the real world, and I provide the guidance you need to do just that.

Marketing through social contacts is sort of like fishing, but it's not bait-the-hook fishing. It's more like chumming, where you toss food into the water to attract the fish. I've never looked at this fishing analogy as being about setting a trap or luring people into doing something that's not in their best interest. It's more of a saving-the-whale approach, where you attract the fishes (I know, a whale is a mammal) to present them with options that solve their problems and present options that are in their best interest.

Discovering what you're passionate about

One of the best and most personally rewarding ways to meet new clients is through shared interests. The more authentic and genuine you are about the activity, the better the results you'll have. Don't overthink this. If you love playing soccer, then find ways to serve and/or participate in your community by spending (or giving) your time to the sport.

To find social activities that you're passionate about, take inventory of things you love to do. Don't think about the average net worth of people that you'd meet in the activity. If you do, you're already spoiling the recipe. This has to be rooted in authenticity — meaning, your genuine interest in the activity.

After you find a community that interests you, here are a few suggestions for getting involved and talking about your work:

>> **Initially, engage in small talk.** You need to break the ice for people to feel comfortable discussing anything beyond sports, weather, news, and entertainment.

>> **Ask personal (but not too personal) questions.** People generally don't care about what you have to say unless they feel that you care about them. Take a genuine interest in others. When people open up to you, they often share their challenges, and if you can help them overcome a challenge, you will earn their trust for life.

>> **Be clear and confident when talking about what you do and when explaining any financial concepts, just as you do with clients.** If someone's looking for a financial advisor, she'll be impressed by the fact that you can talk candidly about finances in a way she understands.

>> **Create a judgment-free, sales-free zone.** You want people to come to you with their problems and questions. Any judgment or sales talk is likely to drive them away. People will come to you when they need your advice; don't push it.

PURSUING MY PASSIONS

I have two passions beyond personal finance — contemporary art and veteran home-lessness. These two highly disparate interests bring me into contact with a diverse pop-ulation and have led to the development of some amazing personal and professional relationships, all in a natural way. The people I come in contact with get to learn about me over time. Often it begins by making small talk, which then leads into a discussion about business and finance or the stock market, which gives me the opportunity to share my insights.

I also enjoy surfing (just started learning), sailing with my dad, and fine dining. This last one is particularly fun, because I can socialize and get to know people well over nice din-ners. I like to share my excitement over a particular dish or presentation, and the joy I feel in these moments is contagious.

REMEMBER

You're most genuine and attractive when you're enjoying yourself. Get involved in something you enjoy and you're passionate about. Otherwise, your involvement becomes drudgery, and that shows through, regardless of how hard you try to hide it.

Getting involved in a charitable cause

A genuine interest in a social issue is a surefire way to showcase your values in a more professional and practical setting. To find a charitable cause that stokes your passions, ask yourself what issues impacted you most in your youth — an event or issue that made a big impression on you or your family. These deeply rooted causes are great to pursue when you're an adult. The deeper the interest, the more passionate and effective you're likely to be.

REMEMBER

You may not find the right fit with the first organization or even the first cause you adopt. Don't let that initial disappointment discourage you. You may need to bounce around to find out what really makes you tick and find the right cause and organization to spark your passion.

Serving on boards

As a financial advisor, you're a perfect candidate to serve as treasurer for any charitable organization. In fact, you're probably qualified for any of the leadership roles — president, vice president, or secretary. Taking on a leadership role in an organization raises your profile and gives you greater opportunities to showcase your abilities and develop new skills.

Nonprofits are always in need of professionals to serve on their boards, especially legal, accounting, and financial professionals. The organization can benefit from your advice without having to pay you. In exchange, the board provides you with the means to network with like-minded professionals.

REMEMBER

Again, don't get your hopes up that board membership will draw a large stream of clients willing to sign up for your services. It simply warms them up, so when the opportunity arises for you to talk about what you do, you're talking with someone who's more receptive to what you offer. If you do call someone to follow up after an encounter, be simple and direct. For example, you may say something like, "I enjoyed meeting you, and I'm glad we share this common interest. I'd like an opportunity to introduce myself to you professionally." Then schedule an office visit.

Developing cross-industry professional alliances

One of the most effective ways to network is by reaching out to other professionals in related fields for collaboration and learning opportunities. As more and more business owners and professionals are discovering, the best approach to being successful in business is to focus on your core competencies and team up with others when they're better suited for meeting a client's specific needs.

Connecting with attorneys

Many of your clients are likely to have legal needs that are outside your wheelhouse, so be sure you have several attorneys you can call on for help and to send business their way. Referrals may not be a great money-making opportunity for you, but they generate good karma and may result in some return favors.

I have dozens of attorneys in my professional network, and they're all sources of limited referrals. When clients or prospects have a legal question I'm not qualified to answer, I send them to the person who's most qualified in my network, and if I'm not sure, I simply ping my network to find out who's the best fit and the most interested in helping out. Pinging my legal network with an opportunity is a great way to subtly remind my network who I am and what I do.

Teaming up with certified public accountants (CPAs)

You should have at least one certified public accountant (CPA) to call on to deal with situations that are outside your area of financial expertise. Start with your own CPA, and if you don't have one, get one. You should have a CPA to manage your finances, so you have an objective third-party looking over everything and providing additional insights. Simply extend this existing relationship to your clients. The supplemental information and education your CPA provides will enrich your interactions with clients.

TIP

Take your CPA to lunch (after tax season, of course). Thank her for sharing her expertise. Ask questions about recent tax law changes or about cases you've encountered and how she would approach the situation. Be genuinely curious. The more authentic your interest and the application of what you subsequently learn are, the more likely your CPA will open up to you and partner with you to raise your clients' success.

REMEMBER

Don't expect treating your CPA to lunch to result in a deluge (or even a single) referral post-meeting. That's nice when it happens, but the point of these meetings is more about establishing meaningful productive relationships, exchanging information and insights, and letting people know who you are and what you do.

TIP

After you meet with your CPA, share what you discovered with clients who can benefit. You may even want to schedule a follow-up meeting with your client and CPA if you think a group discussion would be in a client's best interests. Adding value to your client is a never-ending pursuit. Bringing in other professionals to solve specific present or future problems only adds to your perceived and actual client value.

Building Your Own Sales Force

Marketing and networking require a great deal of time and effort, but as you establish your brand, you eventually put yourself in a position to build your own sales force and outsource a great deal of your marketing and networking. In this section, I present some practical techniques for building your own sales force.

Marketing to fellow financial advisors

After you've been in the business for a couple of years and have proven that you have some staying power in the industry, you're ready to consider another opportunity to grow your practice. Most financial advisors lean toward a generalist practice. However, by developing a unique skill that other financial advisors can leverage, you may never have to prospect for clients again, because financial advisors become your clients, eager to tap into (and pay for) the expertise you have to offer.

The key to this strategy is to develop a skill or innovate a technique that fellow financial advisors want to use — for example, a unique method of introducing disability income insurance to a certain customer profile. You can then offer your services as a coach to train your fellow financial advisors in this new technique. To market the service, simply share your success stories. When other financial advisors become aware of your success, they contact you to request coaching, at which point, you can discuss the arrangement. (Insurance, unlike securities, is much easier and more broadly developed, because you're not restricted by FINRA and broker/dealer rules on joint-work.)

The most common arrangement is a joint-work agreement (see Chapter 20), where you split the compensation earned from using the solution(s) you developed 50/50. I started expanding my business using this method. Typically, a 50/50 agreement is fine at first, but you may need to revise it later, especially if the client is paying only annual fees as with an assets under management (AUM) account, because the introducing advisor's role becomes less and less active.

Your best unique skill or technique will come from a demonstrated and repeatable success to generate revenue in a particular financial planning business line. You may take years to develop it, if you ever do, but as soon as you discover it, you can start marketing it to your fellow financial advisors. This approach is one of the most effective ways to build a business. It's called *building distribution* — a technique that big product manufacturers use to distribute their value proposition to others who can leverage it to their advantage. Think of it as franchising.

I've used this technique by marketing my portfolio management solutions to my broker/dealer, and it's been the most rewarding aspect of being in this business. Becoming an advisor to other advisors is the most significant acknowledgement and indication of your success.

WARNING

Don't approach financial advisors to sell your exclusive technique. Simply tell your success stories and let them come to you for coaching. Too often, advisors who have a certain program or system that they use to sell a specific product type or even a specific manufacturer's product approach me. Though I don't believe this is at all a bad thing, it's just not something that I personally feel is the right approach to putting your best foot forward in the profession. Your skill or technique shouldn't be restricted or trademarked. Instead, it should be treated as an open architecture that people are free to modify to improve it or to make it more suitable to their clientele.

Leveraging home office leadership personnel

If you work for a broker/dealer, reach out for help in promoting your unique value proposition. Your broker/dealer is likely to have personnel devoted to growing the company's revenues, and your broker/dealer will be delighted to have a financial advisor who understands the value of marketing and the important contribution she makes to the company's success. These people are potentially key allies in your efforts to market your unique skill set to clients and to other members of the broker/dealer advisor network. It's a win-win-win scenario.

When approaching key personnel, first identify someone who has the role and responsibilities relevant to your desired outcome. After finding the right person, present your value proposition as it relates to that person, the company, prospective clients, and advisors within the company.

REMEMBER

Describe your skill set in plain English, providing a description of the following:

>> The technique/methodology involved in promoting the type of product/ service that's your area of expertise

>> The typical customer/client target profile

>> The way your technique/methodology is the best economic interests of all parties

Encouraging and rewarding client referrals

It's an embarrassing admission, but I've had many clients over the years tell me they didn't refer a friend or family member to me because they assumed that their friend or family member wasn't high profile enough to be of interest to my firm. The other embarrassing admission is that these clients were probably right. As an individual advisor, I quickly found myself rising in client net worth, where revenues are indeed higher, and the work required to deliver exceptional outcomes remains constant.

Now, after having invested in building a team to serve clients, I'm hearing this feedback less often. At my firm, we've expanded our capacity to serve clients so that no client is too small.

REMEMBER

If you're committed to growth, you need to increase capacity by adding personnel and implementing the latest technologies to improve productivity. Then, you need to let your clients and prospective clients know that you have the capacity for referrals and that no client is too small. The most effective way to demonstrate your capacity to serve clients is to spend time with your most valuable clients and others who are most likely to send referrals your way. Being systematic in your portfolio reviews (I recommend quarterly frequency) provides the most fertile ground for referrals. Prioritizing your time with existing clients is the best method for generating referrals.

WARNING

Don't explicitly reward clients for referrals. Most insurance and securities sales regulations strictly prohibit (or specifically guide) monetary rewards for referrals. Be very careful if you're considering any monetary rewards. What may seem to be a grey area to you may be black and white to supervisors or compliance officers. Always consult your company's supervisory or compliance officer or department before rewarding clients for referrals.

I prefer to acknowledge quality referrals by providing premium treatment. I treat clients who provide valuable referrals like royalty with fancy lunches and dinners and occasional outings to a mutual enjoyable activity like golf or travel to let these clients know how much I value their business and ongoing relationships.

Promoting Yourself over the Long Haul

The best financial advisors don't have to engage in self-promotion. They deliver their clients so much value that word-of-mouth advertising generates more business than they can handle. So the key to promoting yourself over the long haul is to make yourself indispensable to your client. As you're working on that, keep the following points in mind:

>> **Be patient.** Building a successful advisory career takes many years, and you're likely to experience plenty of setbacks along the way. Take time to reflect on why you had those setbacks and how to best avoid them in the future.

>> **Pace yourself.** Don't bombard your client and/or professional advisor network with too many posts and pings and calls. Finding the sweet spot between too much contact and too little is more art than science. If you feel you're being too push or too salesy, you probably are, and you need to back off.

>> **Diligently work your client due diligence process, as you're allowed to do so.** Established industry research shows that seven to nine interactions with prospective clients are necessary before they become a client. This can take days or years.

>> **Be devoted to your client due diligence process.** Your process is the only true measure of successful outcomes — for both clients and yourself.

>> **Don't get caught up in a fad product.** The hot story today is tomorrow's client apology. Save yourself from the grief and the disappoint and beware those financial products that promise big rewards with little to no risk.

>> **Don't use emotional manipulation to sell products** Being authentic and honest with yourself and others is a great way to keep calm emotions. Household finances are fiery enough on their own without you having to throw fuel on the fire. Remember that most divorces come about due to either one of two things — and money is one of them. Tread lightly and carry a big stick.

>> **Visualize where you'll be in five years.** Imagine what your professional accomplishments will be, how you're interacting with your clients, and why you're still so excited to be in this business every day. Visualization may sound corny, but it works. Prospective clients will sense your confidence and be more likely to choose you over less confident and resolute financial advisors.

Chapter **20**

Teaming Up to Build Synergies

One of the draws of having a career as a financial advisor is that you can operate as an independent contractor. You don't have to report to a supervisor. You're the master of your own destiny. Depending on your desired lifestyle and geography, you may be able to make a great living as a sole proprietor.

However, if you're more ambitious and more of a social creature, you may want to follow the latest buzz about advisor teaming. After decades of being dominated by one-person financial advisory practices, the industry is rapidly evolving into team sport. More and more financial advisors are building teams of specialists and delegating their busywork to scale their businesses and reap the benefits of greater efficiency.

In this chapter, you explore the pros and cons of flying solo and take a look at your options. You also get direction on how to leverage the power of a team to grow your business through *synergy* — where 1+1 = 3.

Choosing Your Preferred Role: Lone Wolf or Leader of the Pack

Although this chapter is titled "Teaming Up to Build Synergies," you do have a choice, and it's the most important choice you have to make as a financial advisor — whether to operate your business independently or assemble a team of professionals. In this section, I call your attention to the benefits and drawbacks of choosing to fly solo.

Considering the pros of flying solo

Most people become financial advisors either as employees of large establishments or as the proverbial lone wolf. If you're an employee, flying solo isn't an option, but if you're planning to set out on your own or start your own firm, you need to decide whether flying solo (perhaps with an assistant) is the right fit for you.

In this section, I describe the benefits of flying solo.

Mastering your own destiny

When you're alone in your own practice, you feel the magic of a work-life balance that's unencumbered by other people's agendas and by office politics. You can set your own hours and decide which days of the week to work. You report to no one and have no one reporting to you. You're the captain of the ship without a crew to mutiny against you. Your days are free of petty arguments, broken promises, and betrayals. You answer only to yourself and your clients.

That's the ideal. Unfortunately, reality can fall short of that ideal. When you're your own boss, you may discover that your boss is far more demanding than any other boss you've ever had, and you may have trouble drawing the line between work and life. In addition, you may miss the daily banter and shop talk with coworker. Being master of your own destiny can be a lonely position. Of course, you can overcome all of these challenges, but you should certainly consider them when making your choice.

Benefiting from the consensus of one

Working alone gives you the power to be decisive. You don't need to ask for permission, form a committee, sit through team meetings, rely on input from others, or explain your reasoning for taking a certain course of action. You decide and act, which makes your business responsive and agile.

REMEMBER

Of course, the flip side is that you're at risk of becoming myopic (narrow-minded) and falling victim to your own bias. To avoid this trap, consider consulting a trusted mentor or advisor when making important decisions. The decision is still yours to make, but having someone to bounce ideas off of and provide insight into factors you're overlooking is always valuable.

Capitalizing on your responsiveness

As a lone wolf, you can move fast on opportunities, and you don't have to share your hard-earned revenues. You can say yes when larger, slower-moving firms need to consult with the board and realign their resources. This level of responsiveness is the sort of agility that larger firms can only dream of.

Owning it when you have no one else to blame

In a solo practice, you, and only you, are accountable for your business's success or failure. After all, who else is there to blame? Your ability to survive and thrive in this model is rooted in self-sufficiency and self-reliance, core values that have driven the success of many of the greatest financial advisors.

However, self-reliance isn't for everyone, and it can hold you back. Although you have no one else to blame, you have no one else to support you when the going gets tough.

Considering the cons of flying solo

People who work as employees have a romantic notion of working as an independent contractor. All they think about is the convenience of having their own schedule and the misconception of being their own boss. (I say "misconception," because when you're an independent contractor, every client is your boss, and they're often more demanding and more reluctant to give you a raise.)

In this section, I reveal the dark side of flying solo, so you can base your choice on reality instead of fantasy.

Recognizing that generalists can do only so much

You're one person, there are seven days in a week, 24 hours in a day, and you need about six to eight hours sleep every night to stay healthy. When you do the math, you quickly realize the limitations of operating as an independent contractor.

When you're building your practice, a realistic time commitment is 60 hours a week. This includes meeting with clients and prospects, marketing, networking, staying current through reading and education, handling the paperwork, and keeping the books (or at least organizing financial information so someone else can keep the books).

Having to spend time doing anything other than delivering value to your clients limits you in three ways:

>> **Client capacity:** You can effectively serve a fixed number of clients, which caps your growth.

>> **Product selection:** Ultimately, you'll probably have to focus on one or two product lines, which means other advisors will be able to angle into your client relationships if the solutions you offer fail to meet their needs.

>> **Efficiency:** You end up spending too much time on nonrevenue-generating activities, such as office management and paperwork.

TIP

To improve your efficiency and capacity, consider hiring a full-time or part-time assistant or even a virtual independent contractor with experience in the field to handle the more mundane tasks. This is an added expense, but if you're charging $100 or more an hour and paying an assistant $20 an hour, hiring an assistant is a no-brainer. Besides, wouldn't you rather be spending more time honing your skills and meeting with clients?

Limiting your growth and client impact

As I explain in the previous section, given the natural limitations of time and energy, you can effectively serve a limited number of clients. Before I added team members to support various aspects of my practice, I often had to queue clients many weeks in advance, which resulted in missed opportunities. In today's fast-paced on-demand world, people don't like to wait.

Focus on servicing clients and conducting your initial due diligence — the iron-clad pillars of your practice. You need to develop and master a sharp, crisp due diligence process that's both effective and efficient (see Chapter 13), and this can take considerable time. The catch-22 is that to execute well in these two areas, you must limit the number of clients, which means you need higher revenue clients, but you don't have the credibility at this point in your career to acquire and retain those clients consistently. The solution is to offer a limited number of products to a limited number of mid-revenue clients and start to work your way up gradually.

REMEMBER

Certainly, working by yourself means you can spend time on one client at a time, but you can probably add value in at most two areas effectively — for example, asset and risk management. Such limited impact is better than nothing for your clients and may make for a nice career, but it's not the pinnacle of success for most financial advisors.

Dealing with limited resources

TIP

If you're going it alone, focus on two areas where you can add substantial value to a client's life: asset and risk management, the two core financial planning areas. I often refer to these areas as flip sides of the same coin. To create an even narrower niche, focus on one product line or service in each of these two areas. If you go too broad, you won't be able to provide your clients with effective and efficient service.

ASSET MANAGEMENT

In the area of asset management, strongly consider using a turnkey asset management platform (or program) (TAMP). With a TAMP, you outsource asset management to a firm that specializes in this area, so you can focus more directly on your clients and spend less time managing their investments. This outsourcing technique is an excellent way to deal with your more limited resources, as a one-person band.

Every broker/dealer firm has at least one TAMP that charges an asset-based fee, so you need the FINRA Series 63 and Series 65 (or, the combined exam version, Series 66) licenses. Building this type of recurring revenue base into your practice affords you the opportunity to elevate your practice, by going after the bigger fish, as you gain more experience.

REMEMBER

Outsourcing asset management to a TAMP doesn't absolve you of having to keep current on capital markets and economic trends. Regardless of the means used to manage a client's assets, you must allocate a portion of your time to monitoring economic and market trends. However, by leveraging a TAMP, you outsource the construction and monitoring of the portfolio and ensure that adjustments are made consistently and on an ongoing basis to your clients' portfolios.

LIABILITY MANAGEMENT (INSURANCE)

For insurance, several independent insurance brokerages specialize in wholesaling a variety of carriers to fulfill a client's liability management needs. The best way to find one of these brokerages is to ask fellow financial advisors who they recommend. Referrals are the best way to find a competent and ethical insurance brokerage. At your local Financial Planning Association (FPA) or National Association of Insurance and Financial Advisors (NAIFA) networking meeting, feel free to ask about preferred insurance brokerages.

If you're affiliated with an insurance-owned broker/dealer (as I am), then you're surrounded by a sea of insurance-focused advisors eager to provide guidance. Just be aware that these advisors play favorites — they recommend products that provide them with the best compensation. The good news is the number of high quality carriers is limited, so using any of the recommended products rarely results in your having to apologize to clients later.

Collaborating with Other Financial Advisors

To achieve a level of success beyond self-sufficiency and start building business revenues through synergy, you can collaborate with and serve other financial advisors in a number of ways. In this section, I cover three common options:

>> Joining joint-work opportunities

>> Imparting your expertise to other financial advisors

>> Complementing your skills and personality

Teaming up for joint-work opportunities

A *joint-work opportunity* involves two advisors teaming up, usually temporarily, to meet a client's needs. Either advisor can source the client. Here are a few ways financial advisors engage in joint-work opportunities:

>> Early in their careers, two advisors team up. One is better at finding new clients, and the other is better at office management. They split all their business on a joint-work basis, believing they can source enough opportunities and implement enough product or solutions to generate more revenue (and have more fun) than if they were working alone.

>> A property and casualty insurance advisor teams up with a life and disability income insurance advisor to provide clients with a fuller range of coverage.

>> A health insurance advisor teams up with a company retirement plan advisor to provide businesses with health insurance and retirement plan solutions for a company's employees.

REMEMBER

Joint work is best when the two advisors complement one another in terms of talents, skills, passions, and products/solutions. For example, if your skill set is in asset management, team up with a securities-licensed, insurance-focused (risk management) advisor. If you're an insurance-focused advisor, team up with an investment-focused advisor (asset or wealth manager). The main point here is to determine who you are as an advisor and team up with someone who complements that skill set. If you don't know what you have to offer and what you need in exchange, start taking inventory. (See the later section "Finding your niche: Minder, finder, or grinder?" for additional guidance.)

Don't limit yourself to thinking about product or solution-based skill sets; expand your scope. Other skills include business organization, technical expertise, managerial skills, and marketing savvy. Look for the skills you're lacking and think about how you can articulate the unique value you bring to the partnership. When pitching a joint-work opportunity to an advisor you want to work with, you need to be able to explain exactly how you can add value in exchange for the value the other advisor brings to the table.

REMEMBER

Quantify your relative contributions by estimating your compensation in terms of an hourly rate. Advisors often think in terms of commissions or flat fees, when you ask an advisor to estimate his hourly rate, you're likely to get a blank stare. Be prepared to engage in an exercise to quantify your hourly rate and that of the other advisor.

For commission-based financial advisors, estimating an hourly rate can be difficult, because the advisor may invest the same amount of time and effort making a $1,000 sale as he would to make a $10,000 sale. In a case like this, start with an average monthly income based on the past 12 months and then divide by the average number of hours per month that the person worked to earn that money. For example, if the person earned on average $15,000 per month working about 50 hours a week, the average hourly rate would be $15,000 ÷ 200 = $75/hour.

REMEMBER

As a joint-work partner, you'll be competing with the bread-and-butter revenue that your prospective partner has become accustomed to. Make the best use of your partner's time by being well organized and delivering results quickly. Otherwise, your partnership isn't likely to last very long.

In the following sections, I provide some guidelines for handling joint-work opportunities through all four stages of the joint-work relationship: on approach, developing, operating, and terminating.

On approach: Laying the groundwork

When you have a lead on a joint-work opportunity and someone in mind to team up with, approach the situation carefully, so you get started on the right foot. Here are a few suggestions:

>> **Research your potential joint-work partner's LinkedIn page.** Look for areas of connection or similarity — common ground. By understanding your audience, you'll be better prepared to appeal to their sensibilities.

>> **Don't initiate a full-blown discussion in the hallway or near the water cooler about the possibility of working together.** Instead, mention in passing that you'd like to schedule time to discuss a business opportunity and ask what might be a convenient time to meet.

>> **Schedule the meeting over a breakfast or lunch, but don't schedule it for dinner.** Dinner is too formal, and you're just getting a feel for the potential. Also, alcohol is more likely to be consumed at dinner than at breakfast or lunch. When alcohol is involved, you run the risk of making a new friend instead of a business partner.

>> **Host the meeting in a professional setting.** Do it in your office or in a conference room.

Developing your relationship

After you've agreed that there's potential for synergy, formalize the terms of your agreement and develop a strategy:

>> **Draw up a joint-work agreement.** This agreement should spell out the terms of the relationship, including who does what (and when do they do it), how revenue will be shared, who maintains ownership of the customer or client relationship should the agreement end, and under what conditions the agreement can (or will) be terminated. You also need to have a nondisclosure or confidentiality agreement that you both sign to prevent partners from stealing clients or disclosing trade secrets during the relationship or after it's dissolved.

TIP

Head to RocketLawyer.com for a boilerplate letter of agreement that you can customize to meet your needs (you may be charged a fee). Better yet, hire an attorney from your network to draft a letter of agreement. The latter option gives you the added bonus of a having a potential center-of-influence and referral source witnessing your growth and professionalism. Of course, adding an attorney adds to your costs, but that's offset by the potential opportunities generated by your broader engagement with outside collaborators.

>> **Hold a strategy meeting.** During this meeting, develop your game plan, specifying your responsibilities — what each of you agrees to do and refuses to do. Many partnerships fall apart due to misunderstandings over each partner's role and responsibilities. The more time and detail you each put into this phase, the more invested you'll be, and the better the outcomes.

Operating as a team

When you're working with someone else toward a common goal, you need to be on the same page. Team performance trumps individual performance. To coordinate your efforts and complement one another, follow these two suggestions:

>> **After your first joint meeting, have a debriefing session.** Review how you each think the meeting went and what could have happened to make it better. Be honest about items that confused or upset you. If you think the meeting was perfect, then let your partner know it. Honesty is key.

>> **Welcome any criticism and use it to make positive changes.** I've had partners tell me that they thought a certain meeting with a client couldn't have gone better only to find out much later (after we had acquired the client), that they thought I spoke way too fast for the client to follow, and they had been worried that the client was put off by it. When I get excited and passionate, I can get carried away, which is fine as long as it doesn't make our client or my partner uncomfortable. When I finally received the insight, I was able to make the necessary adjustment.

Terminating the relationship (if it doesn't work out)

I always assume that every new partner will work out great. But that's not always the case. Winding down a relationship or being clear that it's best not to pursue further clients together is just a matter of time.

The tricky part to breaking up is determining who gets to keep the clients. If you signed an agreement letter, that letter should establish the rules for determining who gets to keep any given client. Without a clear agreement in place, determining client ownership is difficult. It's even more challenging when an insurance-focused advisor partners with an investment advisor to manage a client's investment portfolio. Often, the client views the investment advisor as the responsible party and the insurance advisor as the connector or referring party. Without a clear separation clause in your agreement, you're bound to encounter confusion and discord.

WARNING

Never put a client in a position of having to choose between you and a partner. It's unprofessional and makes the client feel uncomfortable. In addition, it's bad for business — for both advisors involved.

Sharing unique techniques and skills

If you've developed a unique technique or skill for handling a certain financial matter, as I explain in Chapter 19, you can use this skill as leverage to attract other financial advisors and offer them something of real value that can improve their practices. Training or coaching one or two advisors in addition to serving as a financial advisor to your other clients is a great way to add a revenue stream and build your reputation as a leader in the field.

No doubt, innovating skills and techniques and training your colleagues on how to apply them is difficult, but the bigger challenge brings bigger rewards and enables you to have a greater positive impact.

Finding your niche: Minder, finder, or grinder?

When you're looking to collaborate with other financial advisors and build synergies, you can benefit by recognizing the three roles that financial advisors play in any firm:

>> **Minders** run the business/practice, organizing, managing, hiring/firing, and setting goals and agendas. Typically, these are partners who've been in the business for many years, made the business-building mistakes, and learned from them.

>> **Finders** source new clients. These advisors are great at filling a pipeline and marketing services and solutions. Finders can be any age and at any level of experience.

>> **Grinders** do research, analysis, illustration, and paperwork. Whether it's the research that drives discussion at investment committee meetings or running several insurance carrier illustrations, these advisors are the worker bees of the business. This is a great position for new college grads, because it gives them the opportunity to figure out the business from the inside-out.

Any thriving practice has a healthy balance of financial advisors to fill all three roles. If a business has too much focus on finding new clients and no ability to run the business and deal with the daily workload, it'll be a short-lived business. The same is true if the business has an imbalance in other areas.

WARNING

Avoid the common mistake of deeming the finders the most valuable of the three financial advisor roles. The reasoning is that they're the rainmakers — without them, there is no work. However, each role is equal in value; without minders, there is no business, and without grinders, nothing gets done. As you expand your business, you need to find partners who accept the fact that all three roles have equal value. Otherwise, the partnership is likely to end on a sour note with growing resentment toward the finder who thinks he's the most valuable.

If you know what you're best at, use that knowledge to find the right fit as you seek out other financial advisors to collaborate with. Maybe you're a natural networker and never have any trouble filling your calendar with 15 prospective client appointments every week. You love connecting with people, anytime, anywhere. You're quick to travel with friends and have a full social calendar. You're not interested in being in an office all day, but you need to roam free. Or, maybe you're more of an introvert who loves conducting research and analysis and running illustrations and portfolio proposals all day. You have a laser focus and hate the interruptions that your finder friend craves. Do a little self-analysis and find out which role suits you best. Then, seek out collaborations with financial advisors who have the skills and personalities that complement yours.

Exploring broader practice partnerships

If you're affiliated with a national broker/dealer, you can be sure that management's focus is on increasing revenues. If you've had local success teaming up with colleagues or coworkers to increase revenues, consider taking that local success nationwide. Call the sales director of the broker/dealer or firm and present to him a slide-deck of what you've accomplished locally.

Ask him to help you identify other opportunities where you could add value. Using this strategy, I've developed joint-work partners in cities across the United States, and I'm not alone. Colleagues have developed extensive networks by making themselves available to deliver presentations at firm-sponsored and organized symposiums and conferences.

REMEMBER

The skills and techniques you've developed and had success with locally won't spread nationally unless your broker/dealer or firm pushes for adoption. It must be a priority on corporate's agenda. You can have the best idea in the business, but if your firm isn't pushing in that direction, then you'll be beating your head against the proverbial brick wall.

5
Running Your Practice as a Business

Make your sole proprietorship a bona fide business to ensure sustainability and lay the groundwork for future growth.

Structure and run your firm as a traditional business, so you can focus your efforts on growing the business and delegate the rest.

Explore the option of taking on partners and do it right if you choose that option.

Leave a legacy of quality financial advice by planning for your succession.

IN THIS CHAPTER

» **Deciding whether you can and really want to start a business**

» **Running your financial advisory more like a bona-fide business**

» **Using a key success metric to stay on track**

» **Fueling growth through mergers and acquisitions**

» **Planning for the future without you**

Chapter **21**

Transitioning from Solo Practitioner to Business Owner

Beyond the joint-work partnerships that I discuss in Chapter 19, you can improve your practice's capacity for growth by transforming it into a full-fledged, fully staffed business. However, make no mistake, evolving your mindset and behavior from lone wolf financial advisor to owner of a financial advisory firm is far from smooth sailing.

I often tell colleagues that sometimes I long for the old days, when I was a grinder, directly educating and reviewing strategies with clients, when client-facing work consumed 80 percent of my time. Today, that's a third of my weekly schedule. Now, I spend more time being a minder. I need to constantly evaluate where my time and the time of my firm's other business assets are best allocated. (See Chapter 22 for more about the three roles a financial advisor can play: minder, finder, and grinder.)

In this chapter, I provide guidance to help you navigate the transition from lone wolf practitioner to owner and manager of a firm.

Gut Check: Deciding Whether Starting Your Own Firm Is the Right Move for You

Prior to deciding to transition from an employed financial advisor practitioner to business owner, you have to answer these two questions that I examine in greater detail in the following sections:

» Do you have any previous commitments that prohibit you from starting your own financial advisor firm?

» Do you really want to start and run your own firm?

Determining how tethered you are to your current firm

To answer the first question, consider your current broker/dealer affiliation. Depending on your broker/dealer affiliation, the opportunity to start your own firm may not even be a possibility. For example, traditional wirehouse firms (for example, Bank of America, Merrill Lynch, Morgan Stanley, UBS, Wells Fargo, and JP Morgan Chase) don't provide their financial advisors the option to evolve their practice into an independent business. (A *wirehouse* broker/dealer is one that sells its own products, as opposed to an *independent* broker/dealer that sells third-party products. See Chapter 4 for details.)

Financial advisors affiliated with a wirehouse firm are typically employees of the firm and subject to noncompete and nondisclosure agreements, which makes leaving the firm to establish a business difficult. Establishing a business is becoming even more difficult as firms abandon the broker protocol, as I explain in the nearby sidebar.

Ideally, after you express your interest in evolving into your own business, your broker/dealer will be receptive to the possibility and discuss it with you. Independent dealers are typically more flexible because they have an affiliated network of financial advisors who are independent contractors, and they compensate them as such. Financial advisors with independent broker/dealers have maximum freedom regarding how to run their practice — they're not required to sell proprietary products or follow a biased agenda typical of the wirehouse firms.

WARNING

All of this is to say, that if have future aspirations to evolve a financial advisory practice into a firm, be careful about the firm you join. If you're not inclined to continue to grow beyond your solo and sometimes joint-work practice, then where you practice is less of a concern.

Considering a change in roles and costs

Although starting a business and having employees generating revenue for you may seem like a great idea, consider how your role and expenses will change. Becoming a business owner is like changing careers. You may face the difficult challenge of having to transform yourself from a finder or grinder into a minder, setting vision, mission, and goals; delegating responsibilities; monitoring performance; and providing leadership and guidance.

Also consider the impact of expenses. At a full-service wirehouse firm, growing a practice comes with all-expenses-paid support from the firm. Although independent broker/dealers provide higher payout (for example, 80 percent versus 40 percent gross dealer concessions), after adjusting for expenses, your *net business income* could end up looking like your previous W-2 income.

REMEMBER

The real motivating factor for building your own business is that you create an asset that can continue to generate revenue for you and your family after you retire or pass away.

Putting All the Pieces in Place

Starting a business is a daunting task. In this section, I help you clear that first hurdle. Here you discover how to achieve optimal broker/dealer platforms, structure your organizational chart, and staff your firm. I also encourage you to focus (at least initially) on finding clients or teaming up with another financial advisor who's better suited to take on this role.

REMEMBER

The way you organize and run your business is a reflection of how your business will handle its client's finances. Organize your business with the same care and dedication you manage your clients' finances.

Structuring your business

The first order of business is to structure your business. You basically have four options:

» **Limited liability company (LLC):** The *LLC* is the preferred structure for most financial advisory businesses because it shields the owner's assets from the business's liabilities, provides for a highly flexible management structure, and offers flexible tax reporting options.

» **S-Corporation:** *S-Corp* is another popular option for financial advisory businesses, because it shields the owner's assets from the business's liabilities and because owners pay personal income tax on profits, but the business doesn't pay a corporate tax. Income and losses pass through the corporation to the owners.

» **C-Corporation:** *C-Corp* isn't a popular option, because not only do the owners pay personal income tax on profits, but also the business is required to pay corporate income tax.

» **Partnership:** A *partnership* is a relatively informal business structure. Partners aren't required to hold meetings, prepare minutes, elect officers, write articles of incorporation, or issue stock certificates. Partners share in the business's profits and losses and are equally responsible for its debts and liabilities. However, partnerships don't shield the owner's assets from the business's liabilities, so they're not a preferred business structure for financial advisory businesses.

As a business owner, you can compensate yourself and other owners through salary and bonuses or through salary and distributions. The second option helps to reduce self-employment taxes and provides more flexibility around business succession planning.

For a great consulting service that'll advise you on your business structure and compensation regimes, check out the resources available at FP Transitions (www. fptransitions.com). I've found them to be highly competent in advising more mature financial advisory practices in the areas of business structure, mergers/ acquisitions, business succession, and business continuity.

Choosing a broker/dealer platform

When you're starting your own financial advisor business, one of the first decisions you need to make is which independent broker-dealer to affiliate with. If you entered the field as an employee, your affiliation was through the firm. You didn't have any choice in the matter, and even if you did, your experience and perspective was probably limited at that early point in your career. With the knowledge and experience you've gained since then, you probably want to switch your affiliation. Rarely does a financial advisor build a practice at one firm and evolve it into a business within the same platform.

For a guide to the top 50 independent broker/dealers, as ranked by 2017 revenues, visit InvestmentNews' annual ranking at: www.investmentnews.com/article/ 20180421/FREE/180429998/top-independent-broker-dealers-ranked-by- revenue. (The broker-dealer my independent business is affiliated with ranks number five.)

When you're shopping for an independent broker/dealer, compare the following traits:

» Platform capabilities, such as hybrid broker/dealer and registered investment advisor (RIA) models

» Platform fees, from assets under management (AUM) platform costs to individual retirement account (IRA) custodian fees

» Grid payout (higher isn't necessarily better)

» Practice management support and education

» Access to diverse financial products

» Financial and balance sheet strength

Sketching your organizational chart

Having one or two consistent joint-work partners provides a good foundation on which to build a financial advisor business. (See Chapter 20 for more about joint-work opportunities.) However, you must clearly identify who does what on a daily basis. I recommend using the minders, finders, and grinders model as a guide to realign a current joint-work partner into a specific role and responsibility.

A list of positions required and tasks that must be accomplished is a good start. You may want to include your joint-work partners in the process, so you're sure to get buy-in. After you have a pretty clear idea of who's going to be doing what, formalize it in an organizational chart with three levels:

>> **Level I:** At the top of the org chart, place the business leader(s): Founder, president or chief executive officer (CEO), chief information officer (CIO), and so on — whichever positions you want to include in this top tier. Segregate the role of CEO or president (or whichever designation you choose). This person is the team member who sets the firm's vision, mission, and goals and holds all the accountability. If you're unsure who this should be, then I suggest you hold off on starting a business and perhaps wait until a colleague invites you to play a role in her business.

Ideally, one of these executives is in charge of mentoring and developing junior financial advisors, which includes attending some client meetings to instill the firm's example of how client acquisition, reviews, and retention meetings should be run. This role is either a combination of minder and finder or pure minder. You could have a few leaders at this level who occupy finder and minder roles respectively, and you may have varied business ownership and compensation structures.

>> **Level II:** At this level, the office manager/administrator/chief operating officer (COO) keeps the business on track toward meeting its goals. In the early years, a highly capable executive assistant to the founder may fill this role. It's all about coordinating the firm's resources and tracking performance. This role is most exclusively a minder.

>> **Level III:** At this level, client service/portfolio management associates focus on delivering to clients the information and education related to the firm's products and service offerings. Some may call these the sales positions, but because I don't believe a real financial advisor ever has to sell anything when in the advice business, I prefer to see these positions as equivalent to the new associates at a law firm or doctors in a residency program. These team members are grinders, doing the rubber-meets-the-road work of a financial advisory practice — running illustrations, analyzing competitive products, and designing and building portfolios.

As your firm grows, you may want to add more levels and positions, but for now, this is a good start.

Staffing your firm

First thing: Hire an assistant to handle your paperwork, which immediately frees up your time to pursue business opportunities. If you're currently in practice without an assistant, don't let it go another day. Start interviewing for the position tomorrow. If paying a market rate salary for a proper employee is an issue, then get one or two other advisors in your firm to chip in and share the assistant. A maximum ratio is 3-to-1 (advisors to assistant). Check online resources like Glassdoor.com for salary and other compensation estimates for the position in your area.

TIP

Focus on hiring someone you like, trust, and respect, but most importantly someone who's energetic and eager to learn. The best candidates come from the service and hospitality industry, where they're looking for a normal business hours career. Good energy and an excitement for the opportunity outweigh experience and Excel spreadsheet skills any day of the week.

WARNING

Don't limit your search to people with industry-specific experience, training, or skills. You're ultimately going to have to train them to use your firm's systems and learn your client on-boarding processes, so experience elsewhere doesn't necessarily help. What does matter is intelligence, energy, and character.

When you've hired your first employee, you've started building the foundation to your business.

TIP

In addition to an assistant, one team member should be in charge of managing the prospects and clients pipeline with the help of customer relationship management (CRM) software. As you grow, you may even want to hire a dedicated client service associate who can master the product landscape and attend to the needs of the client base.

Dotting your i's and crossing your t's

Consult one of the attorneys in your professional network to formalize your business structure and file all the necessary paperwork with the federal, state, and local governments and regulatory agencies. Starting any business involves complex legal issues, even more so when the business involves managing client finances. Don't trust yourself or any of your partners to handle this on their own, unless one of you happens to be a lawyer.

Here's a short list of legal documents you need to start your business:

>> Articles of incorporation.

>> Certificate of assumed name, if you're operating the business as a sole proprietorship or limited liability company (LLC) under a name other than

your own and your partners'. (Refer to the earlier, "Structuring your business" section for more information.)

>> Request for an employer identification number, which you'll need to identify your business to the IRS and may be required by banks before you can open a business account in the business's name.

>> Applications for any business licenses.

>> Letters of agreement or partnership agreements to stipulate the terms of the agreement to work together.

>> Expense sharing agreement, if you and your partners have agreed to share certain expenses. A verbal agreement is okay, but a written agreement is much better. Inevitably one advisor will commandeer more staff time than another, which inevitably creates disagreements over expense sharing. Expense sharing should cover all possible expenses, including those related to employer termination, worker's compensation claims, and unemployment benefits.

>> Noncompete and nondisclosure agreements.

For additional details about starting a business, check out *Small Business For Dummies* by Eric Tyson and Jim Schell (John Wiley & Sons, Inc.).

Getting someone focused on rainmaking

Every financial advisory firm needs financial advisors to fill three roles: minder, finder, and grinder. These roles are all equally important, but when you're getting started, the finder role is the most important because you need to start acquiring clients so everyone has plenty of revenue-generating work. The finder in your business may be you or someone else, or all financial advisors in the business may share that role. What's important is that the role not be neglected, even when everyone's busy.

If you're the designated rainmaker, fall in love with networking. New clients are your lifeblood, so stay visible and socialize every breakfast, lunch, and dinner, if you can afford it. Attend charity events, networking lunches and dinners, and parties. The more time you spend socializing, the more prospects you'll add to your staff's workflow. In my own experience, hiring an assistant immediately provided me exponentially more time. I replaced paperwork and administrative tasks with more research and attention to global economics, which in turn enriched every interaction I had with every person I met.

My rainmaking activity was totally natural to me, never forced, never with a product sales agenda, but with a fierce superior performance service offering. To be a great finder, you must be a master of your field, ready with statistics and information that support your vision and recommendations.

Battling client attrition

To minimize client attrition, continue to acquire new clients while improving customer service for existing clients. For example, my business partner is approaching 60 years old, after a 35-year career as a financial advisor. His clients have children who are my age, and their children have children. When we partnered (originally through joint work), we benefitted from working synergies (I did the business operations and portfolio management, and he focused on relationship building and financial planning). Now, 13 years later, our firm has more than 1,000 client households and a support team to deliver superior client service.

TIP

Train your junior advisors on how to retain and develop clients, so you can dig deeper into existing relationships. The only way to achieve better knowledge of your clients and how to add value is to spend more time with them, and for that you need support staff.

Measuring Success in Terms of Profit Margin

Business valuation is rooted in profit margin. And, just like any other business, financial advisory firms are subject to the same valuation metric. Financial advisory service businesses typically run expenses at 33 percent of gross revenue, so make this calculation when viewing your business profit.

If you're making $100,000 in gross revenues, a 33 percent expense margin (67 percent profit margin) means all operational expenses of your business cost a total of $33,000. This total includes the costs of all travel, social events, meals, entertainment, staff payroll, firm fees, technical and other subscriptions, and so on. However, it excludes the financial advisor's income, which can be taken from the business in the form of either salary or equity dividends, depending on how you structure the business.

REMEMBER

Bottom line, aim for a 67 percent profit margin or better.

Achieving Growth through Mergers and Acquisitions

One of the best ways to grow your financial advisory business is through mergers and acquisitions. A *merger* is the voluntary combination of two businesses. An *acquisition* is the purchase of one business by another. Mergers and acquisitions can drive growth in two ways:

>> **Potential synergies:** Combining two businesses with complementary capabilities or service areas is an efficient way for each business to get the expertise and access to markets that its missing to achieve its full potential. Remember, with synergies, 1+1 = 3. (Chapter 20 discusses how your can create synergy.)

>> **Growth in the pool of clients:** Merging with or acquiring another financial advisor's practice instantly increases the number of clients and the number of prospective clients.

Prior to engaging in a merger or acquisition, perform your due diligence by conducting a business valuation of the other business. If you're a Chartered Financial Analyst (CFA), you can perform this valuation on your own (although it's not an independent opinion, it'll get you started in the right direction).

REMEMBER

Determining a financial advisory firm's value is no small feat, especially because so many of them slowly atrophy, while the owners continue to receive income well into their 70s through recurring renewal and asset-based income. These assets typically experience a certain level of attrition, which increases every year. This attrition doesn't necessarily rule out a merger or acquisition, as long as you can negotiate reasonable compensation and buyout terms.

TIP

Financial advisors are constantly starting new firms and retiring, so plenty of merger and acquisitions opportunities are available. You're likely to hear about opportunities through your professional network.

Planning Your Exit Strategy

When you're starting a business, the last thing you want to think about is eventually leaving the business. However, financial advisors are always encouraging clients to think about their end game, so follow that advice. In this section, I introduce you to a few exit strategies and offer some advice on conducting your own estate planning.

Bailing out with a buyout

If you want a clean break when you retire, a buyout is best; you simply sell your business or your portion of the business. Depending on how you structure the deal, you may receive a lump sum payment, a promissory note, or periodic payments. You and (especially) the buyer must pay close attention to the FINRA regulations that govern payment to another advisor. Specifically, if the advisor being bought out gives up her licenses, that could create challenges in paying securities-based revenues.

Unfortunately, a clean, quick break from the business may not be an option. Savvy buyers typically insist on the seller's continued client involvement for some time after the sale to ensure a smooth and comprehensive transition. This approach is usually a win-win-win, for the buyer, seller, and clients. As a seller, you can continue to earn while smoothing the transition into your golden years.

REMEMBER

Whether you're a seller or a buyer in a buyout, I strongly encourage you to hire a known specialist consultancy in the financial advisor industry. Although the price for such services can give you sticker shock, this third-party expertise may save you a ton of time and money down the road in the event of a regulatory audit or other unsavory event.

Choosing a successor to take over

Selecting a successor to take over your business can be easy, difficult, or somewhere in between. The choice can be obvious; for example, if you've been grooming your daughter-in-law for the past 20 years to take the helm. Or, you may not have anyone in mind at all, in which case the only reasonable option is a buyout.

I have only two suggestions for choosing the right successor(s):

>> Pick a successor you like, trust, and respect. She will be the steward to your business legacy, impacting generations to come.

>> Select multiple successors in the case of multiple business lines and practice specialties. Don't feel as though you have to choose one person to take over the entire operation.

Handling your own estate planning

As a business owner, your most valuable financial asset is probably your business, likely more valuable than your primary residence, savings, and other assets combined. You should protect that value for you and your heirs by planning your estate.

The risks are clear. What happens if you pass away? Will your spouse be able to depend on a stream of income, or will compensation come in some other form; for example, a cross-purchase buy-sell agreement, as I explain in Chapter 8?

WARNING

Don't leave your own family without a proper estate plan. Nothing is more disappointing than when I hear of financial advisors who become disabled or unexpectedly die, and the family has no replacement income or even life insurance proceeds. To add to the tragedy is the fact that the financial fallout could have easily been mitigated with a little forethought — something you give every client you serve.

You and your family are no less important.

Avoiding the "die at your desk" scenario

According to Cerulli Associates, (which routinely publishes reports on financial advisor trends), more than 40 percent of financial advisors are older than 55. This presents a unique challenge to the industry, which relies so heavily on human interaction: Where will all the new advisors come from to replace this population?

REMEMBER

If you're a financial advisor who's nearing retirement, I strongly encourage you, for the sake of the industry, to mentor a younger person who's just getting started. Don't be the financial advisor who dies at her desk. Even worse, don't be the financial advisor who failed to help the industry survive the massive loss of highly qualified professionals. By mentoring a young, upcoming financial advisor, you'll stay fresh as you near retirement, you'll help pass the torch to the next generation to keep the industry alive and thriving, and you won't die at your desk.

If you're a young financial advisor, attrition in the industry is good news for you. You'll have a much easier time succeeding in this industry today and in the near future than at any other time in history. The main reason for this is that you don't have to rely on your own networking and business-building skills, because you can build upon the existing businesses of other advisors who've come before you. As the older generation seeks to avoid "working themselves to death", you become the attractive solution.

The key aspect to success in this arrangement is that both parties understand what they're getting out of the deal. One is happy to leave their clients in mentored, competent hands, whereas the other is happy to be gainfully employed in the continued stewardship of a grateful client's assets.

» **Divvying up the workload by department**

» **Attending to key client development areas**

» **Lightening the workload with client service associates**

» **Delegating administrative tasks**

Chapter **22**

Structuring Your Firm as a Well-Oiled Machine

After you make the mental and operational transition into functioning as a financial advisory business, you need to step outside of your practitioner role. Take off your financial advisor hat, and put on your business owner hat. The time has come to staff your business and organize it around the core operations of a financial advisory firm — business development, client service, and administration.

As I explain in Chapter 21, lone wolves handle these three critical aspects by themselves. In this chapter, you find out how to assign roles and delegate responsibilities to other team members.

REMEMBER

Organizing people, delegating tasks, coordinating activities, and mentoring less experience financial advisors and employees all require a fluency in professional development, behavioral psychology, and other interpersonal communication skills. Like any pursuit, be prepared to discover a great deal and to evolve into your role as owner/operator. Getting your firm to function as a well-oiled machine takes time. Be patient and humble.

Organizing Your Business by Department

Every financial advisory practice requires attention to the following three fundamental areas, each of which is assigned to a specific role within the business (see Chapter 20 for more about the three roles):

Business area	Role
Administration	Minder
Business development	Finder
Client servicing	Grinder

When your firm is just getting rolling, one team member may handle two of these areas; for example, you may want to focus on administration, whereas another team member concentrates on business development and client servicing. As you grow, having one team member dedicated to each critical business is often necessary. More advanced businesses have additional layers of management staff for each business area with several people reporting to director-level managers.

REMEMBER

The success of your business doesn't rely so much on how you organize people after hiring them, but on whom you hire in the first place. Figure out what you love to do, whether it's administration, business development, or client servicing, and then partner with or hire others who are passionate and skilled in handling the other areas. If you're a finder who partners with two other finders, your business will be sailing into stiff headwinds. Just because larger firms push to have all their financial advisors focused on acquiring new clients doesn't mean you have to make the same mistake. Staff your business with financial advisors and employees whose passions and skills complement one another's. When an organization is staffed with the right people, it's much easier to organize and manage.

The following sections discuss these three areas and what type of people you should look for to be responsible for that role.

Minding the business: Administration

Administration is all about the proper movement and maintenance of resources and records. Responsibilities include planning, delegating, scheduling, resource allocation, oversight, and pushing a lot of paperwork, whether the documents are paper or digital. These are the responsibilities of the minder — in larger businesses, the chief operating officer (COO), in smaller businesses, a capable executive assistant or office manager.

The right person for this position is well-organized, detail-oriented, patient, and cordial.

Ideally, your minder will be skilled in implementing a client relationship management (CRM) system for your business to improve customer service efficiency and effectiveness. See the later section "Harnessing the power of client relationship management (CRM) software," for details.

TIP

Tie your administrator's compensation (salary and bonuses) to operational efficiency and overall growth to incentivize the minder to implement technologies and innovate systems that improve the firm's internal operations and client service. With CRM, you can access reports to gain visibility into the firm's performance metrics. Tie compensation to these metrics.

Finding clients: Business development

Business development involves finding clients (who receive services) and customers (who buy products). Finders are often deemed to be the most important people in the organization and are typically rewarded accordingly. However, finding clients is only one of the three key components to a successful financial advisory firm. Someone must run the firm, and others must provide exceptional client service.

REMEMBER

Have your finders focus more on developing clients than on selling products to customers. Many financial advisors give this role a bad name by pushing products to maximize their commissions instead of engaging in the more intimate and impactful delivery of insightful and unbiased financial advice.

The finder's responsibilities include the following:

- » Identifying opportunities where the firm can add value to a client's financial outcomes.

- » Studying market segments where the firm's specific value proposition is likely to find the most fertile ground.

- » Interviewing market constituents to develop insight into what clients value in order to adjust the firm's value proposition, if necessary.

- » Challenging the finder's own comfort zone routinely, especially in relation to contacting prospects — phone calls, referrals, meetings, professional introductions, and so on.

Train your finders on your client due diligence process, as I discuss in Chapter 13. Only with a clear and consistent due diligence process does your business development activity engage new clients in positive and productive ways.

WARNING

When training finders, reinforce the importance of not being too invasive or intrusive and not using emotional coercion to gain clients or sell products or solutions. Developing good client opportunities means taking time to identify where and how you can have the most beneficial impact on the client's financial outcomes. (See Chapter 18 to find out more about earning clients.)

TIP

Tie each finder's compensation to a salary plus a performance bonus. The base salary should be commensurate with industry experience, and the bonus should be tied to a specific threshold of new business acquisition — for example, a base salary of $36,000, plus a bonus of $5,000 for every five new platinum–level clients. Provide clear guidelines on how rewards will be granted upon meeting expectations.

WARNING

Don't pay commissions to a team member who's not properly licensed approved by your broker/dealer.

FOLLOWING THE CHARITABLE DONOR MODEL

Finders are wise to follow the charitable donor model that nonprofit organizations use to engage donors. Most nonprofits have an entire department devoted to converting non-donors into donors and then increasing each donor's contribution level. The department is usually referred to as Development, which usually has a Director of Development.

The development team identifies potential donors and markets to them with the goal of getting them to make a small one-time donation. Over time, the unrelenting marketing messages evolve to gradually align the donor's interests with those of the charitable organization in an attempt to take the donor from that small one-time donation to a recurring monthly or annual gift.

Likewise, taking a prospective client from initial meeting to a top-tier client takes tremendous stamina and carefully crafted messaging to help a prospective client realize that your firm's value proposition is supremely aligned with his financial interests.

Educational communications are most effective in presenting a firm's value proposition in a supportive, nonjudgmental way without aggressive sales tactics.

Grinding out the work: Client service

After prospects become clients, the grinders step in to deliver client service that exceeds client expectations. The goal of a grinder is to establish a lifelong relationship with a client, which requires a flexible approach. Clients' needs and desires change over the course of their lives in response to changing conditions and mindset. They can become more aggressive or conservative depending on life events and experiences and what they learn over time. The grinder must be able to adapt client service accordingly.

To deliver the most effective client service, get to know your clients. Check in with them regularly, which varies according to each client's service level tier, as I explain in Chapter 16; generally, this means once or twice a year for less engaged clients and quarterly (or more frequently) for your more active clients and those who are good sources of referrals.

REMEMBER

Although grinders focus client service on the needs of existing clients, grinders often become finders, contributing to business development. For example, when client service involves portfolio management or financial planning reviews (for example, making sure retirement savings is on target or checking to make sure the client has sufficient insurance), the grinder has an opportunity to find out more about the client and the client's needs, their friends and family, and their needs. The insight gained from these interactions can reveal areas for additional value to be generated for both the firm and its clients.

Tie grinder compensation to a salary plus a bonus associated with a client retention ratio. Start with a base salary commensurate with industry experience, as you did with the finders, and add a flat bonus payable when the business achieves a 95 percent client retention rate annually. For example, you may pay your grinders $36,000 annually with a $10,000 bonus for achieving the targeted annual client retention rate.

TIP

To encourage synergy between business development and client service (finders and grinders), tie the bonuses of both to new client acquisitions and client retention. These positions should be closely coordinated to maximize the complementary nature of getting to know clients better and revealing opportunities for growth.

Identifying Business Development's Focus Areas

If you're one of the firm's finders, you need to know about certain areas that are fertile ground for new opportunities — areas that automatically connect you to a host of new prospects. In this section, I highlight four key areas on which to focus your business development efforts.

REMEMBER

Develop a clear strategy and implementation plan for pursuing these four areas of opportunities. Reaping business from each of these sources takes a disciplined and consistent approach. Without a carefully planned program, you won't achieve the desired level of success. As you pursue these areas, conduct formal weekly evaluations with your team on what's working and what's not to gain the traction necessary to uncover areas where your team can add value.

Getting your firm's foot in the door with 401K plans

In recent years, the revenues associated with taking over an existing, well-funded 401K company-sponsored retirement plan have declined dramatically. Commissions for moving these plans have dried up, and trail-based income has dropped to 0.25 percent range. So, why am I bringing them up? Because, in my mind, the fact that these plans have dropped their revenue-generating potential, makes them even more attractive. As other financial advisors abandon these opportunities, they open the door for others who have a more value-added focus. Acquiring a corporate retirement plan provides you with a fresh pool of potential clients in the form of plan participants.

WARNING

Don't assume that you'll be able to deliver a couple product sales pitches at a breakroom lunch-and-learn event and convert all those plan participants into clients who are eager to sign up for the other services your firm offers. You must approach the plan participants with the same due diligence as you would any other prospect. Taking on the 401K plan simply provides you with a list of leads.

TIP

For best results, hire salaried personnel (not commissioned salespeople) to provide ongoing contact and education regarding the participants' plan contributions and investments and how those tie into their larger personal finance picture. Using this approach, you can introduce other personal finance topics, such as the importance of having health, disability, and life insurance; estate planning; and more. Remember to keep the focus on education and provide valuable information to reflect the value that your firm offers to its clients.

Take a gradual approach over time and make sure your team is capturing all the information collected regarding plan participants through the use of your CRM software. Turnover is natural in the junior financial advisor positions responsible for maintaining contact with plan participants, so you need to capture the information about plan participants and their interactions with your firm to provide continuity of service in the event of turnover. Paying a salary lowers your advisor turnover rate but doesn't eliminate it. The better your business is able to capture the communications and interactions with plan participants and share that information with others in the firm, the better the long-term results. Frankly, this advice applies to all clients, but it's more imperative with a corporate client, which has many more points of contact with the firm.

Expanding opportunities through corporate benefit programs

Just as with 401K plan takeovers and consulting, you can easily diversify your revenues and add value to the same client through other corporate employee benefits programs, including group insurance plans such as life, health, and disability.

If you happen to come in contact with a company's financial manager or HR personnel, ask about their corporate benefit programs, whether they're satisfied with their existing programs, and how their employees have responded to them. If you're already taking over the company's 401K plan, you're in contact with the decision-makers who choose the plan providers.

REMEMBER

Because major players, such as ADP, are already operating in the corporate benefits space, a more customized design and service solution will grab attention. Don't assume that the larger companies have an advantage over your smaller firm.

Networking through trusts and estates

Estate planning (see Chapter 10) often involves numerous people, including the owner of the estate, individual trustees, corporate trustees, trust protectors, attorneys, accountants, and named beneficiaries. All of these individuals provide business-building opportunities:

>> You can showcase your knowledge, skills, and professionalism to fellow professionals, including attorneys and accountants. Trusts and estates often demand greater sophistication and coordination of asset and liability management solutions, which brings together the client's attorney, accountant, and financial advisor.

>> You can coordinate beneficial financial outcomes for all stakeholders, including beneficiaries, the trustee or corporate trustee, and trust protectors.

REMEMBER

Rarely does a trustee fully understand the scope of his duties under a family trust document, which can place the person at risk of a significant liability. For example, the trustee could easily and unintentionally violate the laws governing the management of the trust, subsequently exposing the trustee to a lawsuit from beneficiaries. Your services would provide tremendous value to several parties involved; it's just a matter of educating participants to the risks. Whether they ultimately do anything about those risks is their concern, but at least you've provided the appropriate guidance, and you may be remembered and rewarded for your efforts with future business.

Easing the burden of household's financial manager

The wealthiest households often have their own family offices complete with an administrator who oversees the activities of the household staff (cooks, maids, butlers, household financial manager, and so on). The household financial manager is often overburdened with other nonfinancial work, which increases their challenge to achieve the financial outcomes the family desires.

If you're able to support the household's financial manager, without displacing him, you can secure another source of business. More importantly, the administrator and staff typically are well-connected to organizations with whom they network to discuss all things family office. One such organization, Family Office Exchange (`www.familyoffice.com`) is "the world's largest peer-to-peer network for ultra-wealthy families and their family offices and the leading authority on matters related to legacy wealth management." Early in my career, I had the pleasure of learning from this organization's founder, Sara Hamilton, and it has informed my perspective in this area ever since.

Delegating Responsibilities to Client Service Associates

Client service associates are a cost-effective way to lighten financial advisor workload affordably. The main purpose of a client service associate is to ensure routine engagement with clients and to gather intelligence on what's going on in their lives. By keeping informed about clients, the finders and grinders know how clients are getting on mentally, physically, and emotionally. Whether driven by life events (such as a family member's death) or just growing older, a client's changing viewpoint can create unique challenges and opportunities for their existing financial plan.

To make the most of your investment in a client associate, you may want to assign them additional duties, including the following:

>> Researching and reporting on the competitive marketplace and product landscape.

>> Handholding around new business submissions such as a new investment account application or a new insurance policy to be underwritten.

To delegate as much as possible to your client service associates, make sure they're properly licensed. They should have both a state insurance (health and life) license and have passed the FINRA Series 6 and 63 exams.

Assigning Administrative/Operational Responsibilities

The first person to hire is your assistant as I discuss in Chapter 21. When you're building a business, your assistant serves more as an executive assistant, managing the office, taking ownership of the client relationship management (CRM) software, coordinating new-client workflow, and outsourcing accounting tasks and legal matters.

In this section, I explain these job responsibilities in greater detail.

Hiring an assistant is a landmark moment in your business, leaving you with an ongoing feeling of freedom and joy. Use your assistant wisely to leverage your time on matters that drive more value into your future business pipeline.

Managing the office

In terms of office management, your assistant has the following responsibilities:

>> Updating your calendar

>> Scheduling all routine client retention work and due diligence meetings for new clients

- » Answering inbound calls

- » Running reports

- » Ordering office supplies, including stationery and business cards

WARNING

Always defer to your assistant for scheduling purposes. I've been reminded of this often, when I've short-circuited the system and booked an appointment myself. It throws the whole calendar into disarray and creates more work and frustration for all involved. I have to remind myself that I'm not aware of outstanding dates and times that my assistant has offered to several people, so I really shouldn't be scheduling anything.

Harnessing the power of client relationship management (CRM) software

CRM is a system for tracking prospect and customer interactions with a business for the purpose of staying connected with customers and improving customer service and profitability. I use "CRM" to mean "client relationship management," because financial advisors should be advising clients and not selling products to customers.

A CRM system typically provides the following functionality:

- » Qualifies leads, so finders can focus their efforts on pursuing the most promising prospects and not waste time on prospects who are less likely to be receptive to the firm's services.

- » Collects data on prospect and client interactions with the firm and provides quick and easy access to every client's details, including contact information, transaction history, interactions with the firm, notes about the client, and much more.

- » Forecasts sales for improved resource planning and scheduling.

- » Facilitates analysis to gain clearer business insights by identifying patterns and trends that may impact the business. CRM systems enable data-driven decisions, instead of having to base decisions solely on intuition.

- » Coordinates sales and marketing efforts to optimize the sales cycle.

- » Monitors the firm's social media properties to improve responsiveness to posts and highlight areas for improvement.

- » Automates the process of maintaining contact with prospects and clients in a way that leads them from initial engagement to adoption, as I explain in the next section.

Even though every team member should be using your firm's CRM software to record customer information and interactions routinely and to consult the system to inform their interactions with customers, your administrative assistant should own the system. What I mean by *owning* the system is that your administrative assistant becomes an expert in using the system, training others on how to use it, and ensuring that everyone in contact with clients is using the system to its full potential. In addition, your administrative assistant uses the CRM software to generate reports that provide insight into *how* your business is functioning (for example, too much time in between client due diligence steps) and *what* everyone is doing in the business to contribute to the stated goals and objectives.

Early on, you'll use your CRM software to capture data. Later, after you've collected data, you can run reports that provide insight into clients and into your firm's operations and performance. You may be collecting data for weeks, months, or even years before you can start asking the software questions that only historical data can answer.

REMEMBER

Your assistant isn't responsible for entering into client conversations, calls, or meetings into the system. Those tasks are the responsibility of the person who's interacting directly with the client — usually, the finder, the grinder, or a client service associate.

Coordinating the workflow for new clients

Every new client experience should be the same pleasant, consistent process. The steps should mirror those of your client due diligence process, which then flows into an established client onboarding protocol. (See Chapter 13 for more about the due diligence process and onboarding new clients.)

The workflow for new clients involves collecting a considerable amount of documentation from a client, including a copy of a client's government-issued ID, an emergency contact list, and financial records, just to create a complete file. You may be waiting for certain documents for several days or even weeks. As new clients pop into the queue, older client onboarding often takes a back seat or falls between the cracks leading to bottlenecks later.

TIP

Use your CRM software along with checklists to keep workflow for new clients running smoothly. Dedicate a weekly meeting to tracking all clients in your queue. Using a CRM generated report would help, but I must admit that in my practice we still use a separate tracking report. It's not ideal, but as we develop mastery of our CRM, we're hoping to use it to automate and streamline client onboarding.

Outsourcing accounting and legal

Every business can benefit from professional accounting and legal services. As your business starts to grow from you and your executive assistant to additional partners and employees, you'll need professional accounting and legal services even more. Accounting services can help you evaluate your business's financial success and progress. Legal services can ensure that ownership and compensation terms are understood across all your team members (though specific details are best kept private between you and the specific team member).

Unless you're a larger business (more than 15 employees and revenues greater than $5,000,000 per year), you'll probably outsource all your accounting and legal needs. Only very large firms have in-house corporate counsel and accounting.

Outsourcing accounting and legal to professionals increases your expenses, but the benefits more than make up for the costs:

>> Your CPA can answer questions and provide guidance that increase profits and reduce costs. He can answer questions such as: How much have my business revenues grown relative to expenses? Is profit margin increasing? What's my year-over-year growth rate? Your CPA can also recommend a business structure that provides more favorable tax treatment on your profits.

>> Your attorney can help with compensation agreements, nondisclosure agreements, ownership agreements and exchanges, cross-purchase buy-sell agreements, and so on. You can use an online resource such as Legalzoom. com or RocketLawyer.com for many of these basic agreements, but you may not get the personalized service that a local attorney provides. The more people you negotiate with the greater the likelihood of agreeing to terms that aren't in your favor. Seeking the counsel of a competent business/corporate attorney saves you time and money in the long run. Most financial advisors forego legal counsel to avoid the expense. Just realize that by skimping on this expense, you increase the chance for future unintended and possibly break-the-bank consequences.

Chapter **23**

Divvying Up Your Business: Equity Participation

After creating a business entity, you need to start thinking about whether and how you want to use the business to build wealth. As the business earns more and more money, you could simply pull that money out of the business in the form of higher salary and bonuses. Another option is to leave the money in the business to build equity value.

Like any business, publicly traded or privately held, your financial advisory firm can have equity value. Once determined, this equity value gives a genuine market value to your firm's ownership units (whether LLC units or C-corporate stock shares). Ascribing value to these units enables exciting methods to keep your business operating beyond your own functional career, and even your lifetime.

In this chapter, I describe various ways that building equity in your firm creates opportunity to grow and to compensate key personnel beyond mere salaries and bonuses.

Keeping Some Profits in the Firm

Building equity is a relevant and practical option only if you're a financial advisor who owns a firm and is planning ahead for business continuity or business succession. That is, it makes sense only if you're looking to pass the business along to someone else, sell it, or negotiate a deal with the future owners to play an ongoing role in the firm while you scale back your responsibilities to spend more time golfing, sailing, contributing your time to a heartfelt cause, or starting a new career. If you have the business just to generate revenue so you can pay yourself and your team, building equity in the business may not be important to you.

When I first started to study building equity in a firm and then offering ownership interests to others, I couldn't wrap my brain around the logistics. The big mental hurdle for me was the concept that net profits ultimately drive a firm's equity valuation, as any certified financial analyst (CFA) charter holder can attest. In all the practices I was involved in (including my own), the practice had no explicit profit, because it all flowed through the firm to the people who earned it. Nothing was left in the business to cover distributions (in the form of dividends).

Assuming you decide to build equity in your business, set your own salary first, based on the role you serve in the practice. The more salary you take, the less profit for the business. So, if maximum cash flow is what you want, then you won't be creating equity. Of course, there's no right or wrong way to pay yourself. It's a choice between cash flow and equity. The more cash you pull out of the business, the less equity you leave in it.

TIP

Instead of paying a constant percentage of revenues, based on assets under management (AUM) or product sales, consider using an up-front loaded compensation model; for example, the advisor earns 6 percent up front, and the firm keeps the ongoing trailing revenue. By structuring the compensation this way, you accomplish two things:

>> The financial advisor is rewarded for adding to your firm's revenues and has no limits on how much she can earn, which is great for motivating optimal performance.

You must have reserves (or a financing mechanism) in place to adequately fund the up-front compensation.

REMEMBER

>> The recurring trail revenue creates a differential that can be automatically added to the firm's equity. For example, suppose you have a team member who's bringing in new AUM, and your firm charges 1 percent asset-based fees. If you provide an up-front compensation to the advisor of $6,000, when a new

$1,000,000 account is deposited, then in subsequent years, the ongoing annual fee will become a part of your firm's profits. It's like having an auto deduction that goes directly into the firm's equity account.

This structure is commonly used in the registered investment advisor (RIA) marketplace. By providing a front-end loaded compensation, you're aligning the advisor's work focus with the compensation.

If you're managing money under a Corporate RIA, have your compensation structure approved by your broker/dealer first.

Adopting a Founder Mentality

As the founder of the firm, you have a tremendous amount of responsibility weighing on you, but you also have a tremendous amount of freedom. Assuming you have the firm running like a well-oiled machine (see Chapter 22), you've been able to delegate day-to-day operations to your partners and staff. You can now step back a little and focus on the bigger picture.

Here I guide you through the process of settling into your role as founder.

As founder, envision having built a thriving business, and then remove yourself from the equation. This exercise enables you to envision the legacy you'll leave behind, so you have a clearer idea of the type of business you want to build and the people you want to have in place to continue its operation.

Playing the role of visionary

As founder, one of your responsibilities is to think big and envision your firm's future. You may have no idea how your firm will get there, but you need to have a clear vision of where it will be in 5, 10, or 15 years. Then, you need a clear concise statement that captures and conveys your vision — a *vision statement*.

Qualities of an exceptional vision statement include the following:

>> **Future focused:** Focus on the ideal — where you want the firm to be, not where it's been or where it is.

>> **Purposeful:** Express the positive impact the firm will make on client's lives, the industry, the community, or the world.

- » **Directional:** Provide direction to guide decision-making but enough flexibility to allow for innovation. In other words, point to the destination without giving directions on how to get there.

- » **Unique:** Capture the qualities of your firm that make it exceptional.

- » **Inspirational:** Fill everyone in your organization with the enthusiasm to wake up in the morning eager to serve clients.

- » **Bold but not ridiculous:** Be ambitious, but within the realm of reality. As a small firm, you're probably not going to be the *world's* leading premier financial advisory service.

- » **Short and sweet:** Aim for between 50 and 75 words, definitely no more than 100.

Here's an example of a vision statement that meets all these requirements:

> We will serve as trusted financial advisors to our clients, attending to their finances through all stages of their lives. We will listen carefully to our clients to gain insight into their dreams and aspirations. We will seek ways to optimize the use of each client's assets to achieve their goals while protecting their assets from losses resulting from unforeseeable events. We will continually improve through training and education to provide our clients with increasingly exceptional financial guidance, and we will remain committed to upholding the highest fiduciary standard.

Having started and built a firm I now have the pleasure of running, I can honestly say that nothing is more exciting than envisioning the practice's future. Searching for new ways to add value to new client markets never gets boring. Setting an example for my team on how to achieve business growth ethically and with integrity is also deeply satisfying.

Serving as the primary rainmaker

As founder of the business, you're probably the rainmaker, not necessarily because you have the marketing and networking drive and skills to find and acquire clients. You may just be the idea person — the one person in your firm with the vision and creativity to innovate ways to generate revenue and the passion to get everyone else in the firm revved up enough to execute those ideas. The point is, as founder, you need to find ways to generate revenue — whether by becoming a productive finder in your firm, coming up with new ideas, or figuring out ways to harness other talent in the firm to make things happen.

Take a self-assessment to identify your talents, so you can leverage them to your benefit as a rainmaker. Years ago I took a StrengthsFinder 2.0 self-assessment test and encourage you to do the same. This assessment, administered online, subjects you to a series of rapid-fire questions and then uses your answers to identify your key strengths. My top strength is ideation. I'm an idea guy. My second strength is activator. I like to take ideas and put them into action immediately. Ideation plus activation is a powerful combination for business building.

I've never had an interest in cold calling, or even warm calling. Instead, I set about developing something unique, which I believed in through conviction and passion, and I shared it with clients and colleagues that I thought would benefit most from my value proposition. If I believed I had developed the best client due diligence process in the industry, I made sure everyone I talked to knew about it.

This type of passionate conviction to your value proposition is what enables true rainmaking. Rainmakers are like marksmen. They have a fine bead on their target from a thousand yards away, and they instinctively account for wind speed, the earth's rotation, and gravitational pull. They're certain, when they pull the trigger, that their shot will hit its mark.

Avoiding the temptation to deal with day-to-day operations

The siren's call toward micromanagement is a constant companion. Because most financial advisors begin in solitary practices, they're unaccustomed to delegating and trusting others to deliver quality that meets their high standards. If you've been a lone wolf practitioner for several years, you've probably been telling yourself all that time that you could get it done faster, easier, and more efficiently if you just did it yourself. And yes, that's true, until it isn't. Building a practice to resemble an actual business requires that you not only move emotionally past this limiting mindset, but you also embrace the possibilities that others may be able to do it much better and more efficiently than you. Even if they can't, you really don't have a choice; you can't do it all yourself, so you'd better figure out how to let go.

The two secrets to transitioning from doing it all yourself to delegating without feeling as though you have to micromanage are as follows:

>> Hire great people.

>> Develop great processes.

With great processes in place and great people to carry out those processes, you can confidently delegate.

Offering Equity Buy-in to Team Members

When you're looking to attract great talent and you don't yet have the cash flow to pay them the going rate, consider sweetening the pot by offering them equity in the company. Many tech sector employees (for example, programmers) have enjoyed the benefits of owning their company's stock. Whether shares are privately held or publicly traded, getting in on the ground floor of stock ownership can be a great approach to wealth creation.

You've probably heard of all the multimillionaire administrative assistants that were created by Microsoft in the 1990s. Unfortunately, other than hedge funds and private equity or debt funds, this wealth-creation phenomenon hasn't made its way to the financial sector. However, the financial advisory sector is ripe for equity development, particularly given the breadth of small, independent practices.

In this section, I offer guidance on how to offer equity buy-in to team members.

REMEMBER

Being able to buy ownership interest in a well-run financial advisory firm is a tremendous opportunity, but not everyone sees it that way. Most employees want and need a steady paycheck and may not be interested in being compensated with stock options. However, highly successful financial advisors who have some money socked away may find the opportunity irresistible, making this a great tactic to hire and retain top talent.

Being selective

Allowing for your team members to buy ownership interests into your business doesn't mean *every* team member automatically qualifies. Instead, use the following factors to determine eligibility for equity ownership:

>> **Person has demonstrated exceptional contribution to the firm's operational efficiency, revenue generation, and/or new client development.** These are each correlated to different roles within your organization: administration (minder), business development (finder), and client service (grinder). By offering equity ownership, you're saying that this team member has become part of your firm's fabric.

>> **You like, trust, and respect this person.** One of my colleagues calls this the "Mother's Test." If you'd let this person become the financial advisor (or other responsible role) to your mother, then that's a pretty good indication that person has the likeability and trustworthiness to meet this criterion.

>> **Person has tenure with your firm.** Wait for a period of time that feels right. I won't recommend a standard time frame. Some couples get married after

years of courtship and divorce after a few years (or months), whereas others date for a few weeks, get married, and stay married for 50 years or more. You'll know in your gut. If it feels too soon, it probably is. Generally, after a period of three to five years, you should have a good sense of the person's dedication to your firm and its clients.

» **Person has a shared business ethics and values-based philosophy.** Because the financial sector generally attracts money mongers as opposed to altruists, know where the person's heart and soul are when it comes to doing the right thing.

In short, offering a chance for someone to share in the future profits of your business means you're going to be closely connected with that person. Like a marriage, you'll be bound forever to one another and to all of that other person's problems and other baggage. And like marriage, parting ways can be quite costly, both financially and emotionally.

Putting your agreements in writing

Whether you're forming a partnership, agreeing on compensation, or offering team members the opportunity to buy interests in the firm, put all agreements in writing. Even though verbal and hand-shake agreements are the industry norm, these informal contracts have an unfortunate tendency toward confusion and misunderstandings.

TIP

If you're giving employees/team members an opportunity to buy into the firm, put the criteria for qualifying for the opportunity in writing. This clear guidance motivates team members, because the written document proves that you're not making empty promises. You don't have to be specific on terms and conditions, but your agreement should paint a picture of what the employee/team member must do to qualify and what she'll get in return. In addition, consult an attorney to prepare the necessary agreements.

Proceeding When Equity Ownership Doesn't Matter

If you're not concerned with building equity in your firm, you have other options regarding how you compensate yourself and other members of your firm and how you choose to navigate the evolution of your career as you age. In this section, you find out more about your options in these two areas.

Maximizing annual compensation to advisors

In the early years of my firm, I couldn't afford to pay someone the salary that a certain position would demand. As a result, for a period of a few years, my firm's compensation structure involved passing through the advisor cut of shared revenues from the broker/dealer or insurance carrier directly to my firm's advisors. All of my advisors were earning a constant, recurring percentage of revenues *not* adjusted over time. This model completely eliminates a firm's ability to have a worth of its own.

However, each advisor may develop her own business value separate and distinct from the joint work being conducted within the firm — for example, sourcing her own clients away from any firm client acquisition program. She's able to earn compensation at difference levels depending on how a client has been sourced — either on her own versus through the firm. In fact, this approach is how I've been able to build my own business without modifying the income streams that my advisor team members have become accustomed to.

Now, years later, after achieving a level of scale and sustainable, recurring, predictable revenues, I'm in a position of having to broach the uncomfortable, but necessary subject of an advisor's compensation structure. The reason I'm having to broach this subject now is that with certain team members, I continued to honor old revenue-sharing split agreements, which maximize cash flow to the advisor forever, regardless of whether the client was sourced through the firm. This robbed the firm of an opportunity to build profits, because the revenues were fully allocated to advisors year after year.

Having no desire to ever sell the business

I don't have any intention of retiring. I've always subscribed to the mindset that if you love what you do, you'll never have to work a day in your life. I've had a tremendous career. I've had the opportunity to enhance the financial outcomes of hundreds of clients and the joy of mentoring and training staff on how to enable clients to achieve their life goals and aspirations. What could I possibly want to retire from?

However, if you're on the fence about retirement and leaning toward staying in the game, make sure you're staying in the business for the right reasons, such as the following:

>> Mentoring others in the various skill areas — financial planning, behavioral finance, financial management, and so on.

>> Keeping your mind occupied and sharp, constantly acquiring new information to shape future decision-making.

>> Inspiring colleagues toward their own greater accomplishments, whether that means new joint-work partnerships, considering a merger or acquisition, or doing something else entirely.

>> Serving as a living example to your team members and your community as to how money can become a force of positive change in the world.

>> Building excitement around what's next and discovering how else you can leverage the talents and skills that you and your team have amassed to have an even greater positive impact on the world around you.

Here are two terrible reasons to stay in the business after losing your passion for it:

>> You need the money. Don't stick with any career solely for the money. You can earn money in an infinite number of ways limited only by your imagination. Do something you love *and* can earn money doing.

>> You hate your home life. It may sound crazy, but many financial advisors stay at their desks working well into their 80s because they don't have anything better to do. Maybe they never had the time or opportunity to pursue other interests or to engage in the self-reflection that reveals other interests. One day, they wake up at 65 and realize that they don't have a life outside work and can't even imagine a life outside work, so they stick with what's familiar and, as a result, start to lose what once had made them great financial advisors.

TIP

Don't overstay your welcome. If you've lost your passion for being a financial advisor, exit gracefully and spend some time figuring out who you are and what you love in life.

In order to be a successful financial advisor, you must have other nonfinancial passions to enrich your spirit and, in turn, enlighten your client and business interactions. Automatons need not apply.

TIP

To dive deeper into the topics of building equity in a business and related topics, check out Part 7 for additional resources, including books, websites, and consultancies.

Chapter **24**

Ensuring Business Continuity and Planning for Succession

Whether you're a solo practitioner or owner of a several-member advisory firm, you need to plan for your succession to ensure business continuity and provide for your family (and perhaps for yourself) in the event that you can no longer practice (or you no longer want to practice) temporarily or permanently. If you die or are disabled without a plan in place for taking care of you, your family, and your clients, you may be destitute, your family members may suffer serious financial stress, and your clients may be left without the guidance they need to access their accounts or to transition to a new advisor.

A sure sign you're at the pinnacle of your career is that your clients have tremendous confidence in you and are tremendously loyal to you. If you unexpectedly leave the business (due to a debilitating illness or accident, death, or family crisis; to pursue an incredible new opportunity; or to retire) without conscientiously transitioning your clients to a competent and trustworthy advisor, that accumulated confidence and loyalty dissipates. In addition, an untimely and sudden departure does a disservice to the industry, adding to its challenge of building credibility and trust.

You owe your family, your clients, and the industry the duty of loyalty and care. Should something unexpectedly happen to you, having all the requisite insurance policies to protect your family's financial plan is easy enough. But, protecting your clients' futures is more complicated.

In this chapter, I explain how to plan ahead for your planned or unplanned departure from the business to ensure that your family is taken care of financially and that your clients have a smoother transition from you to their next financial advisor.

REMEMBER

Failure to plan for your succession is irresponsible, placing both your family members and clients at risk. In addition, failure to plan contradicts the sage advice you give your clients. It's the equivalent of being the cobbler whose children have no shoes; your clients have contingency plans and products in place to protect against unforeseen risks, but when you don't plan for your succession, you have no plans and products in place for you or for your family and clients.

Creating a Hit-by-the-Bus Business Continuity Plan

Business continuity involves having a plan in place to prevent any temporary or permanent disruption in income to you or your family and disruption in service to your clients. Think of your business continuity plan as a back-up plan. If anything were to happen to you, where would your family obtain the income you're pulling in, and who would ensure that your clients' assets and liabilities were properly managed? As they say in show business, the show must go on, but how? Your answer to that question helps you to ensure business continuity.

Unfortunately, most financial advisors don't have such a plan in place, which puts their family in jeopardy, creates potential uncertainty among clients, and places their broker/dealer firm into the unenviable position of having to reassign all of that advisor's clients to someone else.

I strongly encourage you to create your own business continuity plan. In your plan, be sure to do the following:

>> **Identify the conditions that trigger the execution of the continuity plan:**

- If you become disabled (mentally or physically) to the point at which you can no longer fulfill your duties as financial advisor

- If you die

>> **State the commitments being made between the two advisors:**

- **Former advisor:** the one who is no longer able to serve the client base

- **Continuity advisor:** The other who is going to be stepping into the role

You may want to include something to the effect of, "I promise, as the continuity advisor, to uphold the standard of care and due diligence executed by the former advisor."

>> **Specify the compensation to the continuity advisor for the commitment to the former advisor's practice.** For example, providing a life insurance policy with the continuity advisor as the beneficiary would provide a lump-sum payment for his continued services.

>> **Specify the compensation to the former advisor's family, for replacing lost income and/or business value.** This clause is especially important, because unexpected events (such as death and disability) usually mean that the former advisor's family is left only with personal life insurance or disability income policies and nothing from the practice.

TIP

Add a promise to pay the former advisor's family a lump-sum payment or an income stream for a specified period of time. Think about this carefully, and involve your spouses, so that everyone understands the liability being managed. You want to be sure that your family is protected when they're at their most vulnerable, dealing with extraordinary loss and suffering.

TIP

A great way to compensate the survivors and ensure business continuity is to use a *fully funded cross-purchase, buy-sell agreement*. With this arrangement, all owners agree to buy the interests of the departing owner when the trigger event occurs. The owners take out insurance policies on one another that provide them with the money to pay the survivors for the departing owner's interests. See Chapter 10 for details.

Create a one-page document to mail to clients after a triggering event. This document should include the signatures of the former and continuity advisors and simple language reassuring clients that their financial matters will henceforth be entrusted to a partner who is dedicated to continuing the ongoing relationship. I recommend that you have the document notarized to convey the formality of the event. Also, share it with your broker/dealer's compliance department, so they have a chance to review it and are aware of the agreement.

Here's a sample draft of the one-page document:

> We the undersigned have entered into a Business Continuity Agreement, which becomes effective as a result of a triggering life event. In such an event, _____ (herein referred to as, Continuity Advisor) commits to the continuation of clients' care and stewardship of _____ (herein referred to as, Former Advisor).

Both Continuity and Former Advisors have determined that in the spirit of ensuring both continuity of their clients' and families' financial outcomes, this document memorializes their completion and full agreement to terms and conditions outlined in their Business Continuity Agreement dated _____.

After finalizing the succession agreement, send a simple letter to clients notifying them of the arrangement and assuring them that it's just a precaution in the event that you can no longer serve as their financial advisor. In your letter, use a more personal and less official (legal) tone. Taking a more casual approach satisfies the requirement of notifying clients while maintaining their peace of mind.

This agreement and the planning associated with it are simple ways to make sure that your clients and family are seen to properly. The agreement between the former and continuity advisor doesn't need to be a lifelong commitment. If you're the former advisor, you're simply naming the person you think is best at this particular point in time. You can choose someone else if conditions change.

See Chapter 10 for additional details about planning for business continuity and succession.

Protecting Your Heirs' Interests with a Buy-Sell Agreement

If your business has recurring revenue, usually in the form of financial planning/advisory fees or asset-based fees, then you have a business that carries significantly more value than one that earns only transaction revenue (for example, investment or insurance product sales commissions). When your business is generating recurring revenue, include a business valuation within the business continuity agreement.

You can hire a consulting firm to perform a business valuation, but here's a simple method that produces a close enough estimate for government work:

1. **Multiply the former advisor's annual Gross Dealer Concession (GDC) by his grid payout (GP).**

GDC is the amount of money generated for the broker/dealer from a sale. For example, if a mutual fund has a front-end load of 5 percent and a client invests $10,000 into the fund, $500 goes to the broker/dealer as GDC and $9,500 is invested in the fund for the client. *GP* is the percentage of the GDC that the advisor keeps; for example, if the broker/dealer pays the advisor 60 percent of the $500 GDC, then the advisor earns $300 of that $500 GDC, and the broker/dealer keeps the remaining $200.

2. **Multiply the result from Step 1 by 2.5 (2.5 is an industry standard multiple in the mid-range).**

   For example, if the former advisor had $100,000 in the past 12 months in GDC, and a grid payout of 60 percent, the total from Step 1 would be $60,000. Multiply that by 2.5 and you get $150,000, which represents the minimum amount the family of the former advisor would receive.

REMEMBER

   To be fair when valuing a business, use simple industry standard multiples in the mid-range, which assumes the business isn't the most valuable or least valuable of its kind.

3. **Multiply the average annual commissions the former advisor earned from any other business lines by 0.5.**

   For example, if the former advisor also sold personal insurance policies (life, disability, and annuities), take the average of those amounts over at least the past couple of years and multiply the average by 0.5. Because this type of business revenue is typically up front, commissions (for any ongoing insurance trail-based revenues, those could be added into the prior AUM figure), those can be valued at 0.5. For example, if insurance revenue was $50,000 in the first year and $100,000 in the second year, then the average over those two years is $75,000. Multiply that by 0.5 and you get $37,500.

4. **Add the result of Step 3 to the result of Step 2.**

   For example, in Step 2, the business valuation came to $150,000 based on recurring revenue. In Step 3, $37,500 was added to account for sales commissions. The total business value then comes to $150,000 + $37,500 = $187,500.

Based on the results from this example, the continuity advisor should buy a life insurance policy on the former advisor with a net death benefit equal to $187,500. This is the amount that the continuity advisor will pay the survivors in exchange for the former advisor's interest in the practice. In reality, business values increase over time, so I recommend buying a term policy that can be converted into permanent coverage over a ten-year period. This would provide flexibility in your household's financial planning as your business scales up.

Planning for Succession

Whether you're preparing to have someone take over your financial advisor business when you retire or you're being responsible and making sure your clients are well served in the event of your demise, you need to have someone ready to step in without missing a beat. You need a successor. Ideally, you have a strong team in place with developing leadership — personnel you've trained and who your clients know and trust. Short of that, you should have a partner, a colleague, or a well-trained family member whom you know and trust and is willing to take over.

REMEMBER

If you've done the challenging work of building a business with equity, as I explain in Chapter 23, you have an attractive asset to offer to a successor. You just need to find the right person. In this section, I describe the criteria for selecting a successor.

Picking a successor with the right credentials

Clearly, the first qualification your successor must have is competency as a financial advisor. After working with a colleague or protégé, you'll know whether the individual has the core competencies to fill your shoes. Here are the basic qualifications:

COMPETING FOR TALENT

When you're recruiting a talented individual to take over your financial advisory practice, more than likely you want someone who you're relatively sure will stay in the business for a decade or longer, so your clients aren't bounced around from one advisor to another.

Unfortunately, given the current employment environment, the financial advisory industry is competing for talent and losing the battle on a daily basis. Many top college graduates are finding their way into technology companies, where the promise of stock options and building equity are par for the course.

Building a thriving business with plenty of equity is one of the best ways to strengthen the financial advisory industry and make it an attractive field for young talent.

>> A bachelor's degree from an accredited college or university, preferably in a finance or accounting field of study

>> Experience in the field, as a financial advisor, accountant, loan officer, or other related position

>> Financial Industry Regulatory Authority (FINRA) licenses, including Series 6, 7, 63, 65, and 66

>> Additional certifications from financial education institutes that show a commitment to continuing education and improvement in the field

See Chapter 6 for additional details about the education and skills required to become a financial advisor.

Addressing personality and values compatibility

As with any job, the knowledge and experience to do the job are the baseline requirements, and measuring them is fairly easy, especially if you've been working with a successor candidate for some time. You can tell whether the person knows how to conduct a thorough client due diligence process and audit an investment portfolio. Those skills are quantifiable.

Personality and values are more subjective but almost equally important. As you observe successor candidates, ask yourself the following questions about them:

>> How do does the candidate interact with clients? As a professional, or more as a buddy? A good candidate is personable but turns professional when the time comes to discuss business. Clients aren't paying you to be their friends; they can get those for free.

>> Does the candidate try to explain complicated financial concepts in simple language or try to impress through the use of jargon and acronyms? The candidate you're looking for wants to be understood, not revered as an enigmatic genius.

>> Does the candidate pick up the check at a business lunch or social gathering without being prompted or asked? Your successor needs to be a natural at being a good host, which is reflected in his comfort at picking up the check.

>> Does the candidate demonstrate a genuine interest in learning the trade? Does he ask intelligent questions about how you would've handled a situation in which he recently struggled? Does he actively seek out learning opportunities? You want a successor who's eager to learn, not one who thinks he already knows everything.

Try to get to the core of the person. Intelligent people can always develop the skills, knowledge, and experience to do a job, but they're born with heart and spirit that's difficult to change. Look for a candidate who "has the right stuff," not necessarily the one who has the most knowledge and skills. Sometimes the subjective qualities are the most important.

Considering transferable skills

Whenever you're recruiting someone for a job or to be your successor, consider not only the skills required for the job but also *transferrable skills* — skills acquired through experience outside of the financial advisory field, such as leadership skills, motivation, the ability to delegate tasks, communication skills, empathy, character, and so on. You probably have transferrable skills that your clients have come to rely on and expect from you, so be sure your successor has the same or comparable skills.

REMEMBER

Your successor shouldn't only replicate what you provide but also be able to take it to the next level. For example, I've developed unique protocols and processes for both portfolio management and client due diligence. I want to be sure that these not only continue but also evolve along with the evolution of technology and capital markets. I know that eventually I won't be in a position to steward that evolution, but my successor certainly can be. I want to be sure that my successor has the same passion and ability to do so.

WARNING

Be prepared for the possibility of investing time and effort into mentoring a candidate only to discover that the person isn't the right fit to be your successor. Mentoring requires time and effort, as does discovering whether someone is the right fit for a position. However, keep in mind that time spent mentoring is rarely time wasted. You're always learning from the experience. More specifically, you may discover that someone isn't the right choice to be your successor, which can be a valuable lesson. Learning is all part of the journey, for everyone involved.

Sizing up a candidate's leadership potential

A wallflower isn't your ideal successor. You want someone with a demonstrated history of contributing to team meetings, someone who frequently visits your office or asks for your time to consult on a matter, and someone who's proactive. The team member who shows up to a meeting with a whole client solution sketched out and seeks your and other team members' feedback is a great candidate.

Keep in mind that although you want someone with leadership qualities, you don't want a control freak. You want someone who has ideas but who is willing and perhaps even eager to have those ideas challenged and to obtain feedback. Be wary of anyone with leadership qualities who is defensive or has a my-way-or-the-highway attitude.

WARNING

Resist the urge to choose a successor whom you just really like and who reminds you of yourself early in your career. You've made a lot of mistakes since then and discovered a lot about how to lead you to the position you hold now. Don't assume that someone who reminds you of who you were back then will follow the same path.

Accounting for loyalty

Loyalty to you, your clients, and your firm is what you're trying to assess here. You don't want blind loyalty, where whatever you say is treated like rule of law. True loyalty is when your successor asks you why you believe what you do. Whether it's about handling a client anxiety or understanding when a certain product mix may be most appropriate, you want your successor to have a deep understanding as to why you've chosen to do things in your practice the way you have. This takes time, of course. Be patient while sharing your wisdom.

TIP

Create opportunities to spend time with a successor candidate away from the office. You can meet after work hours, for happy hour or dinner, or during a weekend get-together on a hike or beach day. Time spent with your potential successor can give you better perspective on who he is, what makes him tick, and what motivates him. You'll want to know that his heart's in it for all the right reasons.

6

The Part of Tens

IN THIS PART . . .

Improve yourself and your business to take them both to the next level.

Discover ten practical tips and techniques to becoming a highly successful financial advisor.

Find out how to grow your business by attracting and landing new clients.

Explore other resources, including trade publications, educational and licensing institutions, and books on specific practices areas.

Chapter **25**

Ten Tips for Being a Successful Financial Advisor

B eing a successful financial advisor requires more than mastering a collection of tips and techniques. It requires education, experience, and dedication. However, reading through a list of tips is a great way to remind yourself of what you need to do to stay on top of your game.

Here, I give you ten tips for being a successful financial advisor. Some are specific action items, whereas others are more like attitudes or behaviors to adopt. All of them are essential ingredients to making you a well-rounded and thriving member of the financial advisor community. Certainly, you need more than ten tips to become truly successful in this field, but I consider these tips to be the ten essentials.

Let Your Conscience Be Your Guide

You have a conscience that has been instilled in you since birth. It's that little voice inside your head that makes you question whether a choice is right or wrong. Pinocchio had Jiminy Cricket to make him mindful of temptation. Others prefer to imagine the conscience as an angel sitting on one shoulder and a devil on the other shoulder debating over the wisdom of taking a certain course of action. However you choose to imagine your conscience, be sure to heed its warning when you encounter temptation. When you're handling other people's money and engaging in commissioned sales, you can expect to encounter more than an average share of temptation, so be particularly vigilant.

Most temptations in this field are the result of commissioned sales. Although nothing is wrong with selling a great product at a fair price and earning a reasonable profit from the sale, you must always put your role as financial advisor above your role as salesperson. You have a fiduciary responsibility to your clients, not to yourself. If you always act in the best financial interests of your clients, you have nothing to worry about in this area.

REMEMBER

Your financial advisory career will lead you to some of the most important and powerful relationships and life experiences you'll ever have. Don't belittle it by taking shortcuts to make a quick buck or to get another referral. Live by the Golden Rule: Do unto others as you would have them do unto you. Better yet, follow the Platinum Rule: Do unto others as they would want done to them. For example, I hate to be harassed and sold to. I prefer to be educated and given the space to make decisions on my timeline, so a salesperson is much more likely to succeed with me if he takes that approach.

Beware of False Profits

A *false profit* is any promise of a low-risk, high-return investment, which is something that doesn't exist. Think of it as a healthy diet that encourages you to consume lots of sugar. Such a diet breaks the laws of nature. It's a contradiction. The same is true of false profits; they break the rules of capital markets.

WARNING

Don't advise or implement capital allocations when you don't understand all the embedded risks. If an investment looks great on the surface, look below the surface by carefully examining the prospectus. If the investment product being pitched has a private placement offering memorandum, be even more skeptical. Remember the old adage, "If it sounds too good to be true, it probably is," which reflects the rules of capital markets — you can't make *more* money while taking on *less* risk.

As a competent financial advisor, you'll be a student of the capital markets and be able to identify for yourself, or through the guidance of others, what thresholds dictate appropriate levels of risk. For my own practice, I keep things simple and use a modified version of the Capital Asset Pricing Model (CAPM) to determine when any asset price is fair relative to its risk.

TIP

Forgetting all formulas, I ask one question: "What's the 10 year U.S. Treasury note yielding today?" Say the answer is 3 percent. The U.S. government, being the largest and most stable in the world, can be expected to honor its debt obligations 100 percent of the time, so the risk-free return would be 3 percent. If an investment product promises a 10 percent return, that's more than three times the risk-free rate, so it has more than three times the risk. It's that simple. If that 10 percent return is touted as risk-free, you should be extremely skeptical, because that rate would severely violate the laws of capital markets.

REMEMBER

When comparing returns on investment products, the only risk to consider is that of permanent capital loss. Other products, such as annuities, have different risks, which are more difficult to quantify, such as liquidity risk, but with a sound insurance carrier, an annuity doesn't carry a risk of permanent capital loss.

Protect Your Clients from Predators

One of your primary responsibilities to your clients is to protect them from predators who seek to scam them out of their money. Encourage your clients to openly discuss any investment ideas they've heard about. The only way you'll find out whether your clients are being targeted is if they tell you. Con artists often discourage their marks from discussing what they consider an opportunity, because greater exposure increases the risk they'll get caught.

Over the years, when I've interviewed my clients during routine portfolio review meetings, I've been alarmed at how many times they tell me, "Oh yeah, my friend just invested in this apartment building fund and asked if I wanted to go in on it with him."

REMEMBER

Predators come in many forms: family members looking for support and cash flow, salespeople looking to make a big commission, and other people who aren't aligned with your client's best interest.

Don't Use Big Words

The world is complicated enough, and it's overflowing with information about everything — thank you, Google. Don't contribute to the confusion or complication. Describe difficult concepts in plain language, and don't leave out any gory details. Every strategy has a downside, and your clients should be aware of those downsides. You're developing a big plan, so explain the upsides and downsides of any investment or insurance product or solution you recommend in the context of the bigger plan.

Every profession has its own terminology that enables people within the profession to communicate more precisely and efficiently. For example, medical professionals communicate in their own language. However, you expect your doctor to explain tests and treatments using language you can understand. In the same way, as a financial advisor, you pick up a lot of specialized terminology, but that terminology isn't appropriate for communicating with your clients. Don't assume that your clients are up on the latest Bloomberg catchphrases or sound bites.

Remember That Good Service Makes Up for Other Shortcomings

Ideally, you want to be the financial advisor who offers the best financial performance *and* customer service available in your area. However, you can still be successful by offering superior customer service and average financial performance. People will want to work with you and stay with you because the level of care, education, and time you offer is worth something to them.

You may lose some clients who expect better performance, but you can easily replace them with clients who value service over performance. Of course, you'll strive for above average performance and above average service, but if performance drags in the short term, your clients won't be quick to judge.

Be Active in a Community Cause

Visibility is key to your success as a rainmaker. It's also a key ingredient to the success of any multi-advisor business. Become involved, giving both your time and money. Seek an issue or cause that's close to your heart and mind, and do something about it — without a hidden agenda, only a will to change the world, or at least your little corner of it, for the better.

Living a life for others is an exciting way to be a human being, and it's great for business too. People want to work with others who inspire and motivate them. Prospects will see you passionately engaged in a common cause, earning you instant trust and admiration. When prospects discover you through your passion, you have a much easier time transitioning them from prospects to clients.

Be Eager to Acquire New Information and to Share What You Know

Inspire the acquisition and sharing of knowledge for the purpose of continuously improving the industry and everyone in it.

Throughout my career, I've benefited from the knowledge that others acquired through their experience and innovation. I continue the tradition by sharing my knowledge and innovations with others. By writing this book, I hope to share on a larger scale.

REMEMBER

The more you discover and find out, the more innovative you become, generating unique knowledge that's valuable to others. If you're not at a point at which you can be innovative, then pick up as much unique knowledge as possible from others and begin to apply it to your own practice, which is yet another way to share what you know.

Focus More on Skills, Less on Tools

A great financial advisor doesn't need a one-of-a-kind financial product that's perfect for every client's needs. A financial advisor who has a thorough understanding of financial fundamentals and asset and liability management can use a variety of products and solutions to create a personalized plan that serves each client's unique needs.

REMEMBER

Focus more on developing knowledge, techniques, and skills than in looking for the perfect products and solutions. If you're not developing financial planning techniques and skills, then you're not evolving into a financial advisor. You'll remain relegated to the more simple life of a salesperson.

TIP

If you believe that all financial concerns can be answered with a quick turn of phrase or product pitch, then dig deeper. Ask yourself why or how a certain product or solution would impact the client's life and her dreams. In the process of answering this question, you begin to uncover and explore more interesting intellectual and emotional connections to the client's money and other assets. The insights gained enable you to make the right recommendation to this client and reveal ways to add value for other clients.

Appreciate the Trust Your Clients Place in You

Advising on other people's money is akin to holding the fate of another's life in your hands. Make no mistake, the gravity of client-advisor relationship is tremendous. You have the power to fulfill or destroy dreams. Be the beacon of hope and financial leader they need to achieve their goals.

Don't thank your clients for their business because that revenue is a small fraction of the wealth that's been entrusted to you, but rather thank them for being open with you and allowing you to do your best work investigating and uncovering uniquely designed solutions for them.

Better yet, show your clients your appreciation by caring for them, as a loving parent cares for her adult children or as a doctor cares for her patients. Remember that their future rests on your shoulders.

Always Ask: What If I'm Wrong?

When he was about to make a major decision or recommendation, Ken Fisher, one of my early career mentors, would always ask, "What if I'm wrong?" Asking this question is a great way to force yourself to analyze the situation more objectively. It always struck me as a relevant, prudent, and truly selfless question.

When you challenge your thinking, you begin to find the source of good advice. Good, unbiased advice is balanced and reasoned without other temptations to sway the final recommendation.

"What if I'm wrong?" is the question that every client wants you to be asking yourself. I've taken to sharing this question with every client. This method ensures clients understand that every financial decision has pros and cons. Finding the best product or solution for each client involves having to reveal every factor and aspect while monitoring the client's reaction and sensitivity to those aspects/ factors. This approach is the best way to develop custom solutions.

TIP

Challenge your own presumptions routinely in full view of your clients and prospects.

Chapter **26**

Ten Business-Building Activities

Every financial advisor knows that the best way to drum up new business is through marketing and networking, but they often don't know how to market and network effectively. Many are too pushy and drive away prospects instead of attracting them.

In this chapter, I offer ten suggestions for meeting new prospects and transforming them into clients.

TIP

Be natural. Instead of thinking of client acquisition in terms of marketing and sales, think of it in terms of meeting and talking with people and serving their needs. Just be passionate about what you do and eager to bring value into your clients' lives. Then, get out in the world and mingle so people get to know you and what you do.

Schedule Client Review Meetings

Early in your career (and throughout your career for your best clients), meet with your clients at least once every quarter to see if anything has changed in their lives that you can help with. This level of frequency has multiple benefits. Chief among them is that these meetings remind your clients who are your natural ambassadors of the great personalized service you offer.

Conduct two or three of these high frequency, best client reviews over lunch or dinner meetings without paperwork or formal presentations. Just engage in conversation about what's going on in the client's life to find out whether anything's changed that would call for modifying the client's portfolio. Conduct a more formal review meeting at your office with charts and documentation once or twice a year.

Keep a Log of Friends and Family That Your Clients Mention

As you talk with clients, they're likely to mention names of people who are important to them — a boss, colleagues, neighbors, friends, family members, and so on. For example, if the topic of vacations comes up, you may find out that your clients have plans to vacation with another couple. When your clients mention names, jot them down along with any details about the people mentioned. After the meeting, add the names to your client relationship management (CRM) system to follow up later.

At the next meeting, you can then ask your clients about their trip with so-and-so. They'll be impressed that you actually listened to them and remembered (or are that organized). Then, you can ask whether they think so-and-so would be a good client for you. If the answer is yes or maybe, ask for an introduction so you can meet with the prospects and judge for yourself whether you'd be able to help them. If the answer is no, you may want to ask follow-up questions to find out why. You still may want to meet with the prospects to judge for yourself.

REMEMBER

Care for the people your clients care about. Too often I've heard from clients about a friend of theirs with financial problems I could have resolved (or helped the friend avoid) had I been the friend's financial advisor at the time. Invariably, the client tells me he wished he had introduced me to his friend. I do, too.

Sponsor One Charitable Event Each Year

Find a cause you're passionate about and want your personal brand associated with, and then sponsor one charitable event annually to generate revenue for the cause.

REMEMBER

This is a charitable event, not a sales event. Don't actively pursue clients at the event or expect anything in return for the sponsorship. Approach this activity as a way to create a more intimate relationship with the organization's development team. The development team may become a long-term source of great referrals.

WARNING

Don't be a one-and-done sponsor. Show up every year consistently. Along the way, share with the charity's development team your charitable-giving solutions, such as charitable remainder trusts (CRTs), donor-advised funds (DAFs), and private family foundations (PFFs) that could benefit their efforts (see Chapter 10 for details). If you don't have any charitable-giving solutions, bring in a joint work partner who does.

Break Bread with Your Best Clients

A long lunch, a festive dinner with significant others, and even a weekend trip all make for great ways to get to know your best clients better. Away from a business agenda, your clients will feel more comfortable sharing details that reveal what's going on in their lives and in their minds.

I've actually gained more by learning from my best clients how to manage my business than I gained from referrals. Don't be surprised; your best clients are most likely to be business owners or senior executives.

Be Responsive: Practice the Same-Day Rule

When clients text or email you or leave a voicemail message, get back with them within a few hours, not a few days. You don't necessarily need to answer a question or resolve an issue immediately, but you should get back with the client quickly to let him know that you received his message and to provide a time frame for when he can expect a more thorough response. The foundation of excellent client service involves establishing consistent expectations.

REMEMBER

If you (or your firm) don't get back with clients quickly, then you're providing fertile ground for a small, benign issue to balloon into a critical, malignant one.

Attend Every Party You're Invited to

Even if you're not a natural finder (see Chapter 20), nothing is easier than accepting an invitation to a party, any party — birthday, graduation, bar mitzvah, wedding, anniversary, retirement, whatever. The community in which you practice probably has dozens of celebrations every week, and if you've met enough people, then you're going to be invited to at least a few of them. When you're invited, go. If the party is with friends or family, you'll have a great opportunity to get to know them in a relaxed environment.

Have an Elevator Pitch

Whenever somebody asks what you do, you should be able to answer the question in less than ten seconds. This terse description of what you do is known as an *elevator pitch*. The idea is that you can tell someone what you do during a short ride together in an elevator. See Chapter 18 for guidance on how to write an elevator pitch.

TIP

When you're composing your elevator pitch, focus on what you do and the value you bring to your clients' lives — your value proposition.

Welcome All Prospects, Large or Small

Even though someone may be too small for your practice (especially if you've been in practice for some time), make him feel welcome and appreciated. If he has questions or concerns that you can address with little effort, do so, and then ask if you can pass his name along to a financial advisor who may be better suited to meet his needs. If your prospects give you permission, call the other financial advisor and give the advisor the prospect's name and contact information.

I recommend calling the advisor instead of simply giving the advisor's name and contact information to the prospects because prospects often fail to follow up. In addition, contacting the other advisor to provide a referral is a powerful networking tactic, making the other advisor a more likely source of future referrals.

REMEMBER

Some of your best big clients are likely to come from smaller client referrals.

Stop Selling and Start Telling Stories

If you're pitching products and solutions to prospects, you're not going to be very successful as a financial advisor. Switch from selling to and start telling stories. Share anecdotes about specific challenges your clients faced and how you helped them overcome those challenges.

WARNING

When sharing stories, protect the privacy and confidentiality of your clients and their families. Obviously, don't mention any names (you can use pseudonyms, if necessary), but also beware of providing any details that would enable the listener to figure out the identity of the person in your story.

Whether you worked with an estate attorney on replacing a troublesome individual trustee with a corporate trustee or just completed a retirement income plan for a newly retired client, highlight the details that made the case most interesting to you. The most interesting cases are usually those that surprised you or that taught you a valuable lesson.

Be Active on Social Media

Social media platforms are great ways to stay in touch with clients while increasing your exposure to prospects. I use LinkedIn to share information and insights with my colleagues in the industry. I'm not so keen on Facebook because lately my news feed has been overrun with ferocious opinions from extremists. Instagram is great, though. I use my account mostly to show the food I eat; people seem to enjoy looking at food. In fact, Instagram has been the best platform for interacting with prospects and joint-work advisors. Now that Instagram feeds into Facebook, the platform has an even greater reach.

TIP

If you have a team, post about them. Share pictures of team members celebrating birthdays, traveling on vacation, or engaging in community service. Convey the idea that your team is about much more than just providing outstanding financial advice. Show team members smiling and laughing. Share your insights or inspirational quotes.

Don't use social media to pitch product or fake articles that promote product sales.

WARNING

Always check with your broker/dealer's compliance department before posting anything on social media. Every firm has its own rules and guidelines.

Appendix

Financial Advisor Resources

Although this book contains most of what you need to start to be successful as a financial advisor, it can't possibly contain everything you need to know, simply because of space and page count limitations. You still need to obtain formal education and on-the-job training and place yourself in continuing education mode.

In this appendix, I provide additional assistance with lists of valuable resources to consult to obtain the additional knowledge that will keep you current and on top of your game.

Professional Licensing Bodies

To engage in any transaction involving an investment or insurance product, you're required to register and pass various exams from one or more of the organizations below.

Financial Industry Regulatory Authority (FINRA)

Website: www.finra.org

FINRA

1735 K Street, NW

Washington DC, 20006

(301) 590-6500

FINRA supervises 629,112 brokers and 3,712 broker–dealer firms (as of June 2018).

To engage in securities sales, you must register with FINRA and meet certain qualifications, including passing licensing exams. FINRA offers many securities exams; the most basic (for financial advisors) are as follows:

>> **Series 6:** Investment Company and Variable Contracts Products Representative Exam (IR)

>> **Series 7:** General Securities Representative Exam (GS)

>> **Series 63:** Uniform Securities Agent State Law Examination

>> **Series 65:** Uniform Investment Adviser Law Examination

>> **Series 66:** Uniform Combined State Law Examination

National Association of Insurance Commissioners (NAIC)

Website: www.naic.org

NAIC Executive Office

444 North Capitol Street NW, Suite 700

Washington, DC 20001

Hours: 8:30 a.m. – 5:00 p.m. (EST) Monday – Friday

Phone: (202) 471-3990

Fax: (816) 460-7493

TIP

Visit www.naic.org/state_web_map.htm and select your state from a drop-down menu to find out more about exams and registration with your state's insurance department.

Securities and Exchange Commission (SEC)

Website: www.sec.gov

SEC Headquarters

100 F Street, NE

Washington, DC 20549

Contact: www.sec.gov/contact-information/sec-directory

The SEC's *Investment Advisers Act of 1940* (www.sec.gov/about/laws/iaa40.pdf) regulates investment advisors. Passing the FINRA Series 65 or 66 permits financial advisors to advise investors on securities.

Securities licensing providers

I recommend the following three (of many) securities license providers:

>> **Kaplan Financial Education:** www.kaplanfinancial.com/securities

>> **Securities Training Corporation:** www.stcusa.com

>> **Wiley Efficient Learning:** www.efficientlearning.com/finra/products

Top broker/dealers lists

>> *Financial Planning:* www.financial-planning.com/slideshow/ranking-the-top-small-broker-dealers-by-revenue#slide-1

>> *InvestmentNews:* www.investmentnews.com/article/20180421/FREE/180429998/top-independent-broker-dealers-ranked-by-revenue

>> *Investopedia:* www.investopedia.com/investing/broker-dealer-firms

>> *On Wall Street:* onwallstreet.financial-planning.com/slideshow/top-10-regional-broker-dealers-by-fee-revenue#slide-1

Professional Development Resources

When you have your FINRA and/or SEC registrations and securities licenses, pursuing education through formal advanced coursework gives you a great competitive advantage. Most successful advisors have at least one of the designations listed here.

CFA Institute

Website: www.cfainstitute.org

CFA Institute

915 East High Street

Charlottesville, VA 22902

Telephone +1 (434) 951-5499

Office hours: Monday to Friday, 8:00 a.m. – 5:00 p.m. ET

24-hour customer service is also available Sunday 5:00 p.m. – Friday 5:00 p.m. ET

Professional designations and programs:

>> Certificate in Investment Performance Measurement (CIPM)

>> CFA Institute Investment Foundations

>> Chartered Financial Analyst (CFA)

CFP Board

Website: www.cfp.net

Certified Financial Planner Board of Standards, Inc.

1425 K Street NW #800, Washington, DC 20005

Phone (toll free): (800) 487-1497

Phone: (202) 379-2200

Fax: (202) 379-2299

E-mail: mail@cfpboard.org

Professional Designation: Certified Financial Planner (CFP)

To find a CFP education provider, visit www.cfp.net/become-a-cfp-professional/find-an-education-program.

Institute of Business and Finance

Website: icfs.com

Contact: http://icfs.com/contact

> Institute of Business and Finance
>
> 4141 Jutland Drive, Suite 330
>
> San Diego, CA, 92117
>
> Toll-free: (800) 848-2029
>
> E-mail: info@icfs.com

Professional designations:

- ❯❯ Certified Annuity Specialist (CAS)
- ❯❯ Certified Estate and Trust Specialist (CES)
- ❯❯ Certified Fund Specialist (CFS)
- ❯❯ Certified Income Specialist (CIS)
- ❯❯ Certified Tax Specialist (CTS)
- ❯❯ Master of Science in Financial Services (MSFS)

The American College of Financial Services

Website: www.theamericancollege.edu

Contact: www.theamericancollege.edu/contact-us

> American College of Financial Services
>
> 270 S. Bryn Mawr Avenue
>
> Bryn Mawr, PA, 19010
>
> Toll-free: (888) 263-7265

Professional designation and degree programs:

>> Accredited Estate Planner (AEP)

>> Chartered Advisor in Philanthropy (CAP)

>> Chartered Financial Consultant (ChFC)

>> Chartered Leadership Fellow (CLF)

>> Chartered Life Underwriter (CLU)

>> Chartered Special Needs Consultant (ChSNC)

>> Financial Services Certified Professional (FSCP)

>> Master of Science in Financial Services (MSFS)

>> Master of Science in Management (MSM)

>> Retirement Income Certified Professional (RICP)

>> Wealth Management Certified Professional (WMCP)

Trade Publications and Resources

To remain in the know about what's happening in the financial advisory industry, sign up for news alerts or email newsletters from these established and reliable industry news publications.

Financial Advisor Magazine

Website: www.fa-mag.com

This site features a bookstore, calendar of events and conferences, continuing education (CE) center, videos, webcasts, and whitepapers.

Financial Advisor IQ

Website: financialadvisoriq.com

A personal favorite, this *Financial Times* company delivers timely editorial and high caliber news reporting.

FinancialPlanning

Website: www.financial-planning.com

Organized by subject matter, this site offers insight, perspective and news that impacts the profession, including Resources, Events, Practice, Portfolio, Industry, and Voices.

InvestmentNews

Website: www.investmentnews.com

Conducting research and studies, as well as showcasing those performed by others, makes this publication a great resource for more technical portfolio related updates.

Journal of Financial Planning

Website: www.onefpa.org/journal/Pages/default.aspx

For members of the Financial Planning Association (FPA), this publication delivers more in-depth, peer-reviewed contributions to the more sophisticated financial planner.

RIABiz.com

Website: riabiz.com

Their tagline "News, Vision, and Voice for the Advisory Community" reflects what this website is all about, highlighting news specific to advisors at independent broker-dealers and independent RIAs.

ThinkAdvisor

Website: www.thinkadvisor.com

Sections on this website include Investment Portfolio, Wealth Management, Retirement Planning, Life/Health Insurance, Practice Management, TechCenter, Instant Insights, Resource Center, Newsletters, and Webcasts.

WealthManagement.com

Website: www.wealthmanagement.com

According to this site, "Over 435,000 financial advisors and wealth professionals rely on *WealthManagement* information, editorial insight, and analysis to assist them in their client activities to improve practice management and gathering of assets."

Consultants and Books

When you arrive at a crossroads or inflection point in your career, you may want to consider hiring an industry consultant or picking up a book. Here are a few resources that I've either used or have learned about over the years.

Consultants

Consult with these consultants:

>> Excellat Consulting (www.excellat.com) provides operations consulting for independent financial advisors, specializing on increasing business efficiency and profitability.

>> FineTooth Consulting (www.finetoothconsulting.com) focuses on assisting independent financial advisors and registered investment advisors (RIAs) who are looking for transition planning, outsourced recruiting, and acquisitions/succession planning.

>> FP Transitions (www.fptransitions.com) is the largest consultancy focused on building equity in your business, succession planning, and acquisition management. With whitepaper publications entitled, "Transforming Your Practice Into a Business", you'll find even more technical details from concepts presented in this book.

>> Pinnacle Advisor Solutions (www.pinnacleadvisorsolutions.com) organizes their advice around your goals, such as growing your RIA, enjoying your lifestyle, or being your own boss.

Books

Check out these books:

>> *Buying, Selling, and Valuing Financial Practices,* by David Grau, Sr., JD (John Wiley & Sons, Inc., 2016) is the definitive guide to mergers, acquisitions, and valuing financial advisory businesses.

>> *Gratitude Marketing,* by Michael F. Sciortino (Advantage Media Group, 2015) reinforces that fact that financial advisors in the relationship-building business and provides tips for making you a better networker through authentic appreciation.

>> *Storyselling for Financial Advisors,* by Scott West and Mitch Anthony (Kaplan Publishing, 2000) gives helpful tips on how to educate your clients on complex financial subjects using stories and metaphors.

>> *The Art of Selling to the Affluent,* by Matt Oechsli (John Wiley & Sons, Inc., 2014) gives great insight to how to position your services to add value and relieve stress from this niche market.

>> *The Ensemble Practice: A Team-Based Approach to Building a Superior Wealth Management Firm,* by Philip Palaveev, who also runs a business consultancy under the same name, (Bloomberg Press, 2012) guides wealth managers through building effective financial advisory teams and profitable/valuable firms.

>> *The Million-Dollar Financial Advisor: Powerful Lessons and Proven Strategies from Top Producers,* by David J. Mullen Jr. (AMACOM, 2009) gives great guidance on how to grow your business to an optimal and manageable size through new target client acquisition and non-ideal client divestiture.

>> *The Monthly Retainer Model In Financial Planning: What It Is, Why It Works, and How to Implement It in Your Firm,* by Alan Moore and Michael Kitces (XY Planning Network, 2016) shows you how to deliver financial planning for a monthly subscription fee, which is particularly useful in acquiring clients who don't currently have large assets to manage or have a need for products that pay commissions.

>> *The Pocket Guide to Sales for Financial Advisors,* by Beverly D. Flaxington (ATA Press, 2014) is a comprehensive resource that you can flip through when you get stuck on different parts of your business, whether you need tips and techniques for client acquisition or management.

Index

A

absolute benchmarks, 229
absolute return funds, 230
accountable plans, 205
accountants
  family, 145
  roles in collaborative approach, 207
  teaming up with, 145, 255–256
  working with client's, 205
accounting
  bookkeeping, 202
  business, 202
  forensic, 203
  outsourcing, 298
  tax, 202
accumulation phase, 227. *See also* benchmarks
acid test, 7
Acorns, 98
acquisitions, 284
action, in due diligence, 20, 179–180
active asset managers, 109–110
active investing, 109
administration. *See also* business development; client service
  client relationship management (CRM) system, 296–297
  coordinating workflow for new clients, 297
  job responsibilities, 295–298
  office management, 295–296
  outsourcing accounting and legal, 298
administration department, 288–289
administrator, 280
advocacy for clients, 29–30
affluenza, 143
Aladdin, 114
Albert, 98
Aligne Wealth, 246
alignment, in due diligence, 20, 180–182
alpha, 74–75

alternative investments, 106–107
American College of Financial Services, 84, 337–338
Ameriprise, 52
amortization, 114
analytical skills, 12
anecdotes, sharing, 331
annual compensation, 306
annual recurring trail revenue, 131
annual revenue, 214
annuities
  defined, 116, 129
  drawbacks, 129
  flexible or multiple premium deferred accumulation, 129
  single premium immediate income, 129
Anthony, Mitch, 341
appreciation, of client, 212
apprenticeship, 38–39
apps, 98
articles of incorporation, 281
The Art of Selling to the Affluent (Oechsli), 341
assessment, in due diligence, 20, 176–178
asset allocation, strategic, 239
asset-based fees, 55, 115, 116. *See also* compensation
asset management
  active, 109–110
  brushing up on, 99–116
  in core competencies, 80–81
  defined, 17, 80, 99
  investment policy statement, 100–108
  passive, 110
  solo practice and, 265
  steps in, 17–18
assets
  financial, 80
  intangible, 80
  under management (AUM), 300–301
  risk assessment of, 80–81
  tangible, 80

attention, to clients, 212
attorneys
  connecting with, 255
  estate planning, 145
  partnering with client's, 204
  roles in collaborative approach, 207
  teaming up with, 145
audits, in due diligence, 20, 178–179
auto insurance, 128
autonomy, 48
auto pay, 98
AXA Advisors, 52

B

Baby Boomers, 9
background check, self
  about, 37
  personal background, 41–43
  personal finance background, 43–45
  professional background, 38–40
Baird, 51
Bank of America, 51, 276
banks
  on-the-job training, 58
  working in, 51
BB&T, 51
behavioral changes, 182
behavioral finance
  about, 19
  defined, 83, 161
  fear and greed in, 167–168
  irrational thoughts and behaviors, recognizing, 162–164
  market cycles and, 167–168
  muting irrational thoughts and behaviors, 165
  rational thinking, 166–167
  recognizing irrational thoughts and behaviors, 162–164
benchmarks
  about, 221–222
  absolute, 229
  blended, 108, 223–224
  index as, 221–225
  personal, 226–229

poor performance and, 231–232
  relative, 229
  tailoring performance to client's needs, 230–231
beneficiaries, naming, 136
best interest, 68–69
Betterment, 74
Blackrock, 114
blended benchmarks, 223–224. *See also* benchmarks
blended portfolio, 102
blogs, 248–249
boards, serving on, 254–255
bond market traders, 40–41
bonds
  coupon rate, 106
  credit quality, 106
  duration, 106
  global market, 106
  market liquidity, 106
  maturity, 106
  risks, 106
  taxes, 114
  yield, 105
bookkeeping, 202
book of business, 49
books, 341
BrightScope, 252
broker/agent
  versus financial advisor, 67
  roles of, 172
  serving consumers as, 172–173
BrokerCheck, 69, 252
broker/dealers
  affiliating with, 25, 59–61, 276
  choosing, 279
  expenses, 277
  independent financial advisors and, 52–53
broker protocol, 277
budgeting
  about, 17
  auto pay/payroll deductions and, 98
  in core competencies, 82
  estimating income, 92
  expenses and, 92–96
  guiding clients on, 91–97

household, 91–99
savings and, 96–97
spending and savings guidelines, 97
tools, 97–98
building distribution, 257
bureaucracy, 67
business
starting or growing, 191
succession plan, 193–194
business accounting, 202
business-building activities. *See also* business
development
accepting and attending party invitations, 330
being responsive, 329
breaking bread with best clients, 329
elevator pitch, 330
keeping log of client's family and friends, 328
scheduling client review meetings, 328
social media, 331
sponsoring charitable events, 329
stop selling and start selling stories, 331
welcoming all prospects, 330
business continuity. *See also* exit strategy; succession
planning
commitments made between former and continuity
advisors, 311
compensation to continuity advisor, 311
compensation to former advisor's family, 311
condition that trigger continuity plan, 310
creating continuity plan, 310–312
ensuring, 309–317
fully funded cross-purchase, buy-sell agreement,
311–313
business development. *See also* business-building
activities; earning clients
client service and, 291
corporate benefit programs and, 293
finding clients and, 289–290
focus areas, 291–294
401(k) plans and, 292–293
networking through trusts and estates,
293–294
supporting household's financial manager, 294
business development companies (BDCs), 116
business licenses, 282

business ownership. *See also* solo practice; starting
own firm
about, 275–276
broker protocol, 277
business structure, 278–279
change of roles in, 277
checklist, 24–25
choosing broker/dealer platform, 279
client attrition and, 283
client's risk exposure and, 119
commitments to current firm and, 276–277
costs of, 277
designating a rainmaker, 282–283
exit strategy, 25, 284–286
growing through mergers and acquisitions, 284
legal documents, 281–282
organizational chart, 279–280
profit margin, 283
pros and cons of, 15
question to ask before, 276
revenue sharing and, 25
staffing, 281
transitioning from solo practice to, 275–286
versus working in firm, 12–15, 47–61
business structure, 25, 278–279
Buying, Selling, and Valuing Financial Practices
(Grau), 341
buyout, 285
buy-sell agreements, 137, 311–313

C

Cambridge Investment Research, 52
capital, 21, 187–188
capital asset pricing model (CAPM), 105
capital gains, 151–152
capitalization, 103
Capital One, 51
careers
changing within industry, 39–40
choosing, 38–40
fresh out of college, 38–39
care standards, 64–65
car ownership, 94
cash, 107

cash flow. *See also* income
  financial plans and, 190
  negative, 190
  net, 190
  positive, 190
cash value insurance, 103
categories of financial advisors
  about, 48
  familiarizing with, 64
  hybrid models, 48
  independent contractor, 59–61
  independent financial advisor, 52–53
  key differences, 48–50
  registered investment advisor, 61
  traditional employee, 50–51
C-corporation, 25, 278
certificate of assumed name, 281–282
certifications, 89, 252
Certified Annuity Specialist (CAS), 86
Certified Estate and Trust Specialist (CES), 86
Certified Financial Advisor (CFA) Institute, 72
Certified Financial Planner (CFP), 54, 65
Certified Financial Planner (CFP) Board, 72
Certified Financial Planner Board of Standards, 86
Certified Fund Specialist (CFS), 86
Certified Income Specialist (CIS), 86
Certified in Investment Performance Management (CIPM), 85
certified public accountants (CPAs)
  family, 145
  roles in collaborative approach, 207
  teaming up with, 145, 255–256
  working with client's, 205
Certified Tax Specialist (CTS), 86
Cerulli Associates, 286
CFA Institute, 84–85, 336
CFP Board, 86, 336–337
charitable donor model, 290
charitable lead trusts (CLTs), 145
charitable remainder trusts (CRTs), 145
charity
  career as financial advisor and, 41
  contributions to, 158–159
  getting involved in, 254, 324
  sponsoring events, 328

Charles Schwab, 74
Chartered Financial Advisor (CFA), 85
Chartered Financial Analyst (CFA), 65, 284
Chartered Financial Consultant (ChFC), 84
Chartered Life Underwriter (CLU), 84, 89
chief executive officer (CEO), 280
chief information officer (CIO), 280
chief operating officer (COO)
  in level II of organization, 280
  responsibilities of, 288–289
childcare costs, 94–95
childhood memories, 42
Citigroup, 51
client base, growing. *See also* business-building activities; earning clients
  by marketing of services, 23
  by teaming up with colleagues, 23–24
  by winning lifelong clients, 23
client relationship management (CRM) system, 206, 281, 289, 296–297
clients
  advocacy for, 29–30
  assigning to service level brackets, 216–217
  attrition, 283
  breaking bread with, 329
  characteristics of, 173–174
  versus consumers/customers, 66, 172–174
  coordinating workflow for new clients, 297
  defined, 171
  demographics of, 212
  earning, 234–244
  families and friends of, 328
  financial capacity of, 101
  financial goals of, 7, 102
  financial plans for, 183–196
  goals and objectives of, 101–102
  guiding, 7
  investment philosophy of, 109
  inviting clients to breakfast or lunch, 218–219
  lifelong, 23
  liquidity needs of, 102
  listening to, 175
  partnering with lawyers of, 204
  protecting from predators, 323
  providing superior services to, 20–22

reducing tax burden of, 200–201
referrals, 258–259
rewarding, 217–219
risk profile, 101, 118–125
scaling services, 210–211
scheduling review meetings with, 328
scoring system for, 212–217
serving as fiduciary financial advisors to, 173–174
tailoring performance to needs of, 230–231
teaming up with, 203–204
winning, 23
client service
about, 291
associates, 294–295
compensation, 291
goals of, 291
responsibilities of, 291
synergy between business development and, 291
clothing costs, 95–96
collaborative approach. *See also* teaming up
acting as central point of contact in, 206–207
aligning compensation model with other advisors, 199
benefits of, 198–203
checks and balances, 201
delivering optimal results with, 199–201
family trust and, 200
follow-through in, 206
partnering with client's lawyers in, 204
power of specialization in, 201–202
reducing client's tax burden in, 200–201
separation among advisors in, 207
serving clients better with, 203–206
shopping for solutions in, 208
teaming up with clients in, 203–204
value-added advice in, 197–208
working with client's accountants in, 205
colleagues, teaming up with, 23–24
collectibles, 107
college funds, 157–158
commissions. *See also* compensation
about, 115
commissionable products, 116
commission-only compensation model, 56–57
conflicts of interests, 116

disclosing to clients, 16
on insurance policies, 56, 131
from product shopping and selection, 55
transparency, 131
up-front, 33–34, 130
Commonwealth Financial Network, 52
communication skills, 12
compensation. *See also* income
aligning with that of other advisors, 199
annual, 306
asset-based fees, 55, 115, 116
for client service, 291
commissions, 56–57, 115, 116
comparison of, 115–116
to continuity advisor, 311
fee-only model, 54–55
flat fees, 115, 116
to former advisor's family, 311
to grinders, 291
investigating, 53–58
to joint-work partners, 267
to managers, 57
portfolio's success and, 56
sales charge, 115, 116
compound annual growth rate (CAGR), 153
compounded total portfolio return, 153
computer skills, 12
concierge care, 211–212
confirmation bias, 162–163
conflicts of interests, 11
conscience as guide, 321–322
consequences, 21, 188–189
consultants, 340
consumer debt, 95
consumers
characteristics of, 172–173
versus clients, 172–174
defined, 171
serving as broker/agent to, 172–173
continuing education, 90
continuity plan. *See also* succession planning
commitments made between former and continuity advisors, 311
compensation to continuity advisor, 311
compensation to former advisor's family, 311

continuity plan *(continued)*
  conditions that trigger, 310
  creating, 310–312
  fully funded cross-purchase, buy-sell agreement, 311–313
copy, 21, 186–187, 188
core competencies. *See also* professional development
  asset management, 17–18
  behavioral finance, 19, 83
  budgeting, 17, 82
  complying with financial regulations, 16
  estate planning, 18, 82
  identifying, 80–83
  liability management, 18, 81
  taxation, 19, 82–83
corporate benefit programs, 293
cost-benefit analysis, 180
coupon rate, 106
credentials, 252
credit default, 106
CRM. *See* client relationship management (CRM) system
cross-purchase agreements, 137, 311–312
customers, defined, 66

D

D.A. Davidson, 51
death, 81, 119
debriefing sessions, 269
deep breathing, 166
demographics of clients. *See also* psychographics of clients
  annual revenue, 214
  areas, 213–215
  defined, 213
  marital status, 214
  multiple solution sets, 215
  net worth, 214
  profession, 214
Department of Labor, 67–68
derivatives contracts, 107
dining out, 96
direct participation programs (DPPs), 116
disability, 81

disability insurance, 127
diversification, 113–114
dividend discount model, 105
divorce, 119
donor-advised funds (DAFs), 143
dotcom era, 66
Dow Jones Industrial Average (DJIA), 224–225
down-market capture ratio, 224
drift rebalancing, 108
due diligence
  action in, 20, 179–180
  alignment in, 180–182
  assessment in, 176–178
  audit in, 178–179
  benefits of, 176
  deciding between clients or consumers, 172–174
  factors that matter in, 174–175
  four A's of, 176
  listening to clients, 175
  performing, 20
  process in, 171–182
  self-promotion and, 259–260
duties and responsibilities, defining, 103

E

earning clients. *See also* business development
  about, 235–236
  asking for referrals and, 236–237
  being humbled and honored to serve clients, 243–244
  five-step approach to, 236–237
  speaking to clients in plain English, 238–239
  value proposition in, 240–242
economic recessions, 81
education
  continuing, 90
  of financial advisors, 12
  formal, 83–86
  professional development, 90
  savings/investments goals of clients, 191
effective federal income tax rate, 154
effective state income tax rate, 154
effective tax rate, 155
elevator pitch, 241–242, 330

emergency reserves, 191

eMoney Advisor, 195

emotional manipulation, avoiding, 260

employee, traditional

  firm owns the business you develop as, 50

  statutory employees, 50

  types of firms for, 51

Employee Retirement Income Security Act (ERISA), 68

employees, traditional

  building business for the firm as, 50

  firm owns the business you develop as, 50

employer identification number, 282

endorphins, 166

The Ensemble Practice: A Team-Based Approach to Building a Superior Wealth Management Firm (Palaveev), 341

entertainment costs, 96

equity, 103, 104

equity buy-in

  eligibility for, 304–305

  offering to team members, 304–305

  selectivity in, 304–305

  written agreements, 305

equity participation

  about, 299

  annual compensation and, 306

  equity building, 300–301

  founder mentality and, 301–303

  offering equity buy-in to team members, 304–305

  staying in business and, 306–307

estate planning

  beneficiaries, naming, 136

  business succession/continuity and, 136–137

  capital market conditions at time of death, 140

  concentrated holdings and, 140

  in core competencies, 82

  defined, 133

  differences over closely held business, 141–142

  essentials, 133–140

  exit strategy and, 285–286

  financial plans and, 193

  heirs, naming, 135–136

  liquidity and, 139–140

  networking and, 293–294

  passing along values in, 143–145

  purpose of, 134

  role in, 18–19

  settlement complications, 140–143

  spirit of giving and, 144

  struggle for control, 142–143

  taxes, 134, 138–139

  tax exemptions, 138

  teaming up with attorneys and accountants in, 145

estate tax, 134, 138–139

Excellat Consulting, 340

exchange-traded funds (ETFs)

  costs, 112–113

  versus mutual funds, 112

  taxes, 114

exit strategy. *See also* business continuity

  buyout, 285

  choosing successor to take over, 285

  estate planning and, 285–286

  mentoring, 286

  planning, 26, 284–286

expected death, 81

expenses. *See also* income

  cash flow and, 190

  childcare, 94–95

  clothing, 95–96

  consumer debt, 95

  dining out, 96

  entertainment, 96

  fixed, 190

  healthcare, 94–95

  housing, 93

  identifying and estimating, 92–96

  personal care, 95–96

  traditional employee versus owning firm, 48–49

  transportation, 94

  travel, 96

  utilities, 94

  variable, 190

expense sharing agreement, 282

F

fad products, avoiding, 259

false profits, 322–323

families of clients, 30

family crisis, 11, 119
family documents, changes to, 182
Family Office Exchange, 294
family trust, collaborating on, 200
fears, 167–168
fee-only model. *See also* compensation
  disadvantages of, 54
  structuring fees in, 54
  switching to/from, 55
  understanding, 54–55
fees, asset-based, 56, 115, 116
fiduciary
  Department of Labor's rule, 67–68
  due diligence and, 181
  pledge, 73–74
  responsibility, 8, 16
fiduciary financial advisors, 2, 173–174
Financial Accounting Standards Board (FASB), 1
Financial Advisor IQ, 338
Financial Advisor Magazine, 338
financial advisor(s)
  asking for referrals as, 237
  assessing performance as, 22
  being true, 16
  versus broker/agent, 67
  case study, 46
  collaborating with other, 266–271
  criteria, 7
  defined, 7
  fiduciary, 2, 173–174
  good time to be, 9
  independent, 52–53
  industry and, 64
  modes of operating as, 48–50
  personality traits, 10
  resources, 333–342
  roles in collaborative approach, 207
  roles of, 8, 10, 172
  versus salespeople, 33
  titles, 71
financial assets, 80
financial challenges
  dealing with own, 42–43
  helping others with, 43

financial goals
  achieving, 7
  of clients, 7, 102
  as motivation, 11
Financial Industry Regulatory Authority (FINRA), 65, 69–70, 87–88, 334
financial planners, 54
FinancialPlanning, 335, 338
financial plans, client's
  alignment and balance in, 197
  business succession plan and, 193–194
  capital and, 187–188
  cash flow and, 190
  client's input, 184–185
  consequences and, 188–189
  copy and, 186–187, 188
  creating, 20–21
  developing, 183–196
  estate planning and, 193
  gaps in, 198
  holistic, 185–189
  insurance and, 192–193
  investment goals and, 190–191
  outlining, 189–194
  personalized, 20–21
  regular review of, 196
  software, 194–196
  taxes and, 191–192
financial position
  evaluating own, 43–45
  gauging financial stability, 44
  recognizing risks of financial instability, 45
financial regulations
  complying with, 16
  fiduciary and, 63
financial technology, 39
finders. *See also* grinders; minders
  charitable donor model, 290
  personality traits, 10
  responsibilities of, 289
  roles of, 270
  training, 290
FineTooth Consulting, 340
fire sale, 139

Fisher, Ken, 326

529 plans, 157–158

fixed expenses, 190

fixed income, 103, 105

flat fees, 115, 116

Flaxington, Beverly D., 341

flying solo. *See* solo practice

follow-through, 206

foolish assumptions, 3

forensic accounting, 203

founder, 280

founder mentality
  adopting, 301–303
  avoiding to deal with day-to-day operations, 303
  primary rainmaker and, 302–303
  visionary role, 301–302

401(k) plans, 68, 156–157, 292–293

403(b) plans, 156

FP Transitions, 340

frauds, 65

fringe benefits, 205

full-service brokerages, 51

fundraising, 41

futures contracts, 107

G

General Securities Representative Exam (Series 7), 87

gold, 107

Goldman Sachs, 51

Gratitude Marketing (Sciortino), 341

Grau, David, Jr., 341

greed, 167–168

Greenspan, Alan, 115

grid payout, 48, 312–313

grinders. *See also* finders; minders
  compensation, 291
  goals of, 291
  personality traits, 10
  responsibilities of, 291
  roles of, 270

gross dealer concession (GDC), 48, 312–313

gross expense ratio, 113

growth portfolio, 102

H

Hamilton, Sara, 294

healthcare costs, 94–95

Healthcare.gov, 122

health insurance, 127–128

health saving accounts (HSAs), 158

hedge funds, 107, 116

heirs, naming, 135–136

herd mentality, 164

highly concentrated holdings, 140

Hilliard Lyons, 51

hindsight bias, 164

holistic financial advice, 8, 16

holistic financial plan, 185–189

home life, 307

homeowner's insurance, 128

hot money, 115

housing costs, 93

humility, 31

I

icons, 3–4

illness, 119

illusion of control, 163

income. *See also* cash flow; expenses
  cash flow and, 190
  estimating, 92
  investment goals and, 191
  as sole motivation, 10–11

income portfolio, 102

income replacement approach, 124–125

independent broker/dealers. *See also* wirehouses
  affiliating with, 25, 59–61, 276
  choosing, 279
  expenses, 277
  independent financial advisors and, 52–53

independent contractors
  affiliating with independent broker/dealers, 59–61
  finding employment as, 59–61
  as statutory employees, 50

independent financial advisor, 52–53

indexes

blended benchmarks and, 223–224

clients' mindset, 222–223

keeping simple with clients, 223–224

measuring portfolio performance against, 221–225

recognizing limitations of, 223

index funds, 110–111

individual retirement accounts (IRA), 68

industry organizations

change from within, 73

fiduciary pledge, 73–74

fiduciary standards and, 72–74

inflation, 81, 106

Institute of Business and Finance (IBF), 86, 337

insurance

annuities, 129

auto, 128

categories, 125–129

disability, 127

financial plans and, 192–193

health, 127–128

homeowner's, 128

liability, 128

liability management and, 125–129

life, 126

researching, 122–123

revenue/compensation models, 130–131

insurance companies

broker/dealers, 51

financial strength of, 122–123

insurance policies, commissions on, 56

intangible assets, 80

interest rates, 106

internships, 59

interpersonal skills, 11

introverts, 10

Investing For Dummies (Tyson), 103

investment adviser representative (IAR), 69

Investment Advisers Act of 1940, 335

Investment Company and Variable Contracts Products Representative Exam (Series 6), 87

Investment Foundations, 85

investment management. *See* asset management

InvestmentNews, 279, 335, 338

investment philosophy, agreeing on, 109

investment policy statement

client's goals and objectives in, 101–103

developing, 100–108

manager duties and responsibilities, 103

performance monitoring/reporting parameters, 108

portfolio selection guidelines, 103–107

rebalancing frequency, 108

template, 100

investments

active, 109

alternative, 106–107

equity, 104–105

fixed income, 105–106

goals, 190–191

hot money, 115

passive, 109

Investopedia (website), 335

IRAs (Individual Retirement Accounts), 68

irrational exuberance, 115

irrational thinking and behaviors. *See also* behavioral finance

confirmation bias, 162–163

herd mentality, 164

hindsight bias, 164

illusion of control, 163

mental accounting, 163

muting, 164

myopic loss aversion, 162

recent exploration bias, 164

recognizing, 162–164

J

Janney Montgomery Scott, 51

job loss, 119

joint-work partners

agreement, 268

compensation, 267

complementary skills, 266–267

criticisms from, 269

debriefing sessions, 269

developing relationship with, 268

laying the groundwork, 267–268

meeting with potential partners, 268

operating as a team with, 268–269

researching potential partner's LinkedIn page, 267

strategy meetings, 268

teaming up as, 31, 266–269

terminating relationship with, 269

Journal of Financial Planning, 339

JPMorgan Chase, 51, 276

K

Kaplan Financial Education, 335

key performance indicators (KPIs), 242

Kitces, Michael, 341

knowledge, 32

L

lawyers

connecting with, 255

estate planning, 145

partnering with client's, 204

roles in collaborative approach, 207

teaming up with, 145

leadership

balancing service and, 34–35

embracing role, 34–35

servant, 34

service-oriented mindset and, 35

legacy planning, 220

legal, outsourcing, 298

legal documents, 281–282

legislation, 63

letters of agreement, 282

liability insurance, 128

liability management

about, 18

assessing client's risk profile in, 118–125

in core competencies, 81

defined, 117

income replacement approach, 124–125

insurance and, 125–129

needs-based approach, 125

as niche service for solo practitioners, 265

plans, 123–124

licenses

business, 282

obtaining, 87–89

professional licensing bodies, 333–335

life changes, 181–182

life insurance

features, 126–127

permanent life, 126

term life, 126

whole life, 126

limbic system, 164

limited liability company (LLC), 25, 278

LinkedIn

do's and do'nts, 249–250

inspirational quotes, 251

potential joint-work partners, 267

liquidity

assessing client's needs, 102

defined, 104

estate planning and, 139–140

risks to portfolio, 80

loyalty, 317

LPL Financial, 52

M

managers, compensation for, 57

marginal tax rates, 155

marital status, 214

market cycles, 167–168

marketing

about, 23

establishing online presence, 245–252

to fellow financial advisors, 256–257

over the long haul, 259–260

real-world connections, 252–256

market instability, 11

marketplace changes, 181

marriage, 119

Master of Science in Financial Services, 86

mental accounting, 163

mentoring, 286, 306

mergers and acquisitions, 284

Merrill Lynch, 276

micromanagement, 303

The Million-Dollar Financial Advisor: Powerful Lessons and Proven Strategies from Top Producers (Mullen), 341

minders. *See also* finders; grinders
  personality traits, 10
  responsibilities of, 288–289
  roles of, 270

Mint, 98

MML Investors Services, 52

MoneyGuide, 196

The Monthly Retainer Model In Financial Planning: What It Is, Why It Works, and How to Implement It in Your Firm (Moore/Kitces), 341

Moore, Alan, 341

Morgan Stanley, 51, 276

Morningstar Advisor Workstation, 114

motivations
  commissioned sales and, 33–34
  commitment to deliver value, 33
  questioning, 32–33
  right, 11
  wrong, 10–11

MSCI EAFE index, 224

Mullen, David J., Jr., 341

multiple solution sets, 214

municipal bonds, 154–155

Municipal Securities Rulemaking Board (MSRB), 154

mutual funds
  versus exchange-traded funds, 112
  gross expense ratio, 113
  redemption fees, 113
  sales charge (load), 113
  taxes, 114
  transaction commissions, 113

myopic loss aversion, 162

N

National Association of Insurance Commissioners (NAIC), 88–89, 334–335

National Association of Personal Financial Advisors (NAPFA), 54

natural, definition of, 37

Naviplan, 196

needs-based approach, 125

net business income, 277

net cash flow, 190

networkers, 41

networking
  about, 245
  clients' social network/contacts, 216
  through trusts and estates, 293–294

net worth, 214

noncompete agreement, 282

nondisclosure agreements, 282

Northwestern Mutual, 52

no-sell zone beach party, 218

O

obligations, 64–65

Oechsli, Matt, 341

office manager, 280, 295–296

Office of the Comptroller of the Currency, 231

1099 form, 92

online directories, 251–252

online presence
  blogs, 248–249
  certifications, 252
  establishing, 245–252
  Facebook, 250–251
  LinkedIn, 249–250, 251
  online directories, 251–252
  websites, 246–248

on-the-job training
  banks, 58
  getting, 58–59
  internships, 59
  options for, 58–59
  regional broker/dealers, 59
  wirehouses, 58

On Wall Street (website), 335

open-architecture solution platform, 208

Oppenheimer, 51

opportunity cost, 120

organizational chart, 279–280

organizational skills, 12

organizing business
  about, 287
  administration, 288–289, 295–298
  business development, 289–290, 291–294
  client service, 291, 294–295
  by department, 288–292
outsourcing
  legal and accounting, 298
  portfolio management, 232
overconfidence, 31
ownership of firm
  about, 275–276
  broker protocol, 277
  business structure, 278–279
  change of roles in, 277
  checklist, 24–25
  choosing broker/dealer platform, 279
  client attrition and, 283
  commitments to current firm and, 276–277
  costs of mining, 277
  designating a rainmaker, 282–283
  exit strategy, 25, 284–286
  growing through mergers and acquisitions, 284
  legal documents, 281–282
  organizational chart, 279–280
  profit margin, 283
  pros and cons of, 15
  question to ask before, 276
  revenue sharing and, 25
  staffing, 281
  versus working in firm, 12–15, 47–61

P

Palaveev, Philip, 341
partnership agreement, 282
partnerships, 25, 278
party invitations, accepting, 330
passions, pursuing, 254
passive asset management, 110–111
passive investing, 109
patience, 29
paying yourself first, 17
payout, 48

payroll deductions, 98
performance assessment, 22
personal benchmarks
  accumulation phase and, 227
  calming client's nerves with, 227–229
  defined, 225
  establishing, 226–227
  required rate of return and, 225–226
  withdrawal phase and, 227–228
personal care costs, 95–96
personal experiences
  capitalizing on, 41–43
  childhood memories, 42
  financial challenges, 42–43
  helping others with finances, 43
personal finance background, 43–45
personality traits
  advocacy for clients, 29–30
  being patient and supportive, 29
  being well-connected, 31–32
  desire to teach, 28–29
  evaluating, 28–32
  humility, 31
  hunger for knowledge, 32
personality types, 10
personalized financial plans, 20–21
personal property, 119
philanthropic mindset, 216
Pinnacle Advisor Solutions, 340
PNC Financial Services, 51
Pocket Guard, 98
The Pocket Guide to Sales for Financial Advisors
  (Flaxington), 341
Ponzi schemes, 65
portfolio management, 8, 99, 232
portfolio selection guidelines, 103–107
precious metal approach, 21–22
precious metals, 107
prepaid plans, 157
present value (PV)
  calculating, 120–122
  of cash value accumulations, 120
  economic loss, 120
  sum of all premiums paid, 120

price multiples, 105

private family foundations (PFFs), 144

problem-solving, as service to clients, 212

profession
  of clients, 214
  defined, 65

professional alliances
  with attorneys, 255
  with certified public accountants, 255–256
  cross-industry, 255–256
  developing, 255–256

professional background, 38–40

professional development
  certifications, 89
  continuing education, 90
  core competencies, 80–83
  formal education, getting, 83–86
  licenses, obtaining, 87–89
  pursuing, 79–90
  resources, 336–338

professional licensing bodies, 333–335

professional networkers, 41

profit margin, 283

profit sharing retirement plans, 205

prospects, 330

psychographics of clients. *See also* demographics of clients
  areas, 213
  philanthropic mindset, 216
  quality of relationship, 216
  social network/contacts, 216
  values advisor relationship, 216
  weighing, 215–216
  willingness to refer, 215

psychology, 41

pyramid schemes, 65

Q

qualifications, 11–12

qualified longevity annuity contract (QLAC), 150

qualified plan accounts, 68

R

rainmaking
  founder mentality and, 302–303
  getting someone focused on, 282–283
  primary rainmaker, 302–303
  starting own firm and, 25, 282–283

rational argument, 166–167

rational thinking
  client's fear and, 166
  deep breathing and smiling, 166
  explaining strategy and, 167
  rational argument and, 166–167

Raymond James Financial, 52

RBC, 51

real estate, 104

real-world contacts
  charitable causes, 254
  cross-industry professional alliances, 255–256
  joining communities of interests, 253–254
  serving on boards, 254–255

rebalancing frequency, 108

recent exploration bias, 164

redemption fees, 113

referrals
  asking for, 236–237
  clients' willingness, 215
  differentiating as trusted advisor, 237–238
  encouraging and rewarding clients for, 258–259

refinancing, 237

regional broker/dealers
  on-the-job training, 59
  working in, 51

registered investment advisors (RIAs)
  becoming, 61
  establishing own firm, 52–53

registered representative (RR), 69

relative benchmarks, 229

required minimum distributions (RMDs), 150

required rate of return (RRR), 225–226

resources
  books, 341
  consultants, 340

professional development, 336–338

professional licensing bodies, 333–335

trade publications, 338–339

retirement, 190–191

retirement plans, 156–157

return/risk tradeoff, 104

revenue/compensation models

  annual recurring trail revenue, 131

  asset-based fees, 55, 115, 116

  commissions, 56–57, 115, 116, 130–131

  comparison of, 115–116

  fee-only model, 54–55, 115, 116

  insurance products, 130–131

  investigating, 53–58

  sales charge, 115, 116

revenue sharing, 25

reverse mortgage, 93

review meetings, scheduling, 328

rewarding clients

  budgeting time and, 219

  by hosting special events, 217–218

  by inviting to breakfast or lunch, 218–219

RIABiz.com, 339

RIA in a Box, 61

right of first refusal, 208

risk profile, assessing, 118–125

risks

  coverage modification, 182

  exposure to, 118–120

  hedging against, 122

  identifying, 81

  insurance, 122–123

  mitigating, 120–121

  profile, 101, 118–125

  return/risk tradeoff, 104

robo-advisors, 74–75

Roth IRA, 147, 156

S

S&P 500, 224

sales charge (load), 113, 115, 116

sales force, building own

  client referrals, 258–259

  leveraging home office leadership personnel, 257–258

  by marketing to fellow financial advisors, 256–257

sales-free zones, creating, 253

salesperson

  asking for referrals as, 237

  commissions, 33–34

  versus financial advisors, 33

same-day rule, 329

savings

  budgeting and, 96–97

  goals, 190–191

  guidelines, 97

  plans, 158

Schell, Jim, 282

Sciortino, Michael F., 341

scoring system for clients

  assigning clients to service level brackets, 216–217

  demographics, 212–215

  psychographics, 215–216

S-corporation, 25, 278

Securities and Exchange Commission (SEC), 68–69, 335

Securities Industry Essentials (SIE) exam, 69

securities licensing providers, 335

Securities Training Corporation, 335

self-assessment

  about, 10, 27–28

  leadership, 34–35

  motivations, 10–11, 32–33

  personality traits, 28–32

  personality types, 10

  qualifications, 11–12

self background check

  about, 37

  personal background, 41–43

  personal finance background, 43–45

  professional background, 38–40

self-promotion

  about, 245–246

  building own sales force in, 256–259

  establishing online presence, 245–252

self-promotion *(continued)*
  over the long haul, 259–260
  real-world connections, 252–256
SEP IRAs, 156
Series 6 Examination, 87
Series 7 Examination, 87
Series 63 Examination, 88
Series 65 Examination, 88
Series 66 Examination, 88
serious illness, 81
servant leadership, 34
service-oriented mindset and, 35
services
  adjusting level to different clients, 209–220
  due diligence, 20
  legacy planning, 220
  marketing, 23
  performance assessment, 22
  personalized financial plans, 20–21
  providing to clients, 20–22
  rewarding quality clients, 217–219
  teaming up for, 21
  tiered client service model, 21–22, 210–212
simple laddered bond portfolio, 116
siphoning funds, 17
skills
  analytical, 12
  communication, 12
  computer, 12
  interpersonal, 11
  organizational, 12
  transferable, 316
Small Business for Dummies (Tyson/Schell), 282
small talk, engaging in, 253
smiling, 166
social media, 331
Socrates, 28
software
  client relationship management (CRM), 206, 281,
    289, 296–297
  financial planning, 194–196
Solo 401(k), 156
solo practice. *See also* business ownership; starting
    own firm
  asset management and, 265

benefiting from consensus of one in, 262–263
  capitalizing on responsiveness in, 263
  client capacity and, 264
  inefficiency of, 264
  liability management and, 265
  limitations of, 263–264
  limited resources in, 265
  limiting growth and client impact in, 264
  mastering own destiny in, 262
  product selection and, 264
  pros and cons of, 14, 262–263
  self-sufficiency and self-reliance in, 263
  transitioning to business ownership,
    275–286
  versus working in firm, 12–15
special events, 217–218
spending
  categories, 17
  guidelines, 97
staffing, 25, 281
Standards of Professional Conduct, 86
starting own firm. *See also* business ownership; solo
    practice
  about, 275–276
  broker protocol, 277
  business structure, 278–279
  change of roles in, 277
  checklist, 24–25
  choosing broker/dealer platform, 279
  client attrition and, 283
  commitments to current firm and, 276–277
  costs of, 277
  designating a rainmaker, 282–283
  exit strategy, 25, 284–286
  financing and, 25
  growing through mergers and acquisitions, 284
  legal documents, 281–282
  organizational chart, 279–280
  profit margin, 283
  pros and cons of, 15
  question to ask before, 276
  revenue sharing and, 25
  staffing, 281
  thinking about, 15
  versus working in firm, 12–15, 47–61

state rules and regulations, 69
staying in business
  right reasons for, 306–307
  terrible reasons for, 307
Stifel, 51
stocks
  about, 103
  in asset classes, 104
  as charitable gifts, 159
  costs, 112
  floor specialist, 39
  indexes, 223
  versus mutual or ETFs, 111
  taxes, 114
story-telling, 331
Storytelling for Financial Advisors (West/Anthony), 341
strategic asset allocation, 239
success
  achieving, 7
  as financial advisor, 2
succession planning
  accounting for loyalty in, 317
  choosing right successor, 285, 314–315
  for clients, 137, 193–194
  failure in, 310
  personality and values compatibility in, 315–316
  sizing up candidate's leadership potential in, 316–317
  transferable skills in, 316
success tips
  acquiring and sharing new information, 325
  always asking "what if I'm wrong?", 326
  appreciating client's trust, 326
  avoiding big words, 323–324
  being active in community cause, 324
  beware of false profits, 322–323
  conscience as guide, 321–322
  focusing on skills, 325
  protecting clients from predators, 323
  providing good service, 324
suitability standard, 181
SunTrust, 51
support, 48
supportive personality, 29

T

tangible assets, 80
taxable equivalent yield, 154
tax accounting, 202
tax advisors, 149–150
tax bracket, 155
Tax Cuts and Jobs Act, 83, 138
tax-deferred accounts, 152–153
taxes
  on capital gains, 151–152
  charitable contributions and, 158–159
  college funds, 157–158
  compounding returns and, 152–153
  estate, 134, 138–139
  financial plans and, 191–192
  health saving accounts and, 158
  identifying key issues, 19
  investments and, 114
  reduction strategies, 82–83
  retirement plans and, 156–157
  tackling, 147–159
  tax advisor, 149–150
  transparency in level of expertise on, 148
tax-exempt securities, 155
tax-free investments, 153–156
tax-light investments, 153–156
tax-loss harvesting, 150
TD Group, 51
teachers, 28–29
teaming up. *See also* collaborative approach
  broader practice partnerships in, 271
  building synergies by, 261–271
  with certified public accountants (CPAs), 255–256
  with colleagues, 23–24
  finding niche by, 270–271
  versus flying solo, 262–265
  for joint-work opportunities, 266–269
  with other financial advisors, 266–271
  sharing techniques and skills in, 269–270
technology, 63
terminology, 323–324
term life insurance, 126

ThinkAdvisor.com, 339
tiered client service model
  about, 21–22
  building, 210–212
  concierge care in, 211–212
  metals model, 211
  scaling services to different clients in, 210–211
time
  for clients, 211
  horizons, 103
tracking error, 111
trade publications, 338–339
training, 12
transferable skills, 316
transportation costs, 94
travel expenses, 96
trustees, 293–294
trusts
  charitable lead, 145
  charitable remainder, 145
  family, 200
turnkey asset management program (TAMP), 8, 18, 103, 265
turnover ratio, 110
Tyson, Eric, 103, 282

U

UBS Wealth Management, 51
unexpected death, 81
Uniform Investment Adviser Exam (Series 65), 88
Uniform Securities Agent State Law Examination (Series 63), 88
up-market capture ratio, 224
US Bancorp, 51
U.S. Fifth Circuit Court of Appeals, 67
U.S. savings bonds, 155–156
utility costs, 94

V

value proposition
  asking clients about past experiences, 241
  defined, 239
  elevator pitch, 241–242
  qualifying value and expectations, 242
  showcasing, 240–242
Vanguard, 74
Vanguard 500 Index Fund Admiral Shares (VFIAX), 110
variable expenses, 190
Venn diagram, 185–186
visionary, playing role of, 301–302
vision statement, 301–302
visualization, 260
volatility, 80

W

W-2 forms, 92
WealthFront, 74
wealth management. *See* asset management
WealthManagement.com, 340
wealth managers, 80
websites, creating as home base, 246–248
well-connected, being, 31–32
Wells Fargo Advisors, 51, 276
West, Scott, 341
whole life insurance, 126
Wiley Efficient Learning, 335
wirehouses. *See also* independent broker/dealers
  affiliation with, 276
  expenses, 277
  on-the-job training, 58
withdrawal phase, 227–228
working in firm
  building business for the firm, 50
  versus building own practice, 47–61
  firm owns the business you develop as, 50
  pros and cons of, 13–14
  statutory employees, 50
  types of firms, 51
  versus working for yourself, 12–15

Y

Yelp, 252
yield, 105

About the Author

Ivan Illán has been pursuing his quest for innovative methods of managing money and risk for more than 30 years. He developed his first investment plan at the age of 12, when he asked his father to let him manage his own college fund. Such early interest was inspired by his grandfather, Jose M. Illán, former Undersecretary of the Treasury of the Castro Revolutionary Government, who, under threat of execution, fled Cuba to eventually lead Inter-American Development Bank initiatives in South and Central America.

Since 1996, Ivan's successful career has included experience at large, institutional asset management companies and boutique, retail financial advisory firms. He has directly raised and/or managed $1 billion AUM. Currently, Ivan is the founder of a top ranked financial advisory firm, headquartered in Los Angeles, with more than 1,000 retail and small-business clients across the United States. His firm has been recognized as a *Financial Times* Top Financial Adviser, Five Star Wealth Manager Award (*Los Angeles Magazine* and *The Wall Street Journal*), and *Investopedia* Premier Advisor.

Ivan is an active member of CFA Institute (Los Angeles, Wealth Management League), and holds the Certified Fund Specialist (CFS) designation from the Institute of Business and Finance. He's frequently interviewed and published on topics related to capital markets and economics, and a member of the *Forbes* Finance Council and *Forbes* Contributor. He has degrees in finance and philosophy from Boston College. His first book *How to Hire (or Fire) Your Financial Advisor: Ten Simple Questions to Guide Decision Making* (iUniverse, 2015) was critically acclaimed by *The Washington Post*.

Dedication

To my first mentor, mi abuelo (my grandfather), whose ethical economic pursuits provided me a lifetime of career passion.

Author's Acknowledgements

First, I'm grateful to the good folks at Wiley. Their experienced team of editors — from acquisitions to copy — have enabled this book to achieve its full potential. Specifically, thanks to senior acquisitions editor, Tracy Boggier; project, development, and copy editor, Chad R. Sievers; and wordsmith, Joe Kraynak, who carefully crafted my content into the patented For Dummies style. Thanks also to technical editor, Maria Erickson, CFP, MBA, for ensuring the technical accuracy that readers depend on.

Special thanks to all those financial advisors who earned my respect and admiration over the years through the productive, collaborative relationships we formed for the benefit of our mutual clients. Chief amongst them is my firm's founding partner, Jonas Lee, who's been serving as a true financial advisor for nearly 35 years.

Thanks to Pablo Fernandez, whose firm represents one of the best financial planning service models I've ever seen. I'd also like to thank Andrew Moore for his inspiration many years ago to boldly diversify my firm's business services.

My firm's team, Madelynne Bent, Jacob Weston, and Jason Veris, deserve a big shout out for ensuring consistently spectacular client experiences and freeing my time and mind to take on projects like this. They remind me every day that sharing knowledge and experience with the next generation is one of the most satisfying aspects of our profession.

Lastly, I want to thank John Rikley, whose patience and support empowered me daily in the writing of this book and continue to fuel my enthusiasm in life.

Publisher's Acknowledgments

Senior Acquisitions Editor: Tracy Boggier

Contributor: Joe Kraynak

Project Editor: Chad R. Sievers

Technical Editor: Maria Erickson, CFP, MBA

Production Editor: Siddique Shaik

Cover Image: © Konstantin Faraktinov/ Shutterstock

Take dummies with you everywhere you go!

Whether you are excited about e-books, want more from the web, must have your mobile apps, or are swept up in social media, dummies makes everything easier.

Find us online!

dummies.com

Leverage the power

Dummies is the global leader in the reference category and one of the most trusted and highly regarded brands in the world. No longer just focused on books, customers now have access to the dummies content they need in the format they want. Together we'll craft a solution that engages your customers, stands out from the competition, and helps you meet your goals.

Advertising & Sponsorships

Connect with an engaged audience on a powerful multimedia site, and position your message alongside expert how-to content. Dummies.com is a one-stop shop for free, online information and know-how curated by a team of experts.

- Targeted ads
- Video
- Email Marketing
- Microsites
- Sweepstakes sponsorship

20 MILLION PAGE VIEWS EVERY SINGLE MONTH

15 MILLION UNIQUE VISITORS PER MONTH

43% OF ALL VISITORS ACCESS THE SITE VIA THEIR MOBILE DEVICES

700,000 NEWSLETTER SUBSCRIPTIONS TO THE INBOXES OF *300,000* UNIQUE INDIVIDUALS EVERY WEEK

# of dummies

Custom Publishing

Reach a global audience in any language by creating a solution that will differentiate you from competitors, amplify your message, and encourage customers to make a buying decision.

- Apps
- Books
- eBooks
- Video
- Audio
- Webinars

Brand Licensing & Content

Leverage the strength of the world's most popular reference brand to reach new audiences and channels of distribution.

For more information, visit dummies.com/biz

PERSONAL ENRICHMENT

9781119187790
USA $26.00
CAN $31.99
UK £19.99

9781119179030
USA $21.99
CAN $25.99
UK £16.99

9781119293354
USA $24.99
CAN $29.99
UK £17.99

9781119293347
USA $22.99
CAN $27.99
UK £16.99

9781119310068
USA $22.99
CAN $27.99
UK £16.99

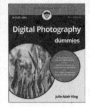
9781119235606
USA $24.99
CAN $29.99
UK £17.99

9781119251163
USA $24.99
CAN $29.99
UK £17.99

9781119235491
USA $26.99
CAN $31.99
UK £19.99

9781119279952
USA $24.99
CAN $29.99
UK £17.99

9781119283133
USA $24.99
CAN $29.99
UK £17.99

9781119287117
USA $24.99
CAN $29.99
UK £16.99

9781119130246
USA $22.99
CAN $27.99
UK £16.99

PROFESSIONAL DEVELOPMENT

9781119311041
USA $24.99
CAN $29.99
UK £17.99

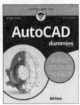
9781119255796
USA $39.99
CAN $47.99
UK £27.99

9781119293439
USA $26.99
CAN $31.99
UK £19.99

9781119281467
USA $26.99
CAN $31.99
UK £19.99

9781119280651
USA $29.99
CAN $35.99
UK £21.99

9781119251132
USA $24.99
CAN $29.99
UK £17.99

9781119310563
USA $34.00
CAN $41.99
UK £24.99

9781119181705
USA $29.99
CAN $35.99
UK £21.99

9781119263593
USA $26.99
CAN $31.99
UK £19.99

9781119257769
USA $29.99
CAN $35.99
UK £21.99

9781119293477
USA $26.99
CAN $31.99
UK £19.99

9781119265313
USA $24.99
CAN $29.99
UK £17.99

9781119239314
USA $29.99
CAN $35.99
UK £21.99

9781119293323
USA $29.99
CAN $35.99
UK £21.99

dummies.com

dummies
A Wiley Brand

Learning Made Easy

ACADEMIC

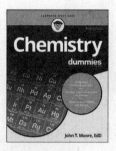

Available Everywhere Books Are Sold

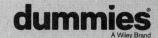

Small books for big imaginations

9781119177173
USA $9.99
CAN $9.99
UK £8.99

9781119177272
USA $9.99
CAN $9.99
UK £8.99

9781119177241
USA $9.99
CAN $9.99
UK £8.99

9781119177210
USA $9.99
CAN $9.99
UK £8.99

9781119262657
USA $9.99
CAN $9.99
UK £6.99

9781119291336
USA $9.99
CAN $9.99
UK £6.99

9781119233527
USA $9.99
CAN $9.99
UK £6.99

9781119291220
USA $9.99
CAN $9.99
UK £6.99

9781119177302
USA $9.99
CAN $9.99
UK £8.99

Unleash Their Creativity

dummies.com